The MASTERS Of Success

INSIGHT PUBLISHING
SEVIERVILLE, TENNESSEE

The
MASTERS
Of Success

© 2006 by Insight Publishing Company.

Published by Insight Publishing Company
P.O. Box 4189
Sevierville, Tennessee 37864

10 9 8 7 6 5 4 3 2

Printed in The United States

ISBN: 1-932863-94-X

Table Of Contents

A Message From The Publisher

Time is a precious commodity in the fast-paced world in which we live today. The amount of information available to us is so overwhelming there's just no keeping up with it all. Reading or word-of-mouth used to be the only way to disseminate information but today we have the Internet, radio, and television giving us instant access to all kinds of information including local and world events as they happen.

With time so valuable, sorting through the vast amount of information out there can be a daunting task. *Masters of Success* has been carefully put together to help you quickly learn tips and the inside information you need to live a full and successful life. This book contains some of the most interesting conversations I have ever had with several of the most successful people I have ever met.

The comparatively small amount of time you spend with this book will reward you with more information about success than you can find just about anywhere else. It is my pleasure to invite you to sit back, relax, and get ready to be inspired!

Interviews conducted by:
David E. Wright
President, International Speakers Network

Chapter One

THE INTERVIEW

David Wright (Wright)
Today we're talking with Steve Lishansky. When senior executives and top professionals commit to realizing more of their full potential, producing much better, more sustainable results, and taking their organizations to a higher level of success, Steve Lishansky is often the person they call. As a leading Executive Coach, organizational consultant, author and respected speaker, Steve brings his 3-Dimensional Effectiveness™ principles and practices to talented executives of top global companies in elevating their professional and organizational productivity, profitability and fulfillment.

As co-founder and principle of Koanetic Consulting, he has produced exceptional results with top executives and companies as diverse as: Johnson and Johnson, PricewaterhouseCoopers, MetLife, Oakley, AT&T, Freddie Mac, Fidelity, Glaxo Smith Kline, State Farm Insurance, the Federal Aviation Administration, Booz Allen Hamilton, and many more.

Steve, welcome to *Masters of Success!*

Steve Lishansky (Lishansky)
Thank you so much David!

Wright

Right up front, let me ask you, what is the key to being successful with other people? Is it inter-personal success and effectiveness?

Lishansky

Well, the essential element of professional success—for any person—is how well they interact with people. That goes for your colleagues, your boss, the people who work for you, your clients— anyone you need to interact with who can affect the outcome of your business. Your ability to be of value to those people and to help them be valuable to you is the most critical factor for creating professional success.

Taken to another level, consider a situation as a leader where perhaps you don't even get to interact directly with those who are part of your organization—whether they're clients or your team. When you start managing large corporations or large divisions it's almost impossible to know everybody you deal with. In that case it becomes even more important to use the same principles of inter-personal effectiveness to be able to create value for the people who are in your business network for success. Whether they're your colleagues, your workers, or your clients, the essential question is this: do you create value for them, and in return do they create value for you?

Wright

As you can imagine, I've asked this question often of people and they say it's being a good communicator or influence, so why is it not one of these?

Lishansky

People often say the essential skill for success is being able to communicate well. I'll tell you a quick story. I was brought in by a company CEO one time who knew me and said, "My board says we need the senior team to communicate more effectively. We'd like to have you help us communicate more effectively."

I looked at him and I said, "Communicate for what"?

He took a deep breath, looked at me, and said, "I'll get back to you in two weeks."

The key issue is that communication is an essential, critically valuable tool, but it is only a tool, and in and of itself it is not as important as what it can build. It is the tool—the bridge—for all the work we do. It is essential to recognize that communication is a means to an end and not the end itself. If we communicate more effectively we become better influencers. If we can influence people, which means being able to move them more effectively, once again, that is a means to an end.

What we contend is the ultimate end result you really want is to be able to create immense value—as much value as possible—with everybody you do business with. Whether they work with you, for you, or they're clients of yours, you want them to value you highly. Ultimately, your value in the market place is determined by the value that others believe you provide to them. Remember, communication is the *tool* to get more influence, but *value* is the ultimate objective we must seek and develop.

Wright

So how did you develop your understanding of what makes people inter-personally successful?

Lishansky

I think I can say I did it the hard way—I made all the mistakes. I started out in sales and marketing, and I started and ran companies. The key issue I always found was that we were in a very competitive business and we had a very hard time differentiating ourselves even though we were highly creative, because our best products got copied all the time. We started asking, how can we separate ourselves from the competition when we're in a viciously competitively market? Basically, within a few months after we would innovate, somebody would copy us.

We started to look at ways in which we could influence our clients; great service is obviously one. We decided that taking care of them better than anybody else, creating more what we might call "added value" or "value above and beyond" the products we provided, could set us apart. What we started to do was ask how we could be more valuable to our clients, and what would be valuable to them?

We had a lot of ideas about what we could do and as we started talking to clients we discovered that they didn't necessarily share the same ideas we had. In conversations, we started to hear from them what would be valuable from their perspective. We started to understand their point of view, which was significantly different from ours as a vendor.

The more we listened to our clients and the more we understood our clients, the easier it was to tailor our products and services to specifically meet what it was that they were looking for, and to do it in ways they found to be the most enjoyable, most advantageous, and of the highest value possible.

By being able to do it in advantageous and valuable ways, totally in tune with what our customers were looking for, we were able to separate ourselves from the competition. People decided they preferred to do business with us, regardless of what we were selling at any given time.

When I left that business, I decided to take this kind of understanding and bring it to my corporate clients. We teach our clients how to build these highly valuable relationships with their external clients, as well as with their internal people. If your people are getting value by working for you and your organization, you've got very loyal and highly productive people. When your people stop seeing that what matters to them is what matters to the organization, then you begin to lose their interest, their attention, and their productivity. Looking to survive, looking to thrive, and then looking to differentiate ourselves from the competition taught us that the best way to do this is to get clarity and understanding about what others really and truly value. That is what led us to develop our high value relationships system.

Wright

Why do you focus on principles and practices rather than techniques and tips?

Lishansky

We always say that there are two ways to fundamentally create better results. Those two ways are: First, you can change what you do (basically your techniques). This is an interesting challenge because under stress you are likely to revert to your habits rather practice the techniques I give you. I can tell you six or eight ways to be a better communicator or to improve your relationships, or to become more profitable. If I tell you better things you could do, in our stressful and overwhelming environment today your chances of *remembering* them under pressure are slight and your chances of being able to *actually do* them under pressure are even smaller than that.

The second way you can actually change your results is to shift what we call "your mindset"—your perspective—your way of thinking about something. I can tell you six actions or techniques to create value, but you may not remember any of them. If you approach an engagement on the basis of asking yourself how you can create more value rather than how you can communicate better, you have fundamentally shifted your approach—your perspective—your mindset.

Shifting your mindset—the questions you operate with and the perspectives that drive your actions—on one hand is often actually much simpler than changing your techniques or your actions, which are often limited by entrenched habits. Shifting the perspective or framework of thinking that drives the actions you choose to take is far more sustainable, even under the pressure and stress experienced in your daily professional life.

Wright

How does inter-personal success relate to the other two dimensions of success that you write and speak about—personal success and organizational success?

Lishansky

In the context of finding how to be most effective with the executives we work with and their organizations, we asked, "What are the critical driving forces and factors that most determine their success?" What we discovered is there are really three dimensions of success and effectiveness:

1. **The personal dimension**—How well are you attuned to what matters most to you? How well are you fulfilled in what is really most important to you? We have consistently found the most fulfilled people are those who live, think, and act consistently with their purpose, their values, and their sense of self. It is obvious that the most fulfilled people are also the most energetic, creative, and talented people who are bringing more of themselves, their talents, drives, and creativity to work. On a personal basis, your fulfillment directly affects your effectiveness and your success.

2. **The inter-personal dimension**—This is the aspect we are talking about here and it has to do with your ability to bring value to the relationships you have. It directly leads to significant increases in your productivity, which is a function of how well you work together with others.

3. **The organizational dimension**—This is about the social structure within which we operate. Organizationally, the driving force of success is actually leadership. The

quality of leadership is fundamentally the single largest determining factor of your long-term success. The interesting thing is that leadership success—the driving force of organizational success—is really intertwined with and built upon personal and inter-personal effectiveness. The three dimensions we talk about—personal, inter-personal, and organizational—address every contingency we've encountered. What we're doing in this particular section is focusing on the element that is most obvious and most in demand today by our corporations for them to be more successful—*inter-personal* success. That's the obvious first step, although the other two are also important.

Wright

What are the stages and steps to inter-personal success?

Lishansky

We have three stages, each containing two specific steps that constitute our principle-based map of the interpersonal effectiveness process. We also need to set the context for an approach to this journey. When you want to create more value in your relationships, which is critical to professional success, what you really need to do is understand your role and responsibility in building that inter-personal success. It starts with your ability to facilitate gaining clarity about what is most important to the other person. If you want to be most productive, most successful, and most valuable in your business and relationships, your job is simply to facilitate what is most important to the other person.

The reason we do that is because most of the people you're talking with are not really clear about what is ultimately most important to them. Look closely and check it out for yourself! This doesn't mean they don't have strong opinions about what they want you to do, but you begin to find that, very often, what they're asking you to do is not directly connected to what matters most to them. Therefore, if you go out of your way, bend over backwards, and do exactly what they asked you to do, and at the end it didn't give them what they really wanted, who takes the blame? Obviously, as the service provider, you take the blame for their not getting what they really needed and valued.

You must make sure that what you're doing is actually going to deliver the maximum value possible. That often means you need to facilitate clarity with the other person about what would be of real value, which is often not clearly stated nor is it even clear to the person making the request of you.

Here are some sobering statistics: We have asked thousands of people, "What percentage of the time is the initial request you receive directly connected to what is *ultimately most important* to the person making that request?" The average response from thousands of people in the U.S. and around the world is *under fifteen percent.* (We've had group responses go as high as sixty percent!)

Here's what that means: If the response indicates fifteen percent it means that eighty-five percent of the time, if you do exactly what someone asks you to do, you're not doing what's really valuable to them! As the service provider you bear the responsibility for that miss in delivering value. That's why they call on you—they assume you have the expertise to do what's really needed. Now even if it's sixty percent of the time that what you're being asked for is what they really value and need, that means forty percent of the time they're not getting what they value and need, even if you do what they ask you to do.

The critical issue here is, you must always start by helping them to gain clarity about what they really need and value *before* jumping into action. The interesting element about this is if you take on the role, in a professional and inter-personal sense, of being the one who facilitates what's most important to the other person, you add value to them before you ever start to deliver products or services. In your initial conversations you are already demonstrating your value to the people you deal with by virtue of the fact that you're helping them gain greater, more important clarity about what would really be important and valuable to them. Recognize that context because it shapes what you're going to do.

Now let's talk about the three stages that constitute the process of building interpersonal effectiveness.

Stage Number 1 — You need to engage them. Enter this stage with the mindset of understanding that your role is to facilitate clarity with the other person. Realize that they are rarely perfectly clear themselves. That requires two specific steps:

    a. **Shift your focus** from yourself, your agenda, and what it is that you came into the meeting with so that you can actually and literally focus on them, their agenda, and what is going on with them. Doing this well gives you the opportunity to make the second required step of the engaging stage:

b. **Build rapport**. Rapport means an empathetic connection with the other person. The thing that's important about our connection with that other person is we often try and do that via thinking, intellectual, analytical, verbal ways which are not the profound movers of inter-personal, empathetic connection. For example: When you go to a meeting and everybody is saying the things you'd like to hear, but you walk out and feel uneasy, we call that uneasy feeling your "gut feel." Which would you trust, their words or your "gut feel"? It's always the gut feel. What you are responding to is non-verbal communication—the tone of voice, the body language, and how congruent that is with the words being spoken. The non-verbal elements represent ninety-three percent of communication. This is based on Dr. Albert Mehrabian's study about how communication happens. Seven percent is words, thirty-eight percent is tone of voice, and fifty-five percent is body language (*Silent Messages*, p. 77, Wadsworth Publishing, 1971). For many of us who work on the phone, body language is no longer part of our equation. This just means that the percentage related to tone of voice and words change proportionately—to close to eighty percent for tone of voice. You can listen to somebody and very often you can hear when people are doing their e-mail while you're speaking to them. Very often you can hear when people are disconnected or not paying attention to you, whether you're there in person or you're just on the phone with them.

These are critical factors to reckon with. If you can engage somebody (which means s/he knows you're present for them) and h/she feels that connection with you (we call that empathetic relationship—rapport), then you're in a position to move forward. Now, this is a natural progression. When you first meet someone, the first thing you want to do is see if you have a connection with him or her. Do I feel anything for this person? Do I feel like there's any connection? Do I feel a resonance of some sort? When you do, the next natural step is to find out more about the person.

Stage Number 2 in building high value relationships: We call this stage **"navigating."** What that means is we need to navigate to find the best path or route to get to what really matters to them. This is the critical factor: we feel a connection with somebody, want to understand him or her better, but the best way to understand someone better is to really understand what s/he values, what's important to him or her, what s/he cares about, and what his or her decision-making and evaluation criteria is. If I'm working with you, for you, or you're a client of mine, the more I understand your decision-making and evaluation process, the more likely I am to know whether or not I can actually provide value to you in a significant way. I also know how to influence your decisions so that you'll see the value that I have for you. If I don't understand your decision-making, it's like throwing darts at a target 100 feet away. Now, most of us have been in business long enough have learned that even at 100 feet we can hit the bulls-eye every now and then. However, if you understand the decision-making and evaluation criteria of another person, to get him or her to be able to perceive your value and the contribution you can make to his or her success is like moving the bulls eye six inches away. So the second stage is really about navigating—understanding what's important to the other person, then discovering his or her evaluation and decision-making process. This means you understand the values by which others make their decisions.

Stage Number 3 — **Aligning** and delivering. Once we have navigated, we're now in a position to move to the stage that we call "aligning." Our actions now align directly with what is important to them and we can now deliver what is most important to them. This means that what we're doing will not be wasted effort. What we're doing will not need to be re-done, and it won't be based on miscommunication, misunderstanding, or misdirection because we've already defined what's most important and we've got agreement that if we do "x" then they will be satisfied.

The summary of the three-stage process is: We've engaged and established a connection with them, then navigated to their decision-making evaluation criteria, and then we're able to make choices that align our actions to deliver what they value most.

Wright

Let me ask you to clear one thing up before we go to the next question. I was fascinated by this eighty-five/fifteen percent finding. Let's say I'm in the business of helping people with their computer problems and the client asked me to fix his old computer and I know for a fact that he should be buying another computer. Are you saying he's wasting my time and his money by trying to repair the old one?

Lishansky

Yes. Let me give you a more specific example. If somebody says, "I need you to fix my computer," or in a more professional sense given our clients, major IT organizations are told, "I need you to write this program so that we can do x, y or z." The real key issue is we need to understand why that program is valuable to them. What they've determined to be the action—repair the computer and write the program—may not actually deliver what they're trying to accomplish, which is perhaps increase their business, improve their profitability, and/or reduce their overhead expenses by virtue of automating some of their services. If we don't understand what generated that request—that particular desire for an action—then we don't understand what's really moving them to ask us to work with them. If we don't understand what's moving them to make the request it's like throwing a dart at a dartboard 100 feet away. The likelihood of hitting the bulls-eye is slim.

Wright

So, as we talk about the practical applications of these principles at work, how do the principles of high-value relationship help us address being overwhelmed at work?

Lishansky

The most predominant emotions at work today are being overwhelmed and stressed. A lot of that is coming from the fact that most people are being asked to do a lot more than they ever did before. Most people are not in a position to be able to do everything that they're being asked to do—whether you're a CEO of an organization or you're just a manager in the organization. The challenge is you're being asked to do a lot of things, many of which have questionable value, even for the people asking you to do them. If you don't have the ability and the skills to be able to understand what's really valuable to the people you're working with, or to your clients, or to your organization, you end up with a to-do list that would choke an elephant!

The problem with that is you feel like a gerbil on a treadmill racing to catch up with your to-do list, which is often getting more and more disconnected from how you deliver value.

Losing clarity and effectiveness about what is really important, and just doing tasks is the fastest way to be overwhelmed. The fastest way out of being overwhelmed is to have clarity about your most important priorities and to make sure that those priorities are directly aligned with what is most valuable for you, for the people you're interacting with, for your clients, and for your organization. If you are clear about what is most valuable to those you interact with, then you can actually trim your to-do list significantly, prioritize it easily, and make sure that everything you do really does deliver value and is not just another to-do to be checked off. Being able to prioritize clearly and quickly what matters most is the fastest way out of being overwhelmed that we've ever found.

Wright

As you consider mistakes that professionals make, based on your years of experience, would you give us two or three of the most common mistakes made in communicating with other people?

Lishansky

We call a lot of these communication mistakes of top professionals "expertise traps." Expertise is a very useful and valuable aspect of professional life today. However, expertise is useful for this fundamental reason: because a person with expertise can add more value by knowing more about useful aspects of business, than somebody else does. However when expertise—a form of having the right answer—becomes your predominant focus, then you have probably lost touch with what people need to use expertise for. What that means is you—the expert—come in knowing the answer to an issue before your clients may even know the appropriate question to ask. That's what experts are about; they are hired because they know more about a specific topic or area. The challenge is that experts are not valued for having the right answer; they are valued for delivering value to the client or person they are dealing with.

If clients don't understand the problem or the issue, then they won't value the expert's solution. Clients only value the expert's answer in direct proportion to the connection they can see between the expert's answer and what is really important to them.

If you provide an answer—even a definitive, correct answer—in a situation where your clients cannot understand the issue, the problem, or how your solution provides value to them, you get little or no credit for your answer or the value of that answer. In fact, that is one of our basic axioms in building high-value relationships: **"Being right is insufficient for being effective."** As we always like to say, "If you want a real life test of that, anybody who's married knows what I'm talking about." That is a great example of a high-value relationship, of how being right is insufficient for being effective.

High value relationships don't mean that there are no disagreements or misunderstandings. What they do offer is a basis for quick resolution and constantly increasing value. Mistaking being right for being effective is one of the critical mistakes that drop top professionals, executives, and technical experts into the expertise trap. In the stress, speed, and overwhelming tasks of work they are often thinking (and worse, sometimes saying), "I know the answer. Just stop your demanding, listen to me, and let me give it to you." The reality is, until the other person understands the value of their issue or problem they won't give you any value for your solution.

Another key issue is that experts tend to assume people either trust them, are willing to defer to them, or think that they know what they are doing. The problem is—especially as we have greater and faster access to resources via the Internet—it's very easy to find experts in any field. Not so many years ago, it would have been difficult for you to quickly find five people who could solve your problem. Today, in minutes, using their favorite search engine they can find dozens of experts who could potentially work on their problem. One important question for you as the expert is: what will differentiate *you*?

This leads us to expertise trap problem number two: Experts talking about what they do—their process or their services—versus the results and value of the results for their clients. Reality is that most of your clients don't care about what you can do, and due to their lack of expertise, they are not in a position to differentiate your expertise level from your competitors'. Most clients cannot tell the difference between your expertise and that of your top four competitors. The real question then becomes: how will they determine from whom they will buy services? If there's not much difference between Companies A, B, C, or D, what is the deciding difference going to be?

The difference comes down to who they believe will be able to understand them, take care of them the way they want to be taken care of, deliver the maximum value, as well as have the expertise they want. It comes down to the fact that the way you conduct your relationship with them is the single biggest determining factor of whether or not they're going to trust you, respect you, and believe you're going to have the kind of communication and collaboration that they really want to have from their professional provider.

Wright

So, what distinguishes the most successful communicators and leaders from the rest?

Lishansky

Following along with what we just discussed, what distinguishes them is their ability to get to the heart of what matters to people, and to bring clarity and connection to what really matters for the people they do business with. They address what people value and care about, and reconnect them to these issues.

We talk about values all the time in business today. Values determine what people care about and focus on. If a leader is clear about the values that are important, whether it is that they want people willing to take on challenges, or be highly responsible, or hold a high degree of integrity, then the basis of decision-making for their people becomes simpler, clearer, and faster. This is a huge asset and competitive advantage at work today. What happens is the more a leader can focus their people on the important values of the organization, the more a leader can speak to and create the culture that supports those values, the clearer and faster that decisions can be made, and the more respected and successful that leader becomes.

Wright

What causes difficulty in communications?

Lishansky

There can only be three sources of problems in communication. It has to be you, the other person, or how you are communicating together. With our professional clients we often ask the question, "What percentage of the time are you effectively communicating?" The average usually runs between sixty to eighty percent. That means that sixty to eighty percent of the time our professionals are effective in their communication, which also means that twenty to forty percent of the time they are not.

The challenge is often they don't know what to do when it's not working, because most of the time it does. An analogy is being in a foreign country where somebody doesn't understand what you're saying. What we tend to do when a foreigner does not understand what we are saying is to say it louder, with bigger gestures, as if that would make a difference. The same thing happens at work. When we are used to being effective eighty percent of the time, when it does not work it must be someone else's fault. Then we just tend to do what we always do, but do it louder, with bigger gestures and emphasis; but of course that won't work.

The process we offer provides a map of what you do when you're successful so you can understand what's not happening when you're not being successful. That explains the issue when you're successful sixty to eighty percent of the time and not successful twenty to forty percent of the time.

Let's examine what is going on when others might be the source of miscommunication. When we ask people what percentage of the time their clients' initial requests are directly connected with what is ultimately most important to their clients, the average is under fifteen percent. Even if it was fifty percent it means that half the time you're in trouble if you do what they ask you to do. You're not going to deliver value and, in fact, you are going to fall short of what's really needed. Often the issue is helping them get clear because they're not any more clear—and perhaps even less clear—than you are.

The third possible issue is: do we understand each other? To illustrate this point we will put five people on a team and ask them to write down the first five things they think of relative to something they have in common, such as: client, leader, information technology, computers, and human resources. Then we ask them how many exact matches they have. We have found that over ninety-five percent of the time there are no matches whatsoever. This means that none of the five people at the table would have any of the words we used in common. If you just took any five people and said the word "client," you would get totally different associations from each of those five people.

The lesson here is that while we may understand what the word means, we don't understand what the person means and it's immensely more critical to understand what the person means. So it's you, it's them, or it's us together. If you don't take on the role of facilitating clarity about what is most important up front, then you don't have an engagement that allows you to navigate to that clarity, which won't allow you to align your actions with delivering what is most valuable. Otherwise, you run the risk of expending enormous amounts of effort with very little value.

Wright

If I decided to buy into what you've been talking about here today—and it has been extremely interesting—how would I get compensated for the value of my work, rather than one of the other less successful ways such as an hourly basis?

Lishansky

There are two critical issues here: your compensation is an evaluation by the person paying you for how valuable you are. Therefore, if someone doesn't know the value you can deliver they're liable to try and find the lowest common denominator form of paying you. This means the person is saying, "I'm going to mitigate my risk by paying you by the hour and I'm going to try and come up with a very low rate." However, if you follow our process and you help somebody get crystal clear about what they're really trying to accomplish, it is a tremendous value for them right from the very beginning about your engagement with them. That means you are helping them to connect what they're asking you for to what supports them and their organization being more successful. An ability to do that in an efficient and effective way is already a demonstration of how you can be of value. The way you get paid for your value is you help the other person who is going to pay you get clear about what would be valuable to them.

Now, if what they're asking you for is what they'd really value only fifteen percent of the time, the obvious situation is eighty-five percent of the time they don't even know what would be valuable, and so they're not likely to pay you for it. If you can get clear and help them see the value up front, you will distinguish yourself from your competition. You will also demonstrate your value to them before they even sign an agreement for work, and you will build a level of trust, respect, collaboration, and communication that leads them to see you can add enormous value to them and their organization. If they can see the value of what you do, it's easier to get paid for the value you offer. Otherwise, they're just seeing you as a service provider, a vendor, one of a faceless mass that they could hire. That hardly distinguishes you or gets you a premium rate for your services and more importantly for the value that you provide.

Wright

Today we have been talking with Steve Lishansky who's a leading executive coach, organizational consultant, author, and respected speaker. I think he knows what he's talking about when he points to his three-dimensional effectiveness principles and practices for talented executives of top companies in our nation, and all over the world for that matter.

Steve, I really do appreciate this. I've learned a lot today and I really want to thank you for taking so much time. I hope that the people who read this book will take a lot of this information to heart. I know that even after so many years of listening to executive management seminars, this is really, really useful information for me personally. Thank you so much.

Lishansky
David, thank you so much, it's been a real pleasure!

About The Author

Steve Lishansky is the co-founder and principle of Koanetic Consulting—formerly called Success Dynamics—one of the first executive coaching firms in the United States, and a leader in the field of executive development, organizational performance and culture, and building high-value client relationship skills. He is also the founder and Executive Director of the Executive Coaching Institute (ECI), the oldest coach training organization dedicated to elevating results by educating top-level executives and coaches in the principle-based, highly effective work pioneered by Success Dynamics and Koanetic Consulting. Steve is also a founding member of the innovative global consulting and executive development consortium, Jellyfish International. Since starting Success Dynamics and Koanetic Consulting in 1992, after a distinguished twenty-year career founding and running companies, Steve works with senior leaders and their organizations producing results through: executive coaching; consulting; customized educational programs and keynotes; and facilitating executive meetings, retreats and strategic planning sessions. Steve is a Master Certified Coach, the highest earned designation with the International Coach Federation (ICF), and a past President of their largest chapter, ICF-New England. He is the past President of the New England chapter of the National Speakers Association, the author of numerous articles on leadership, executive coaching, and building high-value relationships, and a soon to be published book, co-written with partner Al Bhatt, *The Expertise Trap—Why Being Right Is Insufficient for Being Effective*.

Steve Lishansky

83 Whits End Road

Concord, MA 01742

Phone: 978.369.4525

Email: slishansky@KoaneticConsulting.com

www.KoaneticConsulting.com

Chapter Two

KEN BLANCHARD

THE INTERVIEW

David Wright (Wright)
Few people have created a positive impact on the day-to-day management of people and companies more than Dr. Kenneth Blanchard who is known around the world simply as Ken, a prominent, gregarious, sought after author, speaker, and business consultant. Ken is universally characterized by friends, colleagues, and clients as one of the most insightful, powerful, and compassionate men in the business today.

Ken's impact as a writer is far-reaching. His phenomenal bestselling book, *One Minute Manager*, co-authored with Spencer Johnson, has sold more than nine million copies worldwide and has been translated into more than twenty-five languages. Ken is Chairman and "Chief Spiritual Officer" of the Ken Blanchard Companies. The organization's focus is to energize organizations around the world with customized training in bottom line business strategies that are based on the simple yet powerful principles inspired by Ken's bestselling books.

Dr. Blanchard, welcome to *Masters of Success!*

Dr. Ken Blanchard (Blanchard)
Well, it's nice to talk to you, David. It's good to be here.

Wright
I must tell you that preparing for your interview took quite a bit more time than usual. The scope of your life's work and your business, the Ken Blanchard Companies, would make for a dozen fascinating interviews. Before we dive into the specifics of some of your projects and strategies, will you give our readers a brief synopsis of your life, how you came to be the Ken Blanchard that we all know and respect?

Blanchard
Well, I'll tell you, David, I think life is what happens when you are planning on doing something else. I forget whose line that was; but I never intended to do what I have been doing. In fact, all my professors in college told me I couldn't write. I wanted to do college work, which I did. They told me, "You had better be an administrator." So I decided I was going to be a Dean of Men, a Dean of Students. I got provisionally accepted into my master's degree program, and then provisionally accepted at Cornell, because I never could take any of those standardized tests.

I took the College Boards four times and finally got 502 in English. My mind doesn't work. I ended up in a higher university in Athens, Ohio, in 1966 as Administrative Assistant to the Dean of the Business School. When I got there, he said, "Ken, I want you to teach a course. I want all my deans to teach." I had never thought about teaching because they said I couldn't write and you had to publish.

He put me in the manager's department. I've taken enough bad courses in my day; I wasn't going to teach one. So I really prepared and had a wonderful time with the students. I was chosen as one of the top ten teachers on the campus coming out of the chute. I just had a marvelous time. A colleague by the name of Paul Hershey was chairman of the management department, and he wasn't real friendly to me initially because the Dean had led me into his department. But I heard he was a great teacher. He taught organizational behavior and leadership. So I asked him if I could sit in on his course next semester.

"Nobody audits my courses," he replied. "If you want to take it for credit, you're welcome." I couldn't believe it. I had a doctorate degree and he wanted me to take his course for credit. So I signed up. The registrar didn't know what to do with me because I already had a doctorate, but I wrote the papers and took the course, and it was great.

In June 1967, Hershey came into my office and said, "Ken, I've been teaching in this field for ten years. I think I'm better than anybody, but I can't write. I'm a nervous wreck, and I'd love to write a textbook with somebody. Would you write one with me?"

I said, "We ought to be a great team. You can't write and I'm not supposed to, so let's do it!" So thus began this great career of writing and teaching. We wrote a textbook called, *Management of Organizational Behavior Utilizing Human Resources*. It just came out with its eighth edition last year and it sold more than any other textbook in its field throughout the years. It's been more than thirty-five years since that book came out.

I quit my administrative job, became a professor, and I worked my way up through the ranks. I took a sabbatical leave and went to California for one year twenty-five years ago. I met Spencer Johnson at a cocktail party. Spencer wrote children's books; he has a wonderful series called, *Value Tales for Kids: The Value of Courage, The Story of Jackie Robinson; The Value of Believing In Yourself, The Story Louis Pasteur*. My wife, Margie, met him first and told me, "You guys ought to write a book together—a children's book for managers, because they won't read anything else." That was my introduction to Spencer. So, our book, the *One Minute Manager* was really a kid's book for big people. That is a long way from saying my career was well planned.

Wright

Ken, what and/or who were your early influences in the areas of business, leadership, and success? In other words, who shaped you in your early years?

Blanchard

My father had a great impact on me. He was retired as an Admiral in the Navy and had a wonderful philosophy. I remember when I was elected to president of the seventh grade, and I came home all pumped up. My father said, "Son, it's great that you're the president of the seventh grade, but now that you have that leadership position, don't ever use it." He said, "Great leaders are followed because people respect them and like them, not because they have power." That was a wonderful lesson for me early on. He was just a great model for me. I got a lot from him.

Then I had this wonderful opportunity in the mid 1980s to write a book with Norman Vincent Peale, author of, *The Power of Positive Thinking*. I met him when he was eighty-six years old. We were asked to write a book on ethics together and we wrote, *The Power of Ethical Management: Integrity Pays, You Don't Have to Cheat to Win*. It didn't matter what we were writing together, I learned so much from him; he just added to what I learned from my mother. When I was born my mother said, "I laughed before I cried, I danced before I walked, and I smiled before I frowned." So that, on top of Norman Vincent Peale, really made me I focus on what I could do to train leaders. I asked questions like: How do you make them positive? How do you make them realize that it's not about them—it's about whom they are serving? It's not about their position—it's about what they can do to help other people win. So, I'd say my mother and father, and then Norman Vincent Peale had a tremendous impact on me.

Wright

I can imagine. I read a summery of your undergraduate and graduate degrees. I assumed you studied business administration, marketing management, and related courses. Instead, at Cornell, you studied government and philosophy. You received your master's from Colgate in sociology and counseling and your Ph.D. from Cornell in educational administration and leadership. Why did you choose this course of study? How has it affected your writing and consulting?

Blanchard

Well, again, it wasn't really well planned out. I originally went to Colgate to get a master's degree in education, because I was going to be a Dean of Students over men. I had been a government major, and I was a government major because it was the best department in Cornell in the Liberal Arts School. It was exciting. We would study what the people were doing at the league governments.

The Philosophy Department was also great. I just loved the philosophical arguments. I wasn't a great student in terms of grades, but I'm a total learner. I would sit there and listen and I would really soak it in. When I went over to Colgate and got involved in the education courses, they were awful—they were boring. By the second week, I was sitting at the bar at the Colgate Inn saying, "I can't believe I've been here two years for this."

This is just the way the Lord works: sitting next to me in the bar is a young sociology professor who had just got his Ph.D. at Illinois, and his wife was back packing up. He was staying at the Inn and I was moaning and groaning about what I was doing. He said to me, "Why don't you come and major with me in sociology? It's really exciting."

"I can do that?" I asked.

He said, "Yes."

I knew they would probably let me do whatever I wanted the first week. Suddenly, I switched out of education and went with Warren Ramshaw. He had a tremendous impact on me. He retired a few years ago as the leading professor at Colgate in the Arts and Sciences, and got me interested in leadership and organizations. That's why I got a master's in sociology.

Then the reason I went into educational administration and leadership was because it was a doctoral program I could get into. The reason for that was I knew the guy heading up the program. He said, "The greatest thing about Cornell is that you will be in a School of Education. It's not very big, so you don't have to take many education courses, and you can take stuff all over the place." That was a marvelous man by the name of Don McCarty, who ended up going on to be the Dean of the School of Education, Wisconsin. He had an impact on my life, but I was always searching around.

My mission statement is, "To be a loving teacher and example of simple truths that help myself and others to awaken to the presence of God in our lives." The reason I mention "God" is, I believe the biggest addiction in the world is the human ego. I'm really into simple truth, however. I used to tell people I was trying to get the B.S. out of the behavioral sciences.

Wright

I can't help but think, when you mentioned your father, that he just bottomed-lined it for you about leadership.

Blanchard

Yes.

Wright

Years ago when I went to a conference in Texas, a man named Paul Myers said, "David, if you think you're a leader and you look around and no one is following you, you're just out for a walk."

Blanchard

Well, you'd get a kick out of this: I'm just reaching over to pick up a picture of Paul Myers on my desk; he's a good friend. We co-founded the Center for Faith Walk Leadership here where we're trying to challenge and equip people to lead like Jesus. It's non-profit, and I tell people I'm not an evangelist because we've got enough trouble with the Christians we have—we don't need any more new ones. But, this is a picture of Paul on top of a mountain, and then another picture below of him under the sea with stingrays. It says, "Attitude is everything. Whether you're on the top of the mountain or the bottom of the sea, true happiness is achieved by accepting God's promises, and by having a biblically positive frame of mind. Your attitude is everything." Isn't that something?

Wright

He's a fine, fine man. He helped me tremendously. In keeping with the theme of our book, *Conversations On Success,* I wanted to get a sense from you about your own success journey. Many people know you best from the *One Minute Manager* books you coauthored with Spencer Johnson. Would you consider these books as a high water mark for you, or have you defined success for yourself in different terms?

Blanchard

Well, you know the *One Minute Manager* was an absurdly successful book. It achieved success so quickly I found I couldn't take credit for it. So that was when I really got on my own spiritual journey and started to try to find out what the real meaning of life and success was. That's been a wonderful journey for me because I think, David, the problem with most people is they think their self-worth is a function of their performance plus the opinion of others. The minute you define your self-worth like that, every day your self-worth is up for grabs because your performance is going to fluctuate on a day-to-day basis. People are fickle—their opinions are going to go up and down. So, you need to ground your self-worth in the unconditional love God has ready for us.

That concept grew out of the unbelievable success of the *One Minute Manager.* When I started to realize where all that came from, that's how I got involved in the ministry I mentioned. Paul Myers is a part of it. As I started to read the Bible, I realized that everything I've ever written about, or taught, Jesus did. You know, He did it with twelve incompetent guys He hired. The only guy with much education was Judus, who was His only turnover problem.

Wright

Right.

Blanchard

So it was a really interesting thing. What I see in people is not only do they think their self-worth is a function of their performance plus the opinion of others, but they measure their success on the amount of accumulation of wealth, on recognition, power, and status. I think those are nice success items—there's nothing wrong with those, as long as you don't define your life by them.

What I think is a better focus rather than success is what Bob Buford, in his book *Half Times,* calls "significance"—move from success to significance.

I think the opposite of accumulation of wealth is generosity. I wrote a book called, *The Generosity Factor* with Truett Cathy, founder of Chick-fil-A. He is one of the most generous men I've ever met in my life. I thought we needed to have a model of generosity—generosity not only with your treasure, but also your time and talent. Truett and I added *touch* as a fourth one.

The opposite of recognition is service. I think you become an adult when you realize you're here to serve rather than to be served.

Finally, the opposite of power and status is having loving relationships. Mother Theresa is a good example. She couldn't have cared less about recognition, power, and status because she was focused on generosity, service, and loving relationships. She did get all of that earthly stuff such as recognition and status; but if you focus on the earthly, such as money, recognition, and power, you're never going to get to significance. I you focus on significance, you'll be amazed at how much success can come your way.

Wright

I spoke with Truett Cathy recently and was impressed by what a down-to-earth good man he seems to be. He has Chick-fil-A close on Sundays. When my friends found out I had talked to him, they said, "Boy, he must be a great Christian man, but he's rich." I told them, "Well, to put his faith into perspective, closing on Sunday costs him $500 million a year." He lives his faith, doesn't he?

Blanchard

Absolutely, but he still outsells everybody else.

Wright

That's right.

Blanchard

They were recently chosen the number one fast quick service restaurant in Los Angeles. They only have five restaurants here and they've only been here for a year.

Wright

The simplest market scheme, I told him, tripped me up. I walked by the first Chick-fil-A I had ever seen, and some girl came out with chicken stuck on toothpicks and handed me one. I just grabbed it and ate it and it's history from there on.

Blanchard

Yes, I think so. It's really special. It is so important that people understand generosity, service, and loving relationships because too many people are running around like a bunch of peacocks. You even see pastors who ask, "How many in your congregation are authors, how many books have you sold?" or, regarding business, "What's your profit margin? What's your sales?" The reality is, that's all well and good, but I think what you need to focus on is others. I think if businesses did that more and we got Wall Street off our backs with all the short-term evaluation, we'd be a lot better off.

Wright

Absolutely. There seems to be a clear theme that winds through many of your books that have to do with success in business and organizations and that is how management treats people and how they feel about their value to a company. Is this an accurate observation? If so, can you elaborate on it?

Blanchard

Yes, it's a very accurate observation. See, I think "profit" is the applause you get for taking care of your customers and creating a motivating environment for your people. Very often people believe business is only about the bottom line. But no, the bottom line happens to be the result of creating customers who are raving fans. I described this with Sheldon Bowles in our book. Customers want to brag about you, and then create an environment where people can be gung-ho and committed. You've got to take care of your customers and your people, and then your cash register is going to go ka-ching. Then is when you can make some big bucks.

Wright

I noticed that your professional title with the Ken Blanchard Companies is somewhat unique, Chairman and "Chief Spiritual Officer." What does your title mean to you personally and to your company? How does it affect the books you choose to write?

Blanchard

I remember having lunch with Max DuPree one time. He's the legendary Chairman of Herman Miller, Inc. He wrote a wonderful book called, *Leadership is an Art*. I asked him, "What's your job?"

He said, "I basically work in the vision area."

"Well, what do you do?" I asked.

"I'm like a third grade teacher," He said, "I say our vision and values over, and over, and over again until people get it right, right, right."

I decided then I was going to become our Chief Spiritual Officer. I would be working in the vision, values, and energy part of our business. We have about 275 to 300 around the country, in Canada, and the U.K., and we have partners in about thirty nations. I leave a voice mail every morning for everybody in the company, and I do three things regarding that as Chief Spiritual Officer:

1. People tell me what we need to pray for,
2. People tell me about those we need to praise—our unsung heroes and people like that and,
3. I leave an inspirational morning message every day.

I am really the cheerleader—the "energy bunny"—in our company, and the one who reminds us why we're here and what we're trying to do. Our business in the Ken Blanchard Companies is to help people to lead at a higher level, and to help individuals, and organizations. Our mission statement is, "To unleash the power and potential of people and organizations for the common good." So if we are going to do that, we've really got to believe in that. I'm working on getting more Chief Spiritual Officers around the country. I think it's a great title—we should get more of them.

Wright

So those people for whom you pray, where do you get the names?

Blanchard

The people in the company tell me who needs help, whether it's a spouse who is sick, or kids who are sick, or they are worried about something. We've got more than five years of data about the power of prayer, which is pretty important.

For example, this morning my inspirational message was about my wife and five members of our company who walked sixty miles last weekend—twenty miles a day for three days—to raise money for breast cancer research. It was amazing. I went down and waved them all in as they came. There was a ceremony where it was announced they had raised 7.6 million dollars. There were more than three thousand people walking—and a lot of the walkers were dressed in pink—who were cancer victors, people who had overcome cancer. There were even men who were walking with pictures of their wives who had died from breast cancer. I thought it was incredible.

There wasn't one mention of it in the major San Diego papers on Monday. I said, "Isn't that just something." I said, "We have to be an island of positive influence because you know all you see in the paper today is about Michael Jackson and Scott Peterson and Coby Bryant and this kind of thing, when here you have all these thousands of people out there walking and trying to make a difference, and nobody thinks it's news." So every morning I pump people up about what life's about and about what's going on. That's what my Chief Spiritual Officer is about.

Wright

I had the pleasure of reading one of your current releases, *The Leadership Pill*.

Blanchard

Yes.

Wright

I must admit that my first thought was how short the book was. I wondered if I was going to get my money's worth, which, by the way, I most certainly did. Many of your books are brief and based on a fictitious story. Most business books in the market today are hundreds of pages in length and read almost like a textbook. Can you talk a little bit about why you write these short books and about the premise of *The Leadership Pill?*

Blanchard

I really got that during my relationship with Spencer Johnson when we wrote the *One Minute Manager*. As you know he wrote *Who Moved My Cheese*, which was a phenomenal success. He wrote children's books, and I was a storyteller. As I said earlier, my wife told me, "You guys ought to write a children's book for managers. They won't read anything else."

Jesus talked by parable. My favorite books were, *Jonathan Livingstone Seagull, The Littlest Prince,* and *Og Mandino,* the greatest of them all. These are all great parables. I started writing parables because people can get into the story and learn the contents of the story without bringing their judgmental hats into their reading. You write a regular book and they'll say, "Well, where did you get the research?" They get into that judgmental side. Our books get them emotionally involved and they learn.

The Leadership Pill is a fun story about a pharmaceutical company convinced they have discovered the secret to leadership and they can put the ingredients in a pill. When they announce it, the country goes crazy because everybody knows we need more effective leaders. When they release it, it outsells Viagra and all those big gray trucks. The founders of the company start selling off stock and they call them Pillionaires.

Then along comes this guy who calls himself "the effective manager," and he challenges them to a no-pill challenge. If they identify two non-performing groups, he'll take on one and let somebody on the pill take another one, and he guarantees his group will out-perform the other group by the end of the year. They agree, but of course, they give him a drug test every week to make sure he's not sneaking pills on the side.

I wrote the book with Marc Muchnick who was a young guy in his early thirties. We did a major study together of what does this interesting "Y" generation—the young people of today—want from leaders, and this is a secret blend that this effective manager in the book uses. When you think about it, David, this is really powerful in terms of what people want from a leader. Number one, they want integrity. Many people have talked about that in the past, but these young people will walk if they see people say one thing and do another. A lot of us walk into the bathroom and out into the halls to talk about it. But these people will quit. They don't want somebody to say something and not do it.

The second thing they want is a partnership relationship. They hate superior/subordinate. I mean, what awful terms those are. It's a case of the head of the department versus the hired hands. Someone asks, "What do you do?" The reply is, "I'm in supervision—I see things a lot clearer than these stupid idiots." They want to be treated as partners. If they can get a financial partnership, that's great. I if they can't, they really want at least a psychological partnership where they can bring their brains to work and make decisions.

Then finally, they want affirmation. They not only want to be caught doing things right, but they want to be affirmed for who they are. They want to be known as a person, not as a number.

So those are the three ingredients this effective manager in the story uses. They are wonderful values if you think of them. Rank order values for any organization is number one: integrity. In our company we call it "ethics"—our number one value. Number two value is partnership. Partnership in our companies is relationships. Number three is affirmation—being affirmed as a human being. I think that ties into relationships, too. They are wonderful values that can drive behavior in a great way.

Wright

I believe most people in today's business culture would agree that success in business has everything to do with successful leadership. In *The Leadership Pill*, you present a simple but profound premise that being in leadership is not something you do *to* people; it's something you do *with* them. At face value, that seems incredibly obvious, but you must have found in your research and in your observations that leaders in today's culture do not get this. Would you speak to that issue?

Blanchard

Yes. I think what often happens is this is the human ego, you know. There are too many leaders out there who are self-serving. They're not serving leaders. They think the sheep are there for the benefit of the shepherd. All the power, money, and famous recognition all reside at the top of the hierarchy. They forget that the real action in business is not at the top, it's in the one-to-one, moment-to-moment interactions your front line people have with your customers, it's how the phone was answered, how problems are dealt with, and those kinds of things. If you don't think you're doing leadership *with* them, rather than *to* them, after a while they won't take care of your customers.

I was at a store recently, it's not Nordstrom's, where I normally would go, and I thought of something I had to share with my wife, Margie. I asked the guy behind the counter in the Men's Wear Department, "Can I use your phone?"

He said, "No," rather emphatically.

I said, "You're kidding me. I can always use the phone at Nordstrom's."

He said, "Look, buddy, they won't let *me* use the phone here, why should I let *you* use the phone?"

That is an example of leadership that's done to them not with them. People want a partnership. People want to be involved in a way that really makes a difference.

Wright

Dr. Blanchard, the time has flown by and there are so many more questions I'd like to ask you. In conclusion, would you mind sharing with our readers some closing thoughts on success? If you were mentoring a small group of men and women, and one of their central goals was to become successful, what kind of advice would you give them?

Blanchard

I would first of all ask, "What are you focused on?" As I said earlier, I think if you are focused on success as being accumulation of money, recognition, power, or status, I think you've got the wrong target.

What you need to really be focused on is how can you be generous in the use of your time, your talent, your treasure, and touch. How can you serve people rather than be served? How can you develop caring, loving relationships with people? My sense is if you will focus on those things, success in the traditional sense will come to you. But if you go out and say, "Man, I'm going to make a fortune, and I'm going to do this," whatever it may be and if you focus on those kinds of things, you might even get some of those numbers. You become an adult, however, when you realize you are here to give rather than to get. You're here to serve not to be served. I would just say to people, "Life is such a very special occasion. Don't miss it by aiming at a target that bypasses other people, because we're really here to serve each other." That's what I would share with people.

Wright

Well, what an enlightening conversation, Dr. Blanchard. I really want you to know how much I appreciate all the time you've taken with me for this interview. I know that our readers will learn from this, and I really appreciate your being with us today.

Blanchard

Well, thank you so much, David. I really enjoyed my time with you. You've asked some great questions that made me think. I hope my answers are helpful to other people because, as I say, life is a special occasion.

Wright

Today we have been talking with Dr. Ken Blanchard. He is author of the phenomenal best selling book, *The One Minute Manager*. The fact that he's the "Chief Spiritual Officer" of his company should give us all cause to think about how we are leading our companies and leading our families and leading anything whether it is within church or civic organizations. I know I will.

Thank you so much, Dr. Blanchard, for being with us today on *Masters of Success*.

Blanchard

Good to be with you, David.

About Dr. Ken Blanchard

Few people have created more of a positive impact on the day-to-day management of people and companies than Dr. Kenneth Blanchard, who is known around the world simply as "Ken." When Ken speaks, he speaks from the heart with warmth and humor. His unique gift is to speak to an audience and communicate with each individual as if they were alone and talking one-on-one. He is a polished storyteller with a knack for making the seemingly complex easy to understand. Ken has been a guest on a number of national television programs, including *Good Morning America and The Today Show,* and has been featured in *Time, People, U.S. News & World Report,* and a host of other popular publications. He earned his bachelor's degree in government and philosophy from Cornell University, his master's degree in sociology and counseling from Colgate University, and his Ph.D. in educational administration and leadership from Cornell University.

Dr. Ken Blanchard

The Ken Blanchard Companies

125 State Place

Escondido, California 92029

Phone: 800.728.6000

Fax: 760.489.8407

www.blanchardtraining.com

Chapter Three

ED KUGLER

THE INTERVIEW

David Wright (Wright)
Today we are talking with Ed Kugler. Ed is a successful change leader whose work involves both personal and organizational change. The CEO of a $500 million company once named Ed the Senior Vice President of Truth. He is a former Fortune 50 executive, U.S. Marine sniper, and a guy who has never stopped learning from his unique life experiences. He climbed the corporate ladder after his two years in the Vietnam War starting as a mechanic, then truck driver and then, without a college degree, he rose to be a worldwide Vice President for Compaq Computer. He is the author of *Dead Center—A Marine Sniper's Two-Year Odyssey in the Vietnam War* as well as his first novel, *The Well House—A Story of Love, Peace, War and Forever*. Ed is President and OEO (Only Executive Officer, so named by his wife), of his own company and is a popular inspirational speaker who helps people and organizations make real changes that matter.

Ed, welcome to our program this morning.

Ed Kugler (Kugler)
Thank you, I'm glad to be here.

Wright

You have a unique background; will you tell us about being named Senior Vice President of Truth?

Kugler

I sure can. I signed on to help a $500 million dollar tech company. The CEO hired me on a one-year contract to be the Vice President of Distribution. Then he went overseas on a visit to his branches and was there for the next three weeks. His orders were that while he was gone I should come up with a plan of what we should do with distribution.

I spent the next three weeks with people all over the company and came to the realization that they did not need a VP of Distribution. They built everything to order and shipped Fed Ex and UPS, why would they need a VP of Distribution? So when the CEO returned on Monday I sat down with him and explained to him what I found. I said, "Truth is, you don't need a VP of Distribution. I'm not sure why you hired me."

He sat there for a minute then looked up and said, "You know what? I'm going to have a sales meeting in Cleveland and you're going to get on the plane with me tomorrow morning and go up there with me."

I met him at the airport at zero dark early and we flew to Cleveland from Houston without a word on my being the unneeded VP of Distribution. The limo picks us up and whisks us off to the meeting. We go in and he introduces me to seventy-five salesmen as his new Senior Vice President of Truth. He said, "This guy had the guts to tell me the truth that I didn't need a VP of Distribution. But, by God, I *do* need people with the guts to tell me the truth." So I became his right hand man for a year and coached him through a lot of problems.

Wright

That's pretty interesting. Telling the truth is certainly the foundation of what you do today. You say your philosophy is *"NoMore*BS." Can you explain to our readers where that philosophy came from?

Kugler

I sure can. The origin of *NoMore*BS started in Vietnam but didn't crystallize for me for a few years. The experience that was literally burned into my soul came from an event I document in my book *Dead Center*. I was a young nineteen-year-old Marine sniper going on a night operation with a couple of companies of Marine grunts—infantry. We were going down to a difficult area in Quang Tri Province known by the French as the "Street Without Joy." The Marine grunts at that time carried the M-14 rifle and were experts in assembling, disassembling, and fixing it if necessary. I might also add the M-14 was a proven commodity and worked in all conditions.

That afternoon, a couple of hours before we were to take off, the higher ups were forced—history has shown—by McNamara and his "Whiz Kids," to roll out the new M-16 to the troops on a very aggressive timetable. There was a lot of political debate about the weapon and its readiness to see combat and there has been a lot written about this since then, especially in the last fifteen years, but the fact is it wasn't ready for combat. Not only was the weapon not ready, but they took Marines who were highly trained and familiar with the M-14, stripped it from them, gave them two hours of training and practice, and wished them well. As they say, "the rest is history." We were ambushed about midnight and fought all night, were overrun for a period of time, and when daylight took over it was quite a sight.

As the choppers came in for the wounded, some others and I had the task of gathering up the dead and putting them in body bags for the ride home to their loved ones. As I recall, and as I said, this story is described in more detail in *Dead Center*. We put some thirty-five dead Marines in body bags and more than half of them had their M-16s apart in their hands. The piece-of-crap weapon that was forced down our throats didn't work. That was the case for many years throughout Vietnam, all because of faulty leadership and politics.

I've seen the exact same thing repeated throughout my business career. It's just that in business these decisions don't kill people they just kill your career and mess your up your family as they make transition after transition, change upon change, often for no other reason than the whim of a so-called leader. As I saw more and more of this type of thing, it all came together into what I now call *NoMore*BS. Over the years this concept has crystallized into a workable formula for success. It starts with looking in the mirror and being honest about who we really are and where we really are.

Wright

How do CEOs and business leaders respond to a message like that?

Kugler

The answer is indicative of the problem—the higher you get in the organization, the less they respond to it. Hierarchy in most organizations today consists of nothing more than a "good ole boys club" where "you take care of me and I take care of you."

When I speak to an organization I become a folk hero with middle management and down. They agree and tell me I am absolutely right. But my calculation is if we did a Pareto[1] on it only about probably twenty percent of the leaders will really embrace that message. I had a CEO I did a turn-around for who actually hired me because of my *NoMoreBS* philosophy. He was pumped after reading my website and handed me the keys to his biggest operation. He supported me out of the blocks and it was a sweet deal. I thought maybe I had a guy who really did "get it." We accomplished all that we agreed to for the particular part of his business he brought me in to fix and even got the Teamsters out of his organization. We did this all in ten months.

We'd made remarkable changes by going in the trenches and working with the people and letting them do it. But when I sat down with him—the CEO who hired me—looked him in the eye and told him to sustain it and go to the next level, he said he would have to address some serious problems with his headquarters support people who sat next to him and fed him BS all day; that those were "sacred cows" and he wasn't about to address it.

The problem he had was that his problems were always "out there," therefore that very thought was a problem. I looked him in the eye and told him he was the major part of the problem. He doesn't even speak to me today because I confronted him. He leads a company with more than fifty weeks of inventory in a business that should have maybe twelve but he is the only one who can be right. So, a year from now he'll either have more consultants in to fix the results of his lack of seeing the problem clearly or he'll be out—the company may go under and who pays the price? The people in the organization will pay the price for these leadership charades. The people who are just trying to make a living and raise their families will pay the price.

---

[1] In 1906, Italian economist Vilfredo Pareto created a mathematical formula to describe the unequal distribution of wealth in his country, observing that twenty percent of the people owned eighty percent of the wealth.

Leadership today is a tragedy just like back in Vietnam and the leaders rarely pay the price of their debacles. Leaders today rarely want to hear the truth in spite of their insistence on their being open and approachable.

Wright

What's the answer for people out there who want to be successful?

Kugler

There are two parts to the answer. If you are a leader, then you need to seek and receive feedback. Today I think people as a whole are forced into what I call "situational truth-telling." With the leadership we currently have in most organizations people end up telling leaders what they want to hear. I was turning around the debacle of a change project at Pepsi a few years back and we had a disaster regarding a hand-held computer rollout. When asked how this could happen, the guy sitting in the corner on the floor—he was a coder—said, "It's simple—pain avoidance." I think that said it all. I think about eighty percent of the people fall in that category because they are forced there. I think about ten percent of the people like me will tell you how they see it and another ten percent are liars "just because," I guess.

A leader's job is to create an environment where you move that ten percent of truth-tellers to forty or fifty percent or more. Leaders create a "safe" environment where it is okay to tell the truth. I teach this and more as part of my change skills in a workshop entitled "How to Lead Your Organization for a Change." We all need to learn this stuff. It's not complicated and certainly not rocket science but it is hard to do every day because it is so foreign to most people, especially today's leaders. This phenomenon is why the "Enrons" and "WorldComs" happen. Look at all the people and families impacted by this incredible lack of leadership. So, leaders in such a position have to create safe environments in their organizations.

Now the second part of the problem: When you're not the leader but you work in one of these places it's a much tougher challenge.

I think we have to start by having integrity. In the outside world of government we must start by holding our leaders accountable by our votes and our letters and our e-mails. Let's bring down the servers with our e-mails to these folks who are up there taking care of everyone else but us. People need to read about what's happening and be informed, not just in politics and government, but to study what happened in situations like Enron. Understand for yourself the pain these leaders caused to the many, many people involved. I don't know if we'll ever fully understand it but we can try. Then and only then will we start gaining the courage to do what's right and speak up.

It's been said that all we need for evil to conquer is for good men and women to remain silent. I saw this phenomenon first-hand at Compaq. It's one of the reasons I walked out after just three years. I surprised my wife by leaving when I did. She knew I worked my whole life with the goal of making it to the senior level of a Fortune 50 and achieve this with no college degree. But when I got there—to that level—it was disgusting and disheartening to say the least. It really was a good ole boys club and what mattered most was keeping the peace with your peers, sucking up to those above you, and making the numbers every quarter. That was it! And it was a driven by stock options and the perceived opportunity to become rich. I saw good people—people in my church and good citizens—turn their heads with the admonition, "Ed come on, can't you be quiet about these things until our options vest, then we won't care anymore?" It's happening across America for sure, every day. I think that, until we as individuals make a decision to live our lives with real integrity, not situational integrity, we are going to see this get worse.

I had a speech out here in Montana the other day and got into a discussion about leadership; of course, politics came up. I find that people are sick of the Democrats *and* the Republicans because neither one will stand up and vote for *us*—the people who elected them. They vote straight party line to keep the peace which just serves the "good ole boys club" I have been describing. I think we have to tap into our passion on this one. We have to stand up and be counted and do what Gandhi says and, "Be the change we wish to see in the world." We have to stop the BS and make a stand if we are to change this mess. I am a former alcoholic and, quite frankly until I looked in the mirror and said I'm a drunk, I was not able to overcome that. In the same way we can't change things we do not acknowledge. I think as individuals we have to be accountable to ourselves to see we live that way and then maybe other people will see it and then they will do the same which will grow a better tomorrow in our world.

Wright

I see what you mean and it is difficult today. What can the average worker both male and female do out there with your philosophy?

Kugler

First they have to decide what they want out of life. It all begins with us as individuals—we can't change anyone else. I can't change my spouse, I can't change anybody but I *can* be an example of change. Quoting Gandhi again, he said, "Be the change you want to see in the world." The problem is, so many of us go around pointing to all the problems out there: Our boss should do this or our spouse should do that and the government is the problem. Those thoughts are the problem. We have to work within our own circles of influence and take personal responsibility for a change. It all starts when we stop the BS and be honest with ourselves. Make a decision to be a person of integrity. Be a person others look up to—who is a leader. We all have to start by leading our own lives.

Leaders have followers. People follow you because you engage their whole person. You engage their head, their heart, and their hands. I teach this in detail in my workshop. It is normal for organizations today to engage people's heads—their knowledge, and their hands—their skills; but engaging their heart is a rarity today. You can hire these first two traits but you must inspire their hearts to get to their real passion.

To make a difference today, men and women need to tap into their own hearts, their own passions, and demand more from their leaders by becoming people of integrity.

Wright

If one is to become successful, it would seem to me that they would have to define success to know whether or not they achieved what they set out to do.

Kugler

You're right David, success means different things do different people.

Wright

Could you share with our readers how you define success?

Kugler

To me "success" is reaching whatever goals you set for yourself, provided those goals are for the good of the whole. I like to look at things from the standpoint that may sound corny—the Three Musketeers. Their motto was, "All for one and one for all." I think success has to be for the good of the whole—it isn't singular. I try to teach my kids, telling them, "I don't care if you become a carpenter or whether you become a doctor. I just want you to become a productive member of society where you're giving back and treating people with love." Success to me is not only a destination—it is also a journey. None of us know how long we have left on this earth. We're all terminal. We need to live every day as if it's our last and still plan like we'll live forever.

Wright

What steps do you recommend for people who have goals and dreams and want to reach them as you have?

Kugler

For me there are just a couple of steps and then a lot of commitment, resilience, and work. It all starts by figuring out what problem you're trying to solve. What journey are you heading out on and why? Do you want to get married, be president, or lose weight? Decide where you want to go and then make sure you are solving the right problem.

Then you decide what success will look like. That means defining in detail what your vision is of your new tomorrow. When you've done that then you must be honest—*NoMore*BS again about where you are. Then and only then do you know how far the gap is—the leap—between today and tomorrow. If you're trying to lose ten pounds, that may be relatively easy but one hundred pounds will be much more difficult.

There were a lot of things I wanted out of life but when I drank as I used to, you can imagine I didn't have a lot of focus. In that condition I wasn't going anywhere but I was sure going fast. My first step was deciding I had to be different. My second step was deciding how I wanted to be and then where I was today—a drunk—then I could make a start on reaching my goal. I had a starting off point. When you know how far the gap from today to tomorrow is, you begin to see what it's going to take to cross that chasm. Then you have to figure out the pain and the cost of making the change. What is it going to take to reach your level of success and are you willing to pay the price?

One of the problems today—and it includes the person looking back in the mirror at you—is "the people won't pay the price if they can't see the promise." A mentor of mine, Jim Rohn, taught me this through his books and tapes years ago and I have never forgotten it. We must decide the price is worth it and *then* we'll have the commitment to make it.

A great example of change comes from one of my former snipers. He is a guy who was actually raised in Hells Angels, I wrote about him in *Dead Center*. He came home from Vietnam and spent years riding with them without going through all that was involved in a lifestyle that was going to get him killed. Yet today he lives on a ranch in Texas with his Christian wife (his fourth wife but they've been married for more than seventeen years), he raises expensive horses, and has a cement contracting business.

How did he get there? He decided he wanted something better in life, inspired, he says, by the example of his brother Marine sniper— he wanted a stable life. He made a decision about what he wanted, broke free of the Hells Angels, met his current wife, married and started a business. He realized new friends would be required. His wife liked horses so he got involved in order to meet new folks. He realized the price for him would not just be new friends but a complete break with the past. They moved across the country. He somehow knew he'd have to break from the old ways and establish new ones. He is doing great today and I am confident the changes he made will take him to even greater success. He is an unlikely success story such as others you'd read about in my book. He was quite a character but he defined a better tomorrow for himself and went out and got it.

Wright

What does "defining what success looks like" mean to you?

Kugler

I just talked from a personal point of view. Let me answer this from an organizational point of view. When I engage in a consulting project there are two questions I must answer to be successful. The first is "what problem are you trying to solve?" and the second is what you just asked, "what will success look like" when I solve it?

I can best answer this with a story from one engagement I experienced. An international client once flew me to Mexico to help change the logistics organization of their six billion dollar company. It was a two-day gig to simply meet and assess if there was a match before signing on. We spent the first day and a half watching dog and pony shows of what was happening and what everyone was doing and how this business was different than all the others I had seen. The VP who invited me was becoming frustrated with my questions. I was asking questions like, "What problem are you trying to solve and what will success look like when we do?" He was coming back each time with a very emphatic, "I want to fundamentally change the way we do logistics." He kept asking me if I could do for him what I had done for Compaq. I really didn't know since I didn't know what specific problem he was trying to solve and therefore couldn't define what success looked like.

I finally said to him, "If I figure out how to deliver this cement with helicopters it would fundamentally change the way you did logistics but 'so what?' "

That got his attention. He was about to throw me out when I asked, "What will you get fired for?"

That question brought a fiery, "If I don't take two dollars a ton out of our costs I will be fired!" His fist thundered to the table.

I was then able to say, "That is the problem you are trying to solve and what success will look like."

I didn't get the business but that was okay. Defining success is painting a vivid picture of the results your change will bring about; it is painting a picture that will make people want to cross the chasm of change and pay the price we talked about before.

Wright

So, once we know where we want to go, what do we do next?

Kugler

When we know where we're headed we first look in the mirror so we know where we are starting the journey. Then we make a commitment by breaking with the past and committing to the journey— that's the price we pay. Then we decide the action steps that it will take—what steps we must take to get where we are headed. The key here is breaking old habits and making new ones. It is about behavior change one decision at a time. Your changes will come down to this simple concept: *What we do every day is what we believe; all the rest is just talk.* This is where you have to realize "if it is to be it's up to me." There are no magic pills or someone to do it for you. To change, you gotta' change.

Wright

You said an interesting thing, "What we do every day is what we believe, all the rest is just talk." Will you explain that to us?

Kugler

I sure can. It really comes to the forefront at church. I happen to be a Christian and that was a major change—I was once an atheist. This statement "what you do every day is what you believe, all the rest is just talk" makes you confront your own behavior and beliefs. In the Christian sense it makes you confront your Christianity. It also encompasses my philosophy of *NoMore*BS. Think of it this way: You go to church on Sunday and have your "church face" on. We all do, and then you have to go back out in the world and either behave as you have committed to behave by your words and actions and have been taught, or you behave the way whatever is inside of you comes out. It is about "words and deeds"—do they match? So when I say "what we do every day," I mean our actions. When I say "what we do every day is what we believe," I mean our actions reflect what we really believe, not what we say.

When you put it all together it reads, "What you do every day is what you believe, all the rest is just talk," and it means that our actions are what people really believe because our actions reflect our true nature. So our words—what we say—must match our deeds— what we do—or we don't have integrity. This is always important but more so during times of change. People won't follow leaders across the difficult chasm of change—through all the whitewater—unless they are people of integrity.

Wright

What changes have you endured or perhaps made in your life that might be of value to others?

Kugler

The first major change was in Marine Corp boot camp, Parris Island. Essentially four women raised me. I did have a father and a mother, as they say a "nuclear family," back in the fifties and sixties. I graduated high school in the early sixties. My father was a truck driver who then started a business from that and I really didn't see much of him at all. I had a grandmother on his side who lived with us and a sister and an aunt, and of course Mom. They'd call it a dysfunctional family today but I really didn't know that at the time. So I was raised by these four great women who, I found out later, hadn't adequately prepared me for Parris Island.

Wright

Right. I had the same problem—I know exactly what you're talking about.

Kugler

When I hit boot camp I found out I was no longer allowed to eat just whatever I wanted—I got a rude awakening—literally. I tell about this quite honestly in the beginning of *Dead Center*. I never realized this until later; I had never really had to do much of anything in my life and wasn't ready for being a Marine although had I wanted to be one since fifth grade. I disobeyed an order, got locked up, ran away and a mean old grizzled drill instructor changed my life. When I ran away I was gone for three days without food and I hid in the swamp. Eventually the MP's picked me up and I was, quite frankly, a mess. I had scorpion bites—you name it. But this tough World War II Marine, who I thought was going to beat the crap out of me (and he did slap me around a little bit), took me in his office, looked me square in the eyes and said, "Kid, if you can do what you just did and not eat for three days and hang out there in the swamp like you have, the rest of this is easy; because you have to understand it's all in your head."

I made a significant change right at that point, on the spot. That was the first time I felt like someone cared. He believed in me and in what I could do. He treated me as an equal. I changed and left knowing that the battle in life is between my ears.

The second major change I experienced was facing my own alcoholism. My wife was a saint and worked with me for over five years. Then one day she had just had it with me and made it plain, "It's me or the drinking." It was only then, faced with a crisis, that I could get up the courage to look in the mirror and begin the change.

It was also during these two events that I learned significant change happens around events like marriage, birth, death, and crisis. People and organizations change eighty percent of the time around events and crisis or catastrophe.

The third significant event was going from atheist to Christian. That's a bit of a long story and I am not here to preach religion but it was a significant change for me. It impacted the quality of the rest of my life. It was then I began to understand that change also comes from inspiration. I reasoned that change happens for one of two reasons: inspiration or desperation. People change as a result of either the pursuit of opportunity, inspiration, or from reaction to events, desperation, crisis, or catastrophe. I also realized there is no such thing as organizational change; there is only people change, because organizations are simply groups of people together for a common purpose.

We as human beings are blessed with the power of choice. That is the one thing that separates man from animal—power of choice. We have to be honest with ourselves and make choices that will take us to where we want to be. The key to your better future is you. It's not the government, it's not your wife, it's not your boss—it's you. We all need support but if we're going to be successful and going to do anything special we need to make good choices. We must choose to be all we can be and change for the better—it is life's way. Look around at nature for our living example. Mankind is the only living thing that can choose to be less than they were designed to be. It is the power of choice and it works both ways.

Wright

I understand that people must change but is there one key to changing an organization?

Kugler

Actually there is and that key is the same key to changing ourselves—leadership. To change ourselves, each of us must be a leader of ourselves. We must be able to overcome our own habits, and overcome our negative feelings and practices, and build new ones reflecting our future. We must lead ourselves. In changing organizations the person who is highest and in charge of the part of the organization being targeted for change must provide the unwavering leadership necessary to drive the change. That lead individual is the single biggest key to change. They must decide the problem they are solving, what success will look like, assess the gap, and understand and feel the pain the change will wreak upon the organization. Then and only then are they ready to make the decision to act.

Part of that decision must be that when their best "Lieutenant" stands in the way of the change, after all due diligence to get them on board, they will fire that person for the sake of the change. If they are unwilling to do that or face it by saying it won't happen then they shouldn't go forward with the change in the first place.

Leadership is the key to success in driving change whether it is personal or organizational. I have seen this play out time and again. That's why more than eighty percent of change projects fail. I saw it when I was at Pepsi. We had a great CEO who tried a colossal change project involving top consultants and a few hundred million dollars. It all went up in smoke because the so-called leaders surrounding him told him what he wanted to hear and ran the organization the way it had always been run, and the change died. It was a shame. It's about the leadership. While people believed in the CEO, the leaders under him did not have a safe environment and people wouldn't come forward and tell the truth.

Wright

When I can consider your unique background and all the successes I'm aware of in your life today, I'm really interested in what your goals are at this point and what this unique journey you've been on has meant to you.

Kugler

It really means everything. It started with a great wife who was looking to marry anyone but someone like me. I've learned along the way that things happen for a reason and people come into our life for a reason; it's just a question of whether we will recognize the opportunity or not. In this case I did and convinced her to marry me. To marry her I had to agree to work, which I had no intention of doing but figured I'd better if I was going to have a life with her. She was dating a guy going to MIT and I convinced her that while I had no idea what I was going to be doing it would be a lot more fun than being married to an MIT grad.

Wright

In another words you're a smooth talker.

Kugler

Apparently. But as I look back now after a lifetime of changes it was well worth it. I've been married for over thirty-six years to the same woman! I have three great kids and currently have two grandkids with more on the way. Family is what I am most proud of.

I have been blessed with an array of interesting experiences. My story includes life growing up in a town of seventy-five, being a Marine sniper, a small business owner, race track owner, mechanic, truck driver, several corporate jobs, and being a VP of the fastest growing company in the world at the time. I've been lucky in that respect and I've been blessed to have a wife who coached me to learn from all of them. I didn't have the advantage of a college education but I read a book a week and never stopped learning.

I have much more I want to do at this point in my life. My passion is helping people. My passion is writing and speaking and making a difference. I now am fulfilled helping people and organizations make real change that matters.

To make the real change that matters in this life requires leadership. We must lead ourselves and our organizations whether they are large or small. To do that requires starting with yourself—looking in the mirror and admitting where you are is a prerequisite to getting where you want to go. I want to help as many people as I can stop the BS in their lives and others' lives so they can move forward and prevent some of the personal disasters like the M-16 deaths and floundering change projects that disrupt careers and families throughout our working world.

I don't know what impact I can have but I get pumped up trying. I grew up on the wrong side of the tracks, disenfranchised from the mainstream, and I want to give a voice to those folks who don't have college degrees and who don't necessarily march to the same drummer the masses march to. We need to be about inclusion not exclusion. When I lived in Houston they were building entire developments with big brick walls around them that were filled with kids pressured into honors classes and cheerleading schools. What in the world is this all about but BS? I am for less BS and making a difference during the rest of my life's journey. I am in the business of hope—hope for a better tomorrow.

Wright

What an interesting conversation, Ed, it's always great to talk with you, but more than anything, I'm awed by all of your experiences and the way you have been able to use them later on in life.

Today we have been talking with Ed Kugler, who is a former mechanic, truck driver, small business owner, corporate executive, Marine sniper, and a guy who has never stopped learning, as we have found out today from his unique experiences. He's the President and OEO (Only Executive Officer) in his own company. He's also a popular inspirational speaker who helps people and organizations make real change that, in the final analysis, matters.

Ed, thank you so much for being with us today.

Kugler
Thank you. It's always my pleasure.

About Ed Kugler

Ed Kugler is one of America's leading change agents. A former Marine Sniper with two tours in the Vietnam War, he worked for Pepsi and Frito Lay, and climbed the corporate ladder to become VP—Worldwide Logistics for Compaq Computer. He is the author of four books. Today he runs his own company from his home in Big Arm, Montana. He is married (thirty-six years and counting—to the same woman) and has three children and two grandchildren.

Ed Kugler

PO Box 190

Big Arm, MT 59910-0190

Phone: 866.725.5506

Fax: 866.422.2895

Email: edkugler@nomorebs.com

www.nomorebs.com

www.edkugler.com

Chapter Four

Mel H. Abraham, CPA, CVA, ABV, ASA

THE INTERVIEW

David Wright (Wright)

Today we are talking with Mel H. Abraham. Mel is a highly sought after expert. He's a CPA, and a very successful entrepreneur, with multiple business endeavors. Regularly called upon as a forensic expert in financial and valuation issues, he is also a nationally recognized and award winning speaker. Mel's two-fold forte is in providing strategies for financial risk management and personal physical threat management and self-protection.

In the personal protection and financial realm, he is the creator of the much in demand presentation, *Bulletproof Boundaries ™, Safety and Success Strategies for an Unsafe World.* He has received numerous speaking awards and authored numerous books and articles. His authoritative book *Valuation Issues and Case Law Update,* a reference guide, has just been released in a fifth edition. Recently he was co-author of the business valuation industry's best selling book, *Financial Valuation Applications and Models,* released by John Wiley and Sons Inc. Two additional books will be released by mid 2005, *A Healthier You,* with Deepak Chopra and Billy Blanks, and *Valuing Family Limited Partnerships.*

He combines his background as a forensic accountant, business valuation expert and entrepreneur with his experience as a consultant to law enforcement agencies, corporations, and individuals. He brings extensive experience that marries personal safety, protection, and violence avoidance with corporate fraud, identity theft, embezzlement, and other financial crimes.

Mel's unique background gives him the perspective to understand the underlying causes and predictors of the threats that put your person, property and business at risk.

Mel, welcome to *Masters of Success*.

Mel H. Abraham (Abraham)

Thank you for having me.

Wright

What is Bulletproof Boundaries ™?

Abraham

It's a program that I developed based on my years of experience working as a consultant, an entrepreneur, and as a forensic CPA. It is meant to focus on various systems and strategies to assist individuals, business, families in their creation, retention and protection of their wealth and person as they live their lives. *Bulletproof Boundaries™*, is a risk awareness and management system that results a far greater protection of your physical self, including financial, business, and corporate wealth from the numerous, numerous risks that permeate our society today.

Wright

Why is this so important to our success?

Abraham

Consider this: never before have we lived in a time where there are so many adversarial forces that threaten our everyday existence. They range from identity theft, and Internet scams, to corporate corruption, and property crimes. Our financial and personal security is constantly at risk. When you see the statistics and the magnitude of the occurrences of crimes such as these you will see that typically a U.S. organization loses up to six percent of its annual revenue to fraud each year. When you compare that six percent to the gross domestic product for 2003 that's in excess of six hundred billion dollars in losses in a year. The median loss for most organizations is fifty-six thousand dollars a year and for other small businesses it can exceed one hundred thousand dollars a year.

Wright
Unbelievable. You state that all occupational fraud schemes have four key elements in common. Would you share those elements with our readers?

Abraham
Yes. Let's first define occupational fraud. Occupational fraud is defined as the use of one's occupation for personal enrichment through the deliberate misuse or misapplication of an organization's resources or assets. In other words, it is based on taking advantage of the relationship between an individual and an organization. The four elements that are typically associated with this type of fraud are:

1. It's clandestine in a sense that it's secretive and cloaked,
2. It violates the perpetrator's (the person who's committing the crime) fiduciary duty to the organization. So the individual is taking advantage of the relationship of the organization,
3. It is a fraud committed for the purpose of direct or indirect financial benefit of the perpetrator themselves, and
4. It typically costs the organization either revenues, assets, or some sort of reserves.

Wright
You also say that all occupational frauds fall into one of three major categories. So how would we define those?

Abraham
There are three primary categories that we typically see:
- asset misappropriation,
- corruption, and
- fraudulent statements.

Let's look at those for a moment. Misappropriations typically involve the theft or misuse of an organization's assets. The crimes that will fall under this category include skimming of revenues, stealing inventory, or payroll fraud.

Corruption is the wrongful use of influence in a business transaction to achieve some sort of benefit for the perpetrator or someone else. It's typically contrary to their fiduciary duty to the employer or the rights of some other party. A typical crime such as this would include kick-backs, or those types of situations that we have been seeing a lot of in the press lately—conflicts of interest.

Fraudulent statements typically involve the falsification of financial statements by over-statingrevenue, or understating liabilities or expenses, depending on what the desired result or goal is. Once again, we as a society have experienced an increasing occurrence of these types of events and the resulting shareholder lawsuits. As a society, we have entered into an era where, because of events like WorldCom, Enron and even Krispy Kreme, we have cause to reconsider the credibility and dependability of the very pillars of our economy. The financial reporting mechanism has failed miserably in providing the needed comfort levels from an investing publics view.

Wright

What other types of risks are you talking about?

Abraham

There are other risks that impact us as individuals, as family members, as a society, and as businesses. They range from check fraud, to credit card fraud, to identity theft, as well as other types of frauds, crimes, or scams. Fraudulent insurance claims come into play here, so there are a whole variety of different types of fraud or theft that are committed on a regular and daily basis.

Wright

These things really happen then?

Abraham

Actually the statistics are staggering. It's mind boggling to realize how much of this is going on around us without us realizing it. For instance, take a look at check fraud. The Office of the Comptroller of the Currency estimates that more than 1.2 million fraudulent checks are written every day. Break that down and that's thirteen fraudulent checks written per second of every day. And the losses are going to exceed twenty billion dollars. Then there is identity theft for instance, which is probably the fastest growing crime that we're facing today. *The Wall Street Journal* recently reported that 700,000 Americans have been victims of identity theft and that has an accumulated cost of five billion dollars. Now that is a small cost when compared to check fraud, but identity theft is growing extremely fast.

What many don't realize is how far reaching the impact of identity theft can be, both from a financial perspective and a psychological perspective.

I myself was victimized just this past year. Someone had fraudulently changed the addresses on my credit cards. It is not clear as of yet how it came about, but because of the strategies of Bulletproof Boundaries™ we were able to catch it before any damage was done. We caught it, we shut it down and there was no financial loss, but there was still time involved. Some estimates say that the typical victim of identity theft can assume that it will take upwards of two hundred hours of time to reverse all of the problems caused by an identity theft. I have known some instances where it took almost four years to unravel the loss of their identity

One of the oldest crimes that is still going strong today is embezzlement. For the past twenty-five years KPMG, an international accounting firm, has prepared an annual survey of companies around the United States that asked them to rank the crimes that hurt the company the most both internally and externally. They didn't ask about the dollars that were lost, but just the ranking of the crimes. Since the survey began twenty-five years ago, embezzlement has ranked number one among all these companies. Check fraud, incidentally, didn't make the list until about ten years ago, when it ranked ninth. To give you an idea of how fast it is moving, ten years ago it ranked ninth, today check fraud ranks number two, right behind embezzlement.

The last category would be counterfeiting. Counterfeiting corporate checks is something that has existed since the beginning of time, it seems. And now with all of the technology that exists today with desktop publishing, color printers, digitized printing and color copiers, it is far easier to replicate checks than it was in the past. We can purchase blank check stock on the Internet. Using these other technological tools, we can replicate payroll checks, accounts payable checks, refund checks, cashier checks—there's a variety of ways to do it that didn't exist years ago.

Wright
What does Bulletproof Boundaries™ entail?

Abraham

It is a system, process, and mindset that is meant to raise the level of awareness of the various threats to our person and family as well as to our business and wealth.

Focusing on the financial and business segment (there is a separate program for the personal and family protection segment), we look at a variety of factors and elements. On a very basic level it entails a number of objectives with a much more detailed set of strategies and tasks underneath each objective. We will only discuss the objective at a broad level here.

Much like any risk, the first step in eliminating it is to gain an acknowledgement that you, your business, and your family are exposed to financial crimes. Unfortunately, too many of us try to go through life sitting back thinking that, "it's not going to happen to me, it'll happen to my neighbor," or, "it'll happen down the street, it'll happen in the next town, but not to me." Regrettably, this is happening all over the place, in all types of communities, by all types of people and through all types of means. It truly does not matter where you live, what you do, or how you do it, *everyone* has exposure. The sooner we accept this exposure and accept the responsibility to eradicate it, the sooner we will find ourselves living a life of abundance that has a veil of protection and confidence because we have taken precautions and are not susceptible to these crimes.

The second step is to understand and establish a level of financial literacy and understanding of financial matters, to understand what the impact is, and how to control and identify these things.

The third step is to set a plan in place—a control mechanism—to achieve better financial literacy, wealth, and growth.

And then lastly, if we're going to achieve the wealth and the growth and literacy in the process we need to set up the protective boundaries, the *Bulletproof Boundaries™* to try and protect those. So we don't take on undue risk, and we don't have these risks impacting us on a regular basis.

Wright

What do you mean when you say financial literacy?

Abraham

Too often we look at the accumulation of wealth, as a destination instead of more like a journey. It includes an understanding of all the choices that we make at different stages of our life cycle—even as a child—understanding the value of money and understanding how it works.

When my son was in fifth grade, the teacher put together a program, she called the "Betty Boop Box." Each student had a Betty Boop checkbook and, depending on how they did in class or how they did on the test, they got paid in Betty Boop bucks. They would then make a deposit in their Betty Boop checkbook. Once a week they could go to the "store" and buy candy or something for themselves. The purpose of the program was to teach them, in a fun way, the process of earning, the process of spending, the process of budgeting, and the importance of controlling it and how it can impact one's future. Our kids should start to understand these elements at a younger age. They need to know what money management and wealth savings is as they start into their higher school years and go on to college.

When people have completed school they need to have the ability to manage and plan for the other stages of their lives as they begin looking to a profession, marriage, a family, retirement, and putting their kids through school. If people wait until they are ready to enter the workforce it is too late because too many erroneous perceptions and bad ideas have become engrained. All of this takes planning, goal setting, task setting, and timelines, as well as a process to revaluate the whole plan on a regular basis.

Remember, "If you fail to plan you plan to fail." This has never been so true than in the financial realm and business realm. Consequently, if you achieve success or achieve wealth and growth financially, without a plan it is purely coincidence or luck, and coincidence and luck are fleeting.

Wright

How big a problem is the lack of financial literacy?

Abraham

For the kind of nation that the United States is as a world power and a world financial center, I think it's a huge problem if you look at the statistics. Recent statistics show that forty-four percent of Americans live above their means and sixty percent of them carry debt in excess of $4000 each month. In 2003 alone, 1.6 million Americans filed for bankruptcy, which is the highest in history. Four out of five business start-ups fail within the first five years.

There was a national survey, in 2002 on high school student seniors' financial knowledge. The high school seniors scored an average of 50.2 percent. We are doing a disservice to our children in allowing them to graduate high school with little to no financial literacy. The problem permeates society as they get into college, and all of a sudden they obtain credit card offers from credit card companies. They think it's found money and start start spending it. The whole vicious cycle begins during the college years.

Wright

How does Bulletproof Boundaries™ affect us?

Abraham

The focus becomes one of protecting ourselves, our family, and our finances. It's important to understand the various risks and define the various risks that may exist to ourselves as individuals, as family members, as members of society, and to our businesses. The better understanding we have of these risks, the better we will be in taking the necessary steps to identify, avoid, and eliminate these risk from our lives. This is the first and most important step to take great strides in not having to worry about some of the elements that can impact ourselves and those around us.

Wright

I read something before this interview that really fascinated me and made me sad at the same time. You were talking about how financial literacy keeps us from meeting our life goals. Two out of three American households will probably fail to realize one or more of their major life goals because they fail to develop a comprehensive financial plan. That's a little scary, isn't it?

Abraham

It absolutely is. Unfortunately, we take on a victim mentality and yet we all have greatness inside of us. That greatness is in different facets of each our lives, but it is greatness nonetheless and needs to be nurtured, cultured, and harvested. If we can identify the dormant greatness in each of us, we can make the right choices to achieve our hopes, dreams, and goals. Additionally, if we make the wrong choices but can recognize that we made the wrong choices, we always have the ability to make different choices, which will ultimately change the course of our future.

We all need to understand that each moment we have the ability to change our futures forever by making a different choice. It's never set in stone and that's one of the things that happens. We set a plan, we don't follow the plan, we don't reevaluate it, we don't refocus, and we stop making the choices.

Wright

For those people out there who are reading this book and who want to know about protecting themselves, what are some things that they can do to protect their businesses from check fraud?

Abraham

There are a lot of steps we can take. We need to consider the ever evolving, higher technology environment we live in today. For instance, counterfeiting checks existed for a long time but it was perpetrated in a different way than it is now.

Desktop publishing is probably the largest threat to our check paying system that exists. Counterfeiters perpetrating check fraud have the ability to alter, replicate, duplicate, all kinds of checks, from payroll checks, to accounts payable, to refund checks, to money orders, and gift certificates. Gift certificates are no different than cash when they get out there on the street. So we need to understand that with access to scanners, personal computers, color digital copiers, and laser printers and that type of technology, it is much easier to commit this type of crime. It is also much faster than it used to be. They still use some of the older means, though, including the use of cotton paste, chemicals, or things of that nature.

The reality is that we used to be able to only get our checks by ordering them directly from the bank; and we had to go pick them up directly from the bank when they were ready. That is just not the case anymore. We all get coupon packs in the mail that allows us to order checks by mail. All I need is an address, a phone number, and an account number and I can order someone else's checks and start writing them. It's not that difficult to do and many people become victims because of these types of crimes.

There are steps that we can use to try and reduce the exposure to that. First off, there's a program called "Positive Pay" or "Match Pay" (banks use different terms for it). This is a wonderful program, especially for businesses. It's the probably most effective check fraud prevention tool that exists. It is a check matching service that allows the check issuer to transmit a file to the bank listing the checks once they are issued. Through the Positive Pay/Match Pay system compares the account number, the check number, and the dollar amount of the checks against the list of checks that was issued by the company. If any of the information doesn't match, then it gets kicked out as an exception. The exception gets stopped—it doesn't get processed. If someone has tampered with the check number or the account number, or it's not on the list at all, then the person trying to do the forgery gets stopped. It's a wonderful system, especially for businesses and those companies issuing volumes of checks.

The second important thing to do, which surprisingly doesn't happen on a regular basis, is to perform regular bank reconciliations. Balancing the darn checkbook, is really what it's all about. Many of the banks require us to notify them of any discrepancies within thirty days.

I can't tell you how many businesses and individuals I have seen with unopened bank statements—they've never even opened them, let alone looked at them. It reminds me of that old T-shirt that says, "I still have checks—I still have money." It does not work that way, obviously. Regular systematic bank reconciliations can identify a fraud that may have occurred quickly, can eliminate any future fraud from occurring, and can get it resolved before any further losses are experienced.

The other concern here is who does the banking reconciliation, especially in a business; because it is extremely important to have a separation of duties. The people who are issuing the checks shouldn't be the same people who are reconciling the accounts.

When you leave an opportunity open for someone to commit a fraud, and if you look at the statistics, you will find that they actually believe they are justified in committing the fraud and will say, "What harm is it?" Typically the reality is greed gets most people who commit fraud or crimes of this nature caught. They start with fraud for a dollar, it goes to two, to four, to eight, snowballing until it gets so large they can't control it.

Wright

What about identity theft?

Abraham

Before we go there, let me touch on a few other things that I think are important to related to check fraud. There are a lot of ways to prevent check fraud beyond what we just talked about. They include controlling the check paper and using thermal chromatic inks or void pentagraphs on the checks. Many of your checks come with some of these precautions anyway. If someone tries to make a copy of the check or scan the check in any way, it has "void" written all the way across it. This can't be seen with the naked eye. We need to look at the Xerox copy, watermarks, or holograms.

Micro printing is another thing. Most of the lines on a check, such as the borderlines or signature lines, are created with a process called Micro printing. If you view these areas under magnification, you will see that it's not a just a line, it's actually micro printing of various types of words. It is not possible to copy something micro printed. Micro printing exists on our currency as well.

The last thing about check fraud is if someone has embezzled money and taken money from you legally (or illegally), it is considered income for them according to the Internal Revenue Service. Rather than dealing with it yourself, you can actually issue a 1099 form to them. This will notify the IRS and you can allow the IRS to deal with "waving the big stick."

Let's look at identify theft, since you asked. It was something nonexistent previously, but has grown exponentially in recent years. The ease of committing these crimes—stealing and making a fair amount of money while merely sitting at a computer desk somewhere has made this a very popular crime. The criminals no longer need to be an armed robber in a bank under cameras risking stiffer penalties and their lives—they simply sit in some remote location where it is difficult to be detected. Five hundred to seven hundred thousand Americans are victimized each year and it continues to grow.

Wright

How does *Bulletproof Boundaries™* help us in preventing all this?

Abraham

It's a process of protection. For instance, using it can guard your social security number. Many medical and other types of companies have used your social security number as your plan identification number, but most have now done away with this practice. You need to protect your social security number at all costs. Once others have your social security number, they have access to your credit report, and they have access to your bank accounts. How many times does a bank or credit card company ask, "Give *me the last four digits of you social security number?*" Once this information is given, no other identification is requested and the thief has access to your bank account and/or your credit cards.

Another step you can take is to monitor your credit report. They may not be committing theft and fraud on your existing accounts, credit cards, and checking accounts because that is usually caught quicker, but if they have your social security number and access to your information they are able to get loans in your name without your knowledge. I have seen instances where a criminal was able get house loans, car loans, boat loans and personal loans, which are in someone else's name and the victim didn't have any knowledge of it (until they stopped making payments, that is). A good way to protect yourself against this is by looking at your credit report on a regular basis.

We laugh about it at times but shred all your old bank statements and credit card statements. Shred them all. And don't use a regular strip shredder, use a confetti shredder. This way, it comes out in small squares and they cannot go through and try to piece together. You need to even shred the junk mail that comes in. These criminals are not above dumpster diving. If they find the right documents they've got your name and your information. They can then fill out a credit card application and just change the address. Now they have a credit card in your name.

You can also put a fraud alert on your credit report, so if someone tries to establish credit in your name, the person who is going to give someone credit in your name is going to contact you directly. The fraud alert forewarns them to do that before allowing credit to be granted.

As for your social security card, I wouldn't keep it in your wallet if I were you. Don't keep it in your wallet with your credit cards; if you lose your wallet you've lost *everything*. They've got access to your credit card, your driver's license, and your social security number; they don't need anything else—they have access to your whole life.

Wright

That social security number is really important isn't it?

Abraham

It actually is. I remember back years ago when I worked in a retail clothing store. I had some customers who had their social security number and their driver's license number printed on their checks!

Watch out for how you make your bill payments. Remember the old time mailboxes that are probably still around in some areas? You don't see them in some developments anymore. If you have outgoing mail you put the little flag up and the mail carrier comes and takes the mail. This is like an advertisement for criminals. They understand that around the first of the month, mortgage payments and other bills are mailed. They will go by a mailbox and grab the mail before the mail carrier gets there. Now they have access to your checking account because they now have a check you mailed paying the bill. Drop your mail in a postal slot somewhere rather than putting it out there where someone else can get it.

Wright
What should we do if we become a victim?

Abraham
There are a couple of things. The first thing is to report it as a crime to the police immediately. You want to give them as much documentation as you possibly can. Some police departments have been known to refuse to write a police report on some of these things. But I would suggest and really urge the victim to be persistent with them and say, "I need this, I need it for my records." Your credit card companies, your bank (and your insurance company in many cases) are going to require that report to verify a crime actually was committed. You need to first and foremost report it as a crime to the local police department. If checks were stolen, notify the bank immediately and shut down the accounts. You're going to have to put stop payments on the uncleared checks, but it this is a minor cost compared to what you're going to have to deal with if someone gets your financial information. Shut the accounts down, start them fresh—go to your bank and deal with it. Put a secret password on the new account. Instead of, for instance, using your mother's maiden name, ask them to use a secret password that's not related to a child, a parent, a family member, or something of that nature. Have the bank ask for the secret password for all transactions that are above a certain scope or within a certain category you will designate. Most banks and some of the credit card companies will ask you to sign an affidavit stating that you were not the one who committed these charges; you have been a victim of fraud and to call the credit card companies to verify the transaction. Again, shut the affected account down. Tell the credit card company to process the request as "closed at the consumer's request," not that the card was lost or stolen. It does have an impact on credit bureaus and reports. Do everything in writing, keeping dates

and copies of all correspondence. Then contact the fraud unit of the three credit reporting bureaus: Experian, Equifax, and Trans Union. (Experian is formally TRW.) If you contact one of these companies they will typically contact the other two for you. Report the theft of the cards, report the fraud, put a fraud alert on your account and request a victim statement be added to your report. You can add a statement to the report as it relates to the fraud and if the report is run, what happened will be understood.

These are some of the basic steps that should be taken if you become victimized. It is a time-consuming, aggravating, frustrating processes.

Many people have automatic debits to their credit card for various items that will need to be changed. When I shut things down on my credit cards, as time went on I had to recall whether the charge was an automatic charge to the card or not. I had to notify several companies that they couldn't use that card anymore. It is a time-consuming, aggravating, frustrating thing to go through; but unfortunately, it is an issue in society today and we just have to deal with it.

Wright

Is embezzlement a big problem?

Abraham

Yes, it is. As I said, it's one of the oldest crimes we have seen and in the last two decades. It's been ranked number one on the KPMG survey of a thousand companies ever since the beginning of the survey. When you look at this, under the revised *Uniformed Commercial Universal Code*, employers are going to have sole responsibility for the actions of their employees. Employers are in a far better position to avoid losses by being very specific and very careful about selecting and supervising their employees. Employers should put controls or fraud prevention measures into place, making it clear what their position is on this and that it is not going to be tolerated. That's a big, big step. An employer needs to call a prospective employee's references and gain an understanding about why they left their previous job (believe it or not this is seldom done). If we have employees who are handling money and account receivables, we really do need to check into it and understand the dynamics of the individual employee's personality.

I know some employers who are running credit reports. Law enforcement agencies run credit reports because they want agents who aren't going to be in a financial bind. Financial stress can make a person predisposed to accepting bribes, embezzlement, or theft, or anything of that nature. I think this is unfortunate, but it is the reality of the nature of our society today and we need to look at it in that context.

Wright

So how does *Bulletproof Boundaries*™ assist in preventing this?

Abraham

It increases our ability to protect ourselves and it reduces our exposure to these types of crimes. So you consider actions ranging from controlling check stocks, to hiring practices, to bank statement reconciliations, audits, and separation of duties. But the biggest factor is that it focuses on identification and raising your awareness as an individual, family member, member of society, and as a business owner, to understand that you do have exposure and where that exposure comes from. Knowledge is crucial when it comes to your vulnerability. The source of the exposure gives you an opportunity to eliminate that exposure from your life.

We need to live with the realities of today's societal climate and acknowledge that every day we are exposed to numerous. We live with continual threats to us as a person in a post 9/11 society. We really never even considered that the kind of atrocious act that occurred on 9/11 could have happened to us as American citizens on our own soil. If that can happen, we must believe that these more minor, less atrocious crimes (although not minor or less atrocious to the victim) can also happen. It is time we learned how to live in that reality and how to reduce our exposure.

The kinds of crimes that are committed today have increased tremendously over the years. The occurrence of crime has increased as our economy has experienced a downturn. We are likely, therefore, to see a continuing rise in financial crimes. There are going to be constant risks and threats to our person, our family, our businesses, and our financial future and they can paralyze us if we choose to do nothing. They can paralyze us; they can prevent us from thriving, and they can prevent us from achieving our goals. They will threaten the very ideals and values we live and stand for. We spend at least a third of our lives trying to create wealth and give a life of abundance our loved ones and ourselves only to have it threatened by what are preventable scams, crimes, embezzlements, frauds, identity thefts, forgeries, and other financial, as well as physical, crimes. So by understanding them and knowing what to look for, we can avoid them in the future, or at least hopefully minimize the impact they may have on our life.

Bulletproof Boundaries™ is where we create a means to recognize threats as they are revealed and take action before they have a negative, potentially disastrous impact on our lives. Truly, *Bulletproof Boundaries*™ is there helping individuals and families to protect their hopes and dreams.

Wright

Mel, I really appreciate your taking all this time with me this afternoon to discuss this really important subject. I've learned a lot. I plan to make some changes when I get back to the office based on some of the things you've said.

Abraham

Thank you for taking the time out to speak with me today.

Wright

Today we have been talking with Mel H. Abraham, CPA. Mel is a highly sought after expert and successful entrepreneur with numerous business interests. In the personal protection realm, he's the creator of the much in demand presentation *Bulletproof Boundaries*™: *Safety and Success Strategies for an Unsafe World*. I think we've found out today that he knows a lot about what he's talking about. Thank you so much, Mel, for being with us today on *Masters of Success*.

Abraham

Thank you.

About Mel H. Abraham, CPA, CVA, ABV, ASA

Mel is a highly sought after expert (CPA) and a very successful entrepreneur with multiple businesses. Regularly called upon as a forensic expert in financial and valuation issues, he is also a nationally recognized and award-winning speaker, having addressed professional conferences on local, state, and national levels. Mel's two-fold forté is providing strategies in financial risk management and in personal/physical, threat management, and self-protection. His clients span the country. In the personal protection realm, he is the creator of the highly requested presentation, "Bulletproof Boundaries"™—Safety and Success Strategies for an Unsafe World." This enlightening program provides intellectual tools for living with confidence and security in a risky world through awareness and recognition of threatening situations. Drawing on Mel's diverse expertise, this dynamic program addresses both personal safety and presents measures you can take to protect your financial corporate security against financial crimes. He has received numerous speaking awards and has authored numerous articles. His authoritative book, *Valuation Issues and Case Law Update—A Reference Guide*, has been released in a fourth edition. Recently, he was co-author of the business valuation industry's best selling book, *Financial Valuation: Applications and Models*, released last year by John Wiley & Sons, Inc.

Mel H. Abraham, CPA, CVA, ABV, ASA
543 Country Club Drive, Suite B-543
Simi Valley, CA 93065
Phone: 805.578.1515
Fax: 805.293.8950
Email: mel@melabraham.com
www.melabraham.com

Chapter Five

DIANE HANSON

THE INTERVIEW

David Wright (Wright)

Today we're talking with Diane Hanson. Diane brings thirty years of experience in performance-improvement consulting, training, executive coaching, and team building to her work for large and small businesses, governmental agencies, and nonprofits. Her wealth of knowledge in developing effective teams has helped her clients dramatically improve their productivity. Her clients include AstraZeneca, Wyeth Pharmaceuticals, The Wharton School, McDonald's Corporation, Playtex Products, and the Department of Homeland Security. She has addressed groups such as the Society of Pharmaceutical and Biotech Trainers, International Society for Performance Improvement, and The American Society for Training and Development.

Diane, welcome to *Masters of Success*.

Diane Hanson (Hanson)

Thank you.

Wright

You've worked with teams for nearly twenty years. How did you become known as "The Team Doctor?"

Hanson

It started many years ago when the president of a small technology company called my office to ask for emergency help for a team working on a strategically critical project that had a tight timeframe. In fact, this team had reached such a serious level of conflict that members even had a fistfight in the office! As I worked with the team, its members began calling me their "Team Shrink." Over time, I began to use the name "Team Doctor" and adopted it for my website and email address.

By the way, I was able to help that team to successfully complete their important project on time. However, when teams reach such severe conflict I can help them heal the wounds, but scar tissue usually remains and can often prevent the team from truly reaching top performance. During this interview I hope to explain how to avoid this potential problem.

Wright

Will you tell me what a team is and what types of teams there are?

Hanson

Yes. A team is basically a group of individuals working collaboratively. And the key word is *collaboratively*. The word "team" can be a misnomer if it is used to refer to a group of people who happen to work in the same department or at the same office location, but who do not need to work together. What is important is that they're people who depend upon each other to achieve desired results.

Wright

I see, so each team member has his or her own talent?

Hanson

Yes. Team members often have valuable talents in common, but on some teams members may have completely different skills and areas of expertise. Let me explain. There are five types of teams: work teams or functional teams, cross-functional teams, project teams, virtual or cyberspace teams, and self-directed teams.

Work teams might be established in finance or marketing departments. These teams function in areas where everyone has similar
skills, or at least skills within a similar area of specialization. Sometimes team members happen to work together, but it's incorrect to
call their group a team if they only work in the same department. If
they work collaboratively, however, they constitute a "work team" or
"functional team."

The next type of team is "cross-functional," meaning the team includes workers who have many different talents and areas of
specialization. For example, say an automotive company is designing
a new car. A cross-functional team assigned to support this undertak-
ing might include people in manufacturing, engineering, marketing,
and finance. All of them might be involved in designing the new car
from the standpoint of manufacturing considerations, design, customer needs, and cost.

A "project team" may be cross-functional as well, but it becomes a
project team only when its members are challenged with a particular
task that has a finite beginning and end, such as planning a new
marketing campaign. Or it could be a team assigned to improve a certain process or work on a particular problem, such as improving
customer satisfaction, planning strategic growth, or something of that
nature.

The next type of team is the "virtual—cyberspace—team" where
team members work at different locations. Examples might include
an international team where employees work in different countries, a
team at a company with offices in several locations within the same
city or country, or a team that's located at a single location but works
in different buildings. Virtual team members don't see each other
physically very often and must communicate primarily by e-mail and
conference calls. This is rapidly becoming the most common type of
team.

Finally, "self-directed teams" manage themselves. They have a
particular project or outcome for which they are responsible and they
accomplish their objective close without the management of someone
at a higher level.

Wright
It sounds like that would have to be a responsible team.

Hanson

It would have to be, absolutely; members must be very responsible *and* organized.

Wright

So what's the ideal size of a team?

Hanson

An ideal team size is usually five to eight people. This number fosters enough creativity but should not immobilize members when they don't agree. As you can imagine, the more people assigned to a team, the harder it is to get everyone to agree on issues. When groups get too large, progress may become very difficult. The absolute maximum size for a team would be twelve. Beyond this, I recommend breaking groups up into smaller teams or sub-units all connected by a greater whole. Representatives of the subgroups can attend meetings of other teams or communicate with them as needed to maintain consistency and pass information and work along.

Wright

What stages or transitions do teams go though in their development?

Hanson

Teams usually pass through five definable stages in their normal development. I would like to discuss each phase as well as those issues that need attention during each phase.

The first phase is called the "orientation" or the "forming" phase. When a team first forms, members are occasionally uncertain about how they will operate. Team members may look forward to the idea of being on a team, but are often unsure about what is expected of them. At this point members may not be totally willing to commit themselves to the team's goals until they know for sure what the team is expected to do. To all appearances, members may seem very positive. However, they may actually adopt a wait-and-see attitude to determine if this new way of getting things done is really going to work and if the team will be able to accomplish its goals. This is the time when a team's leader needs to help members master the basics of developing shared goals, creating a plan of action, clearly defining team members' roles and expectations, and developing cohesive relationships. Team leaders must serve as positive role models while actively encouraging involvement of others.

The second team stage is called the "dissatisfaction" or the "storming" phase. That happens because a team often starts to experience internal conflict at this point in its development. While the storming phase is almost unavoidable, training in team building and developing an effective structure and foundation can minimize unproductive conflict and help team members succeed. This is when members need to develop plans and revise them when necessary to redefine gray areas of responsibility. The team needs to establish procedures for how members are going to do their work and live by ground rules for fair and productive interaction. Members have to start encouraging each other to speak up and to overcome diversions inadvertently caused by more extroverted members who may tend to take over meetings. This is the time for members to work on improving their communication skills.

The third stage of team development is the "resolution" or "norming" phase. Here team members continually improve trust and comfort and begin to work more effectively with each other. As the team continues to work on communications issues and problem solving, members begin to see noticeable results in achieving their goals.

The fourth phase—the "production" phase or "performing" stage— is the reason organizations start teams in the first place. This is the time when team members become a smoothly functioning machine and can achieve very high levels of productivity. As they work well together, members share a clear vision of what they're trying to accomplish. Meetings become less frequent and more efficient. Members learn to share team leadership, become more self-managed, and willingly trust each other.

The last team-passage phase is what's known as the "transforming" or "transition" phase. This may occur when a team is disbanded, when the team recruits new members, or when a new leader takes charge. If participants are completing a project as the team disbands, they usually want to feel a sense of closure. If a team is adding new members, the group needs to assimilate those new participants by reviewing the basics with them. It's everyone's responsibility to make sure new members know the team's goals and its plan of action for achieving goals. The team needs to revisit everyone's roles and adjust them to make sure the team has all the talent it needs to get its work done. Each individual may need to find out what other team members can do to pick up the slack and, in some cases, the team may want to go outside to seek extra skills, competencies, or counsel. Outside assistance may come from a contractor or an advisor who has a particular skill to lend to the team on a full- or part-time basis.

That's a really compressed explanation of the five stages of team development and how to manage each phase.

Wright

When you were talking about the second stage you mentioned conflict as something teams usually experience to some extent. Will you talk about some of the causes of team conflict?

Hanson

Causes of potential conflict are numerous and varied. However, I've found in working with teams over the last twenty years conflict usually centers on five specific areas. I call them the "Components of Productive Teams." These include shared goals, clearly defined roles and expectations, effective communications, established procedures and ground rules, and cohesive relationships. Let's look at each one.

A very common cause of conflict is unclear or unshared goals. A team does not necessarily have to decide what its goal is. A company can start a team with a specific goal in mind, but everyone needs to understand what it is and to agree to work toward it. I call that a shared goal. Once team members agree on a goal, they need to develop a plan for how they're going to achieve it.

Conflict can seriously escalate when roles, responsibilities, and expectations are left unclear. Team members need to understand and define who will perform certain tasks, who should be responsible for seeing jobs through to completion, and what team members' expectations are of each other and of their team leader.

There's an expression, "Talk is cheap, it's the misunderstanding that gets expensive!" This adage is certainly indicative of some of the challenges in team communications. When team members fail to keep each other in the loop, the team can suffer from unproductive activity, mistakes, duplicated efforts, and conflict. Teams need effective communications on all angles—360-degree communications. Workers should keep other team members informed, but they also need to communicate well with their team leader, customers, other departments, and outside sources.

Frequent sources of conflict that members don't always anticipate are procedures, policies, and ground rules. These three team fundamentals often get overlooked. So do discussion and agreement about how team members should enforce them. The result is that members often find themselves in arguments about how they're going to do something. Commonly overheard statements may be, "This is the way we did it where I worked before," or, "This is the way we've always done it." Much of a team's conflict can be redirected into creative energy if members agree up front how they're going to do certain tasks and if they have written policies that help members get tasks done.

Personalities—the personal relationships among team members—represent my last common area for potential conflict. Combine personalities with workplace politics and major conflicts can boil over with amazing speed. Conflict can come from egos, relationships, or rank. Discord may be particularly damaging when an ambitious team member who wants to get ahead steps on somebody else's toes, or when one worker gets the promotion another team member thought he or she deserved.

Personality issues like these can drastically reduce a team's effectiveness since team members must trust each other to be able to work with each other. Personal issues may often interfere or destroy with mutual confidence.

Occasionally a team may have one or two members who may be very difficult to work with. In such cases, a team's leader may suggest that these individuals should receive team coaching or counseling. In other cases, it's the team's responsibility to address a problem team member's behavior head on. In severe situations, members may actually ask a troublesome team member to leave the team.

Wright

How significant are personalities in team conflict?

Hanson

Obviously, personalities can pose significant challenges and opportunities. In my experience, however, teams often overemphasize personality as a *root cause* of conflict. I find in most situations the real sources are the other four factors that I just covered: 1) a lack of shared goals, or plan for achieving them; 2) lack of clarity on roles and responsibilities; 3) ineffective communication; and 4) lack of policies and procedures. Without these four factors in place, an organization may very well establish an environment in which conflict will thrive.

Many times, conflict gets blamed on personalities. Yet, when I'm called in to an organization to analyze a team, I often determine that it's not anyone in particular who is a problem or at fault. The underlying problem is a lack of structure. Basically, anyone who joins a team that has a lack of structure may eventually find himself or herself in conflict. Imagine a team where no one can agree on what its goal should be. What happens is that everyone rows the boat in a different direction, so the boat winds up going nowhere. At best it's going to drift around in circles. If it heads into a wave the wrong way, the boat can capsize.

My belief is that personalities often get a bad rap. It's a common misconception that teammates have to like each other to work together effectively. A lot of team-building efforts are directed towards personality profiling and warm and fuzzy games to get people to know and like each other. That has its place, especially when you have a newly formed team whose members don't know each other. But it's not going to help people work together as a team if warm and fuzzy is all the team accomplishes.

In fact, when people like each other too much, members might be reluctant to challenge each other's suggestions and ideas. Even worse, team members may mistakenly put favored friends in charge of tasks that other team members who have related experience and skills should really be doing. Although team members don't have to like each other, they should certainly respect each other and the skills others bring to the team. This will help everyone work together.

Wright

What are the main obstacles to a team's success?

Hanson

Lack of management support tops the list. Without it, a team faces serious difficulty getting the information and resources it needs. If members sense they don't have management support, they may not agree on what their goals should be or how to reach them.

Wright

But why would management initiate teams and then withhold support?

Hanson

Management may not have clearly defined its own roles and responsibilities in supporting teams. Middle management may not have authority to budget funds to provide training or resources to the company's teams. Finally, management may not have thought the team concept through thoroughly enough for teams to really succeed.

I mentioned politics earlier and I'll get into that a little bit more here. Take this example of a cross-functional team. Management may actually prevent members from contributing to a team when supervisors establish departmental priorities they feel are more important than team goals. Sometimes, when individuals responsible for teams fail to build sufficient allies for their cause, others in the company are unenthusiastic about supporting the effort. They may feel it's not going to be successful and don't want to be affiliated with it. Often, different company divisions or sections have historically conflicting goals that hinder effective, collaborative teamwork. Finally, many companies suffer dysfunctional interpersonal, managerial relationships that are related to past negative interactions among individuals, perhaps in the political realm.

Sometimes managers refuse to support teams because teams threaten supervisory authority. Some supervisors actually fear losing their jobs. If a team truly becomes self-directed, a manager might fear that the company could find him or her superfluous. In some extreme cases, managers have actually sabotaged a team's work.

Wright

Let's look at the positive side. What then would be factors that make teams more productive or more successful?

Hanson

Management support, along with the five components of productive teams that I reviewed earlier, are the most important factors in creating motivated teams. Another important element is thinking through and providing the rewards or consequences associated with teamwork. Many managers who expect workers to participate on teams do not give adequate consideration to whether or how members should be rewarded for teamwork. If team members are rewarded primarily as individuals and their performance reviews don't even mention teamwork—which is common—no one will feel a strong incentive to work with others on teams. In fact, some companies base their bonus structures on a process called "forced ranking," in which managers rank workers by performance level with no tie scores being permitted. A manager might have one employee who excels in one aspect of his or her job, and another who's very good in a second aspect of the job. Although these employees' performances are comparable, managers must rank one employee as number five and another has to be number six. Such a ranking system is counterproductive to teamwork.

Wright
What special factors affect the success of an international team?

Hanson
Actually the same factors that affect success of any work team apply to international teams as well. However, international teamwork faces complications that I'm sure everyone can well imagine. One of the most important dynamics on international teams is personal bonding among individuals. I said earlier that sometimes there's too much emphasis placed on personality. However, since members of international teams may rarely physically see each other, it is absolutely essential that they get together face to face, at least once, early in the team's development. Separation can be a tremendous obstacle because of travel expense and the logistics of getting people from many different countries together. If team members who cannot see each other must talk to each other by e-mail all the time, they are at a great disadvantage in communication. Members need time to physically meet and get to know each other and bond.

International teams also need special resources, such as cross-cultural interpreters to explain how body language may signal very different messages in different countries. We know that in Islamic countries it is an insult to show the bottom of one's shoe. In our American culture flashing a middle finger is a tremendous insult. But in other countries identical gestures may mean something innocent. Team members need to understand body language as much as spoken or written language.

Furthermore, international team members usually also need more equipment than other teams. They definitely require computers, tools to do the job, and supplies like any other team; but international teams also require video conferencing capabilities. Some companies have installed conferencing that lets team members sit at a table in front of a screen where they can see the teammates in another country or at another location. This gives everyone the feeling that the team is together physically. Conferencing equipment can certainly enhance communication across hemispheres.

Wright
So how can teams overcome time and resource constraints?

Hanson
If an organization fails to support its teams' goals and the teams themselves, members may not successfully overcome critical obstacles. That's why some teams fail; and that's why management support is one of the main factors in a team's success. Here's a worst-case scenario: A company's management starts teams for a political reason, say, to make it appear that the organization is addressing a problem. Since no one has any real expectation that teams will succeed, the team effort is probably doomed.

On the other hand, with full management support and sufficient resources, teams can jell and members can bond to achieve a common goal. These teams can sometimes overcome massive obstacles by applying their own creativity, resourcefulness, and willingness to work hard. That's the best reason for organizations to start teams in the first place. The key is that team members must enthusiastically support their team's goal and feel that there's a definite reward in achieving it.

When I was a sales manager, my unit director gave my section a sales quota that was astronomically high for a particular product. Because the company was planning a major television advertising campaign, management wanted to make sure the product was stocked in retail stores. I found it extremely difficult to assign a specific quota to individuals because sales professionals understood the quota was a real "mission impossible."

Instead, I assigned the overall quota as a collective challenge to my sales personnel, and asked them to work on it as a team. Whatever percentage of the quota they achieved as a team would be what each individual sales person received on his or her performance review and bonus evaluation. As a result, everyone sensed they were playing in the same game and team members would win or lose as a team. The result was that our unit was the only team in the nation to achieve the "Mission Impossible" quota. I think this case history shows what a team can do if members have a common goal and are rewarded for achieving it.

Wright
So do teams need special training?

Hanson

Yes. One of the most important elements teams need is coaching in team skills, concentrating on the five components of a productive team mentioned earlier. I work with teams to develop a clear team goal that members all agree to and then create a plan of action to achieve it. That might seem fairly basic, but it's not. Goal setting and action planning are skills that teams have to learn. Teams often benefit when an outside facilitator provides assistance to help them define and clarify what needs to happen, how it will be done, who's going to do it, and on what schedule. Team members should also clearly define their roles and expectations, work on skills and methods for communicating with all their different stakeholders, and establish policies and procedures for working together and with others. Teams need leadership and management skills training so that everyone can give feedback, conduct meetings, manage change, and interview people.

As an aside regarding conducting meetings, it's amazing how today's professionals spend nearly half their time in unproductive meetings. It's very frustrating for people working sixty to seventy hours a week to misallocate any amount of time to ineffective meetings. Yet companies rarely train employees on how to plan a meeting agenda or facilitate a discussion. I'm amazed at exasperated managers or team leaders who tell me they are too busy to pull an agenda together. They could have saved at least an hour of meeting time by taking five minutes to plan the meeting agenda ahead of time. Instead they spend two hours in an unproductive meeting. Where's the sense?

Teams often also need cross training. Members ought to learn what kinds of tasks the person sitting next to them is doing and how they do it. Cross training can help team members fill in for each other and move projects forward when someone is out on vacation, sick, or traveling. Training also develops understanding and empathy for fellow team members. Depending on the team's purpose, training in problem solving, creativity, and decision making can also be very helpful. Training in technical skills, such as operating equipment, using different types of software, or executing job procedures should also be very helpful. For international teams, training should include awareness of cultural issues such as the body language of different cultures.

Finally, team training should be conducted in a timely manner. Giving a team weeklong, marathon training on teamwork usually doesn't work well. It's much more effective when trainers provide coaching in small increments which have been specifically designed to help team members with their immediate needs.

Here's an example: Say a team is interviewing candidates to become new team members. Training that includes interviewing skills and legal issues in hiring just before members conduct their first interviews can be very well received and highly effective. Here's another thought: Trainers should try to start conflict-management training just as the team members enter the storming phase of team building, when they start experiencing their first internal disputes.

Wright

So what can an organization or, more particularly, what could I do as CEO of my own company to provide a good support structure for teams?

Hanson

First, a CEO needs to be sure the organization has a realistic compensation system that rewards teamwork. Often companies don't sufficiently deliberate how they're going to reward people who serve on teams. Management habitually retains compensation systems that primarily reward individual performance. Then managers scratch their heads, wondering why people aren't volunteering to work together on teams.

Second, CEOs should support their teams. They should tell team members why their work is important, that management believes in what teams are doing, and then publicly recognize team progress and successes. CEOs should mandate top managers be responsible for teams in the workplace and report team progress directly to the CEO. These managers should also be charged with providing the human resources and financial support members need on a regular basis.

Sometimes, very simple obstacles hinder team productivity. Here's an example. Members of a manufacturing team got into pitched battles with each other because they had to share a ten-dollar tool everyone needed practically all the time. Productivity took a nosedive when tempers flared. However, all it took was a twenty-dollar investment to buy two more of the tools, and the team's productivity and willingness to work together could have been far better. A workplace culture supportive to team progress can eliminate these kinds of petty problems quickly and easily.

Wright

That's like three people using one stapler.

Hanson

Exactly. Then they run around interrupting each other to find out who has the stapler. It's crazy, but I see this sort of thing all the time. A CEO should insist that every team has funding for the training and tools members need. A CEO should also take time to listen to feedback from team members about the resources they need and, particularly, their suggestions for more productive processes.

Wright

What special communications challenges do teams encounter?

Hanson

The most common challenge for any team, whether it's international or not, is the "right- and left-hand syndrome." Members should keep all other stakeholders informed about what their team is doing. They should also remember to include others in decisions that will affect the work and end products of other divisions or sections. All too often, one team's solution becomes another team's problem. Without clear and constant communication, conflict can erupt, even from seemingly simple oversights.

When organizations lack consistent procedures, employees face major problems in communications and interpersonal relationships as the following case demonstrates. A dozen Ph.D. scientists had been embroiled in such severe conflict that when I interviewed the team members individually, more than half the members confided that they were concerned about their own personal safety at work—someone had threatened to burn a team member's house down! Another threatened to kill someone's cat. They all feared one of the members of the group was going to "go postal" and blow them all away one day. It's hard to imagine that these were Ph.D. scientists!

Political issues further escalated the conflict. Although one of the team's members wanted the manager's position, it was given to another employee—and of all things a woman—a first in the scientific world at that time. The passed-over team member was highly resentful. When he noticed that some money might be missing from his project funds, he immediately blamed the new manager. He also whispered to everyone in the office that she was using his project money for her pet projects. Eventually team members divided into two factions and ceased speaking to each other.

I coached them all individually. Then I brought the main combatants together to work out their differences. When the two key individuals met to discuss the missing project money, the accusatory scientist discovered that he had been on sabbatical in Japan and his travel and other expenses came out of his project funds. Because he didn't know the facts, he pointed his finger at someone else. In this case, we established procedures for turning in expense receipts to an administrative assistant with codes allocating expenses to specific project funds. Problem solved—demonstrating how a lack of procedures can sometimes lead to tremendous levels of conflict.

Wright

So let me ask you a final question. How do these communication challenges differ for virtual or international teams?

Hanson

All teams have to find ways to communicate. Everyone must know who's in charge of which tasks and what their progress is over time. International teams, and even virtual teams working in the different geographic areas of the same country, face the problem of working in different time zones. The logistics of setting up a meeting with people all over the world in different time zones is daunting. A team member may have to awaken at three a.m. to join a conference call or a virtual meeting because his or her teammates on the other side of the world have just arrived for work.

Global teams must also meet the challenge of language and cultural differences. These issues obviously add complexity to team productivity. Add to this the difficulty of communicating by e-mail, especially if team members haven't had the chance to bond and get to know each other a little better. Now toss in the need to communicate by e-mail in a second or third language. A misspelled word could send a message with an entirely different meaning, leading to problems. This demonstrates why it's very important for international teams to get to know each other on a personal level. When members know each other well, a teammate may be more likely to say, "Oh well, I know Mary and it's unlikely she would have said that. I'm sure she must have meant something else." But if they don't have that chance to get to know each other, Mary's e-mail is just another message from cyberspace and can lead to unintentional reactions and even emotional outbursts.

In addition to existing within national or religious cultures, each company also has its own culture that makes it unique. When teams from several collaborating companies work on a project, there's always the chance for communication and political obstacles.

Creating effective teams can be very challenging, but the potential for success makes teamwork obviously worth it. It's essential to have strong teams that can enhance productivity and creativity in today's competitive business world.

Wright

Well, what a great conversation. I can see why you're in the *Masters of Success* book. Today we have been talking to Diane Hanson, who brings thirty years of experience in performance-improvement training, executive coaching, and team building to her work with both large and small businesses. Today, we have also found out why she was selected to be featured in this book. She certainly is a master of the topic of teams.

Thank you so much, Diane, for being with us today on *Masters of Success.*

Hanson

Thank you. It's been an honor.

About Diane Hanson

Diane Hanson is an authority on teams, teamwork, and organizational change. She has published articles on these and numerous other topics. Diane was an editorial board member of *Today's Team*, a publication for team members, facilitators, and team coaches. She holds a Bachelor of Science degree from Cornell University and graduated with distinction from the University of Pennsylvania with a Master's in science in organizational dynamics.

Diane Hanson
Creative Resource Development, Inc.
Email: hanson@team-doctor.com
Phone: 1.877.692.5146
www.team-doctor.com

Chapter Six

MARGARET J. SUMPTION, MSED, CSL

THE INTERVIEW

David Wright (Wright)

Today we are speaking with Margaret J. Sumption. Margaret grew up on a farm near the small town of Frederick, South Dakota. She's married and has an eleven-year-old son, Raymond. She holds a Master's of Science degree in Education, Counseling, and personnel services from Northern State University Aberdeen, South Dakota. She owns and operates her own consulting business, Sumption & Wyland, in Sioux Falls, South Dakota.

Within her business, she provides executive coaching, staff training, board development and strategic planning services. She serves as adjunct to the faculty at the University of Sioux Falls, teaching grant writing and other courses. In addition to her professional responsibilities she is an active volunteer in the Sioux Falls community, acting as member of the Executive Committee for Leadership Sioux Falls with the Sioux Falls Chamber of Commerce. Margaret is chair of the Regional Emergency Management Authority, past chair of the Center for Women at the University of Sioux Falls and is a member of the local chapter of Business and Professional Women. She was the 1998 recipient of the YWCA Leader Award for Education, 1999 Sioux Falls Sales and Marketing Executives (SME) Award for Innovation in

Business and is a 1990 graduate of the Chamber of Commerce Leadership Sioux Falls Program.
Margaret welcome to *Masters of Success.*

Margaret Sumption (Sumption)
Thank you.

Wright
We're going to talk about style, since style matters. Could you define "style" for us?

Sumption
Style is often identified as personality type, profile, and basic indicators of temperament. For those familiar with some of the most common tools like the Myers-Briggs Type Indicator or the Gregorc Styles Indicator or perhaps the TeamDynamics™ Profiling System in Human Dynamics, style is defined as those characteristics that identify how we approach the world, how we gain our energy, how we problem-solve and make decisions, and how we generally interact with others and our environment. Essentially those are the elements of style; and style does indeed matter. We look for those characteristics of style, and especially diversity of style, among participants in any team or organizational group because those variances of temperament and approach and problem-solving result in better decisions by a group of people working together toward a common end.

Wright
How does understanding your own style give you leverage for leadership?

Sumption
First and foremost we have to understand how we think, problem-solve, perceive information, gather information, and assist in supporting communicating our view to others in order to influence how others think, respond, and communicate.

It's important, as we look at those elements of style, to understand ourselves well and understand how we approach situations. We will also have a better basic framework on which to support and relate those characteristics and to see the differences in how others relate, see problems, and problem-solve. Once we understand how we behave and act in particular situations we can then apply that knowledge to see the differences in the way others see and view information.

More importantly we can then go forward and help to fashion our communication, fashion our argument from the other person's viewpoint and, using that viewpoint, then assist them to more effectively hear what we have to say and relate to our viewpoint in a common decision-making pattern.

Wright

How does one find out the characteristics of their style?

Sumption

In finding that out, again, there are several tools that are identified. I happen to find the Myers-Briggs Type Indicator as one of the tools I find most user-friendly. It's also well documented and a well validated tool that works very well to help people to gain an understanding their style. The Human Dynamics Indicator and the Gregorc Styles Indicator (which is more of a screening tool than it is a diagnostic tool), can give us an insight into who we are. How we use that information then is by understanding ourselves and seeing how we interact with the world. We can then apply that to how others view organizational priorities and how they organize their environment; we can pick up those cues and then fashion our communication effectively.

The Myers Briggs in analysis uses an interesting tool to help us understand style. They ask you to take your dominate hand and write your signature. People can usually do that without even thinking— they can scrawl their signature and it always looks generally the same—it's very common and simple to accomplish. Now take your non-dominate hand and write your signature; notice how difficult it is to fashion each letter. By using that simple example we can help people to understand how we commonly approach our world without thinking, without pondering, without being aware, or self-aware. By looking at our writing left-handed we can see that others may look at the world very differently. We might perhaps fashion our arguments more effectively by simply crossing over those common, almost automatic approaches to our world by looking at our world in a different way.

91

Wright

How does knowing your own style and preferences impact your ability to read others?

Sumption

Let me tell you, it's very helpful to be able to understand style by looking at how we think and perceive the world. One of the interesting characteristics about style is that as we organize our decision-making process—what gives us energy, what excites us, how are we coordinating our problem-solving kinds of skills sets. By understand those important characteristics we can then look to fashioning our communication processes in such a way that others will hear what we are saying, respond to what we are saying, understand what we are saying, and understand our viewpoint more effectively.

I want to make one point very, very clear though—there is no such thing as a bad style. Often we find that people tend to gravitate toward people who are a lot like themselves. If a person is highly ordered and sequential in how they problem-solve, they may be attracted to others who are highly ordered and sequential in their problem-solving style. That can result in a bad outcome—a less evaluated outcome—and in a less thoroughly analyzed and effective result for a team working together.

One of the things that understanding your style can do is help you to appreciate and honor the styles of others and their differences so that a better outcome can be fashioned for a team of people working together.

Wright

Once you understand the styles of others, how can you best use this resource to get the best out of people you supervise or team with?

Sumption

Being able to speak in their language is the most effective use of this knowledge and resource. As we understand our own selves we become more effective. Let's take for example an individual who is highly ordered and sequential and you can tell which person that is. They are always the people who consistently have their desk clean and their files set up in an orderly fashion and usually have nothing on the top of their desk—everything is very neatly filed and orderly in the drawer. Next to them might be an office where a person has piles all over; there's an automatic disconnect between those two kinds of people.

Understanding your own style gives one the awareness to be able to respect the randomness in the thinking process and the intuitiveness of the thinking process of, what it may appear to be on the outside, a more scattered person who thinks, "My gosh, this person with a neat desk never does anything because there's nothing on his desk." The less organized person can honor how a more organized person thinks and how he or she arranges information in order to be effective.

Using this example, that person who is very orderly in his or her style may be able to effectively make a minor shift in his or her approach to problem-solving or communication and draw in that more random thinker to get a better outcome. Alternatively, someone who is a little bit more random in his or her style can become more intuitive in how he or she thinks and processes and might be able, by putting things in folders, provide a communication strategy to help that more sequential, orderly person to respect and appreciate others' views on a particular issue.

Essentially, understanding the styles of others can be facilitated by writing left-handed, looking at how you do business and then attempting to adjust your style to accommodate characteristics you see coming from another person. That comes first and foremost from knowing yourself well and then seeing how other people think differently than you do and then fashioning your argument from their viewpoint, from their mindset, and from how they communicate and problem-solve.

Wright

We hear a lot of talk about "soft skills." First, what are they, and secondly what impact does one's soft skills have on the ability to be identified for leadership?

Sumption

Soft skills are all of those skills that make us a comfortable person to be around. You hear phrases like, "that person is a team player," "that person always has a smile on their face," or "that person always knows the right things to say." Soft skills are those interpersonal, social, and communication skills identified by what some might term "emotional intelligence" (if you're a devotee of that element of understanding of how people think and process). But essentially, soft skills are those skills that create an environment that draw other people to us.

Let's say, for example, a man starts out in the world as an engineer—a structural engineer. His first job in the market place is going to be a skill set assessment—does he really understand engineering and understand his craft and the production of products, resources, and services that exercise his craft? Just because he is a really good structural engineer doesn't mean he is going to be able to manage the engineering division of an architectural firm well, because that requires an entirely different set of skills—people skills. People skills are the ability to communicate, the ability to draw out the best in others, the ability to problem-solve, to be empathetic with regard to the needs of individuals and their viewpoints and perceptions. Just because you're a really good engineer doesn't mean you have the skill set for leadership.

The literature is very clear on one of the things we find regarding this issue—the higher you move in level of management, administration, and leadership in an organization, the less important your technical skills become and the more important your people skills become. It is your people skills that are called—or identified in the literature—as your "soft skills." If you do not have soft skills, you might be the best structural engineer in the architectural firm but you're never going to get to be the leader of your architectural division or, praise be, the leader within that firm as a whole.

Wright

How does a person gain soft skills? Can these skills be learned?

Sumption

Soft skills *can* be learned and they are most often learned by practice—the practicing of those continuing, interacting kind of skills that come first and foremost from self-understanding; being able to understand style issues and also, frankly, honoring the importance of relationship building, networking, and communication with others as an important characteristic for success in the workplace.

What often happens with highly technically talented people, is they fail to honor the importance of having those people skills that lead them into opportunities for leadership and management and moving up the chain of command. Honoring the fact that these are important skills for success in the world is the first step in being able to learn those necessary soft skills that will allow one to move up in an organization. Again, people need to be reminded that the higher they go in levels of leadership and management in an organization, the less important their technical skills become—the more of the generalist they become.

The higher you move up in management, more important your people skills, your communication skills, your ability to interact effectively with people, your abilities to work effectively with others, and being able to bring out, mentor, or build the skills of others become as you move forward in that leadership capacity.

Wright

How can you help those you supervise or with whom you work on teams to build their soft skills?

Sumption

There are several resources that are now coming into popularity. We're seeing an explosion of new materials on the market that are really looking at the issue of assessing your soft skills and building those skills. Many of them are based on the issues of mentoring, providing networking resource opportunities, and assisting and supporting people through an experiential kind of self-understanding, team-building, and team development.

I believe very strongly that when one looks to build the skills of others it requires an advanced level of leadership. People have to go to the point in their leadership of finding their own voice as a leader where they are able of stepping aside from being the person identified as that person in power. They literally have to give up their power to others and by mentoring and supporting and valuing the leadership potential and the leadership resources others bring to the table, they automatically become that leader, that mentor, that supporter, by moving away from being "the one in control" or "the one in power" to being the one in wisdom and responsibility and leadership. To be a good leader one must stop being a good manager or controller. One must translate to another level of interaction and relationship in the work environment in order to be able to transcend those same skills to another level of leadership with those whom they supervise.

I had an interesting experience that taught me so well, before I became self-employed as a private consultant and started my own firm. I worked in a wonderful organization with a very, very smart executive—CEO—who lacked quality leadership skills. He lacked those inherent qualities that would identify him as leader. One of the things that told me this was his unwillingness to allow any his staff people to "take credit" for work that they had accomplished. In fact, he would tell his subordinates—the managers among us—that we were not allowed to take credit for work we had accomplished, that it was important to bring those accomplishments to him and he would then in turn present those accomplishments to others and essentially take control of them, to make them a *team* outcome as opposed to any individual contribution.

My reaction to him at one point in time was to say, "What you are doing in this process is stopping individuals from demonstrating their skills and leading. Wouldn't it be better if you simply took credit for having been smart enough to hire us in the first place?"

One characteristic I find in people who are unable to learn the soft skills necessary for leadership is a sense of personal self-security. If one lacks a sense of personal self-worth he or she will be less likely to be able to mentor leadership and excellence in others.

Wright

We hear a lot about mentoring as a professional development strategy. Mentoring programs have received very mixed evaluations and many believe they don't work. Are they a good strategy? If so, what are the elements that make them successful?

Sumption

The best mentoring programs are programs that don't assume people know how to do it. One of the biggest mistakes organizations make when they present a mentoring program as a strategy for professional development is they fail to teach those prospective mentors how to do it—how to set it up, how to carry it out and how to evaluate results. Just as importantly, they don't help the mentee understand how to gain from that experience, how to ask the right questions, how to seek out relationship building opportunities and get the best out of that relationship.

What happens then is two people get paired together and they get told, "You're the mentor—you know a lot. You're the mentee—you have a lot to learn." Then several months later someone comes back and says, "How did that work for you?" That's the wrong way to do it, and it's a negative way to do it. The resulting outcome is the belief that mentoring programs don't work.

To be effective, a well-defined mentoring program has to have a training feature where mentors and mentees are trained to understand the role of the mentoring relationship and trained to understand how to access and deliver information in an effective way. It's a very high quality assessment mechanism to evaluate that relationship over time.

A second element of a good mentoring program has to be the match. There has to be a match between the skill set—the skills—of the mentor that you want to convey and the mentee who has a skill set in development. There has to be a style match for those two people which has to be very carefully evaluated and very carefully aligned.

A good mentoring program can be very cost efficient for an organization and can be a very effective way to build the skill set of leadership within an organization; but only if an investment is made in these important characteristics.

Wright

Let's say a company wants to increase its employees' performance and they believe soft skills development is a part of their need. How do they go about evaluating those needs and setting up and evaluating the benefit of a program? Is an executive coaching program an effective option?

Sumption

There are many approaches to assessing need. I believe one of the most effective strategies is for organizations to truly step back in their personnel management systems and take a look at the level of the job descriptions and performance descriptions they are defining and devising for their organization. With that they need to use the evaluative structure, begin to put on paper those characteristics that they would wish to see—both the hard skills—the technical skills that they want, which are often conveyed well in job descriptions—and the soft skills that they want and would like to see evolve. Using that tool then, they need to build a human resource development strategy that will move them toward those performance objectives.

If you go back to some of Steven Covey's very important "Seven Habits," he talks about "beginning with the end in mind." You have to look at the outcome you want in the level skills, both in the technological or skill set area—hard skills of an individual and the soft skills as well, which are really a structure of a culture of an organization—and be able to articulate them effectively. Then, using that framework, you can assess where your deficits are, where the gaps are and then begin to build appropriate mentoring kinds of programs to effect change in some of those important skill areas, as well as consider developing perhaps a coaching strategy as an alternative.

This is one example: I do a lot of executive coaching in my consulting practice and I work both with executives who are wishing to build their own skill set as well as dealing with a "problem manager" or administrator who is at risk of losing employment. I see it from both sides of the coaching practice.

Again, one of the things I find most effective in a good coaching program is fit. I'm not the best coach for every person out there and it is necessary to look again at assessing the skill set and fit. If a coach is identified and comes to you in a contractual relationship and doesn't admit that they might not be the best choice for every person in the organization, then you know you have a problem. You need to look at that style and fit. A coaching program, if done well, can be extremely positive—an extremely effective and cost efficient way to deliver service.

I work a lot with chief executive officers and high-level management and well as administration officials to essentially customize training for them. They come to me either with an understanding of the skill sets they want to attain or by saying, "What is it that I need in order to move up?" We then assess together and I then build a customized program.

An example of that is: for a $6,000 to $8,000 one-year project, during the course of that one year I can deliver an excellent customized resource skill development plan for a CEO that would cost three times as much if he or she were to go to seminars held in various venues across the country. So the assessment and coaching program really becomes a very cost efficient way for the highest level executives to get the advanced leadership development training they need, including the information and technical skills necessary to assess the needs of their organizations in a very safe and confidential kind of environment.

Wright

Wow! What a great conversation. You've given me a lot to think about today.

Sumption

I appreciate that. Style *does matter*. It is a very important part of understanding the effectiveness of businesses and organizations as they move forward. It's really very important that understanding your own style first is not only gratifying in realizing that this is why you make decisions the way you make them but it's also extremely helpful to give you the insight to know that not everyone thinks, organizes, communicates, or problem-solves in the same way. By simply writing left-handed we can get a whole lot more done and bring out the best in people.

Wright

Today we have been talking with Margaret J. Sumption. Within her business she provides executive coaching, staff training, board development, and strategic planning services. As we have found out in this conversation, she knows what she talking about.

Thank you so much Margaret for being with us today.

Sumption

Thank you so much.

About Margaret J. Sumption, MSED, CSL

Margaret Sumption is the senior partner of Sumption & Wyland, specializing in strategic planning, executive coaching, and training and facilitation. Her passion, hard work, and imagination help organizations and executive clients fulfill their missions and realize their goals. She has consulted with the CEOs, boards, and executives of 200 hospitals, universities, associations, government agencies, and businesses since beginning practice in 1990. She is a sought-after speaker and trainer whose energy, humor, and practical wisdom inspires as well as informs her audiences.

Margaret J. Sumption, MSED, CSL
Sumption & Wyland
818 South Hawthorne Avenue
Sioux Falls, SD 57104-4537
Phone: 605.336.0244
Phone: 888.4SUMPTION
Fax: 605.336.0275
Email: margaret@sumptionandwyland.com
www.sumptionandwyland.com

Chapter Seven

JONAH MITCHELL, PH.D.

THE INTERVIEW

David Wright (Wright)

Today we are talking with Jonah Mitchell. Jonah has been a licensed Realtor® since 1974. He has earned his reputation by being an extremely knowledgeable and passionate salesman. Simply put, he closes the deals. Jonah brings a creative, assertive, and unique perspective to sales leadership.

Jonah was the 2004 president of the Lexington Bluegrass Association of Realtors and remains on the Board. He was the first president and is a life member of the Lexington Realtors® Million Dollar Club.

He is the president and CEO of Jonah Mitchell Real Estate & Auction Group, supervising all levels of marketing in real estate sales, property management, subdivision development, and consulting. His company specializes in residential lot marketing and sales.

Jonah is a national speaker, consultant, and president of Jonah Mitchell Speaker & Seminar Leader. He is also a national expert witness for Fair Housing and Standards of Practice. He is a certified instructor for the Kentucky Real Estate Commission, and is certified by the Professional Standards Committee of the National Association of Realtors as a mediator. His earned accreditations include the Accredited Buyer Representative (ABR), Certified Real Estate Consultant (CREC), and the Graduate of Real Estate Institute (GRI) designations.

Dr. Jonah Mitchell has earned two Bachelor's degrees, one from Asbury College in Kentucky and one from Circleville Bible College in Ohio; a Master's degree from Valdosta State University in Georgia; and a Doctorate of Philosophy from Georgia State University.

Jonah, welcome to *Masters of Success!*

Mitchell

Thank you very much, David.

Wright

Reading your biography, it seems you are the poster boy for success in real estate and business leadership. So before we go any further, would you tell our readers how you define and measure success?

Mitchell

Success is the privilege of doing well that which you are passionate about. It is the right mix of passion and hard work. Success is best understood and appreciated if we agree that success is a living, ever-changing process.

To be a top producing multi-million dollar Realtor®, you must begin by passing the real estate exam—that is success. You must then aggressively network, continue your education, and affiliate with a winning company—that's success. Eventually, you must close deals— that's success. Ultimately, you want to make a lasting difference and leave a legacy—that's success.

I characterize this ever-changing process as "seasons of success." We can have different or multiple successes during any or all of the four seasons concurrently.

In the *spring* of each success, we plant and we plan. Those bright spring days and nights are filled with goals, desires, and dreams that are the beginning of any success.

In the *summer* of each success, we toil and we train. Those long days and long nights are filled with work, discipline, and preparation. Summer is our most important time and hardest work.

The *fall* of each success, of course, is the harvesting and the preserving. Those days and nights are filled with professionalism, fine-tuning, and excellence.

But there is always that wonderful *winter* of each success. Those happy winter days and nights are filled with bounty and sharing. Three things happen during our winters of success:

1. We understand and acquire an unquestionable taste for great service.
2. We fully realize that excellence truly matters.
3. We start linking our legacies with people and contributions that will stand the test of time.

I believe those who are passionate and hard working can be successful in every season. Some will measure our successes in concrete objective terms. Others, many of whom we may never know, will proclaim our personal, professional, and community contributions.

Each of us must find that delicate balance of work, family, and service. The true meaning to any season of success is to know that we have lived every hour, every day, and every season to its fullest.

Wright

Jonah, how do we recognize success? Better yet, how do others recognize our success?

Mitchell

Success comes in any of these three forms: 1) Material, 2) Proclaimed, and 3) Personal.

Material success is very measurable: sales volumes, shareholders' dividends, units rented, attendance records, patent approval, conversions, election tallies, and bank account totals. But material success is also very relative. Suppose I close twenty million dollars of sales annually. What about the Realtor of the Year who closed forty-two point seven million, or what about the National Association of Realtors team that closes over two hundred and fifty million? Material success is only true success when it is fully realized and appreciated. The snare in material success is that the goal is seldom satisfied—especially if we accept the ever-moving stick-and-carrot belief that our goal is always more than what we possess now. The appropriate philosophy of material success should be that we continually look forward with confidence and back without regret—that is success.

Proclaimed success is reflected in rewards, honors, hit songs, press releases, civic contributions, memberships, number one best-sellers, or political victories. There are a great many of us who enjoy as much pleasure from a standing ovation as we do from our cashed commission check.

Personal success is self-acknowledged and is not necessarily found on the busiest of roads; who says success has to come on a four-lane highway? Success could be on a private drive with no accolades or headlines. Personal success follows your passions and personal beliefs. I understand that Van Gogh, whose paintings now sell for millions, died broke; but he died a passionate painter. I doubt anyone outside her extended family of eight children raised on Muddy Branch in Eastern Kentucky ever ate my Grandma Cornelia Mitchell's homemade-from-scratch buttermilk biscuits, but regretfully you all missed the privilege of knowing one of the world's finest cooks. She did her personal best and served it all up with love. That is success—very personal—but still success.

Part of your question was how I measure success. I measure success just like Ralph Waldo Emerson—by how often and how much I laugh; by earning the respect of intelligent people and the affection of children; by gaining the appreciation of honest critics; by enduring the betrayal of false friends; by appreciating beauty and the best in others. How I measure success, just like Emerson said, is to leave the world a better place—whether by a garden patch, a healthy child, a cure to a social ill, or a job well done.

Wright

Your biography tells about your obvious success in business. Do you think that to be successful one must always be successful in all areas of life, or can we sometimes fail as we continue to work toward our goals?

Mitchell

I'm not sure, but I think you have been sitting in on my "Mitchell's School of Lessons Learned" classes. As a matter of fact, Chapter One is entitled, *Failing to Find Success*. If you are not failing, you are not moving forward. I teach every new real estate agent that it takes ten prospects to make one good customer; and four ready, willing, and able customers to make a client prepared to list or to buy. That is a lot of rejection, but it's not permanent failure. I should hope that we could find success in all areas of our life, all of the time. But if you are one who is unafraid to pursue your call to greatness, then you understand there are going to be failures along your path to success.

I find that we are either in a crisis, near a failure, in a period of weakness, or we are soon going to be. Almost every time, success is just down the road from doubt, embarrassment, and stress. I believe that darkness has a purpose—to be a canvas for our light.

Wright

Jonah, we both believe that learning something meaningful from painful experiences is a lesson on success. In *Conversations on Success* Randall Bell wrote, "Problems create lessons, lessons create value, and values create achievements." Was he right?

Mitchell

Absolutely. My name is Jonah; in psychology there is a phenomenon known as "The Jonah Complex." It's an abnormal behavior of running from your calling or your greatness. The cure for it is to understand that God has no other you. Galatians 6:4 says, "Make a careful exploration of who you are and the work you have been given and throw yourself into it; don't be overly impressed with yourself and don't compare yourself with others" (*The Message® Bible* translation). Each of us must take responsibility for doing our creative best even when success is temporarily denied.

Wright

Are there specific guidelines for achieving our "creative best" success?

Mitchell

Yes. Long ago Cicero wrote these guidelines and here are my interpretations:

1. I will not worry about the things that can't be changed or corrected. My interpretation is *I am going to concentrate on my strengths, not my weaknesses.* Learn to accept compliments graciously. List your successes and refer to that list often, especially when you are down.

2. I will not refuse to set aside trivial preferences for things of permanent good. I interpret this as *I will care enough to change.* If you think what you are doing is difficult, it's time to elevate your level of expectation. Difficult can be

achieved. People who change the world accomplish the impossible.

3. My individual advancements will not be made by crushing others. I interpret that as saying *I'll greet this day with a great attitude in my heart.* I'll use affirmative language; one can't think in a positive way using negative words, so constructive and encouraging words are essential to the quality of life. As the song says, "And I think to myself, what a wonderful world!"

4. I will not insist that things are impossible because I cannot accomplish them. *I have to learn to be a team member and to inspire others,* and to make them feel important by attentively listening to them. "Nothing that is truly great can be achieved in our lifetime," says Reinhold Niebuhr, "therefore, we must be *saved by hope.* Nothing that is true or beautiful or good makes complete sense on any one day of history; therefore, we have to be *saved by faith.* Nothing we do, however virtuous, can be accomplished alone; therefore, we are *saved by love.*

5. I will not be compelled by others to believe or to live as they do. In other words, *I will exercise great confidence in myself and in my faith.* In life's race, I want to compete only with my own past records. An inner-directed person doesn't always look to others for leadership and certainly doesn't try to please others all the time.

6. The last guideline is *I will not neglect to develop or to refine my mind nor forget the habit of reading and studying daily.* Read, listen to, and attend anything available to continue your development plan.

Wright

I'm always interested in how people arrive at a successful life. Can you tell our readers a little about your early years and what principles were forged into your childhood?

Mitchell

This gets a little personal. I am truly a mountain boy. My mother birthed thirteen children. I was born on Lower Kings Creek in Letcher County, Kentucky. I attended a two-room grade school and carried my lunch in a pail.

Later, I spent two years in orphanages. (That story will be told in *The Rocks Come with the Farm*.) I remember some of the good times, of course—the sound of that out-of-tune piano accompanying us when we sang *Froggy Went A'Courtin'*, the glasses of milk and gingerbread cookies we received on Sunday afternoons, and the pie socials. I can still hear the old mountain songs, fiddles, banjos, the cloggers, and the auctioneer. Every man was expected to bid on his wife's or girlfriend's pies and to give the money as a donation. Every orphan was invited to share a delicious homemade meal with a community family.

However, the most vivid memory of Buckhorn Orphanage is the long, cold winter nights in a narrow bunk bed on the second floor of the wood-framed dormitory. A little seven-year-old boy awakes shivering, crying, and saying, "June Bug, June Bug, I'm cold." My big brother, all of twelve years old, would roll out of the top bunk, cover me up with one of his worn quilts and find an old coat or something else to wrap himself in. Then I would fall asleep, warm and loved.

Wright

What a story. What lessons of success did you learn from these childhood experiences?

Mitchell

I embraced five success principles that still lead me today:

1. We need to *lead by example and to give more than we take.* June Bug died when he was thirty years of age from Hodgkin's Disease, so naturally the scripture means a great deal to me that says, "Greater love hath no man than this, that a man lay down his life for his friends [or a brother]" (John 15:13 KJV).

2. I learned that *you can choose to be successful.*

3. I learned *the rocks come with the farm.* I now live in beautiful Lexington, Kentucky. Every acre of the Bluegrass is sitting on solid limestone, which comes in layers. You can either hate it or you can make these world famous rock fences. It all depends on your attitude. "The rocks come with the farm" means you work with what you have. *You can change lives.* You can transform a malingering, out-of-touch, self-obsessed company into a profitable cutting-edge powerhouse.

4. I also learned this great principle: *let no one steal your joy.* "Hard times are inevitable but misery is an option," says Pastor Wayne Smith. I love to work and I love my work; I don't apologize that my wagon stays full. I don't want anyone to steal my joy.

5. *I am humbled by success.* Hanging on one wall in my office is a picture of our family as children standing in front of my dad's board and batten store next to our four-room home; on another wall hangs my accolades.

Wright

You are known as a proven motivator and excellent instructor. Do you think that you have a responsibility to pass the knowledge you have obtained on to the next generation and your industry, or is it simply part of your job?

Mitchell

It is certainly not only a part of my job, David. I am committed to teaching and to instructing. I experience as much joy teaching as I do closing real estate transactions. I believe that we must pass on the knowledge. I wish we could pass on our wisdom and help young professional sales leaders smooth out the inevitably volatile learning curve.

There is a great deal of remodeling going on in the real estate industry.

Today's prospects have a new way of doing business; they have a new number and it starts with www.com.

Today's relationships are built with new materials. It's no longer, "What can I sell you?" Today's question is, "What does it take for me to build a sustainable and profitable relationship with you?" The greatest marketing plan in the world that does not result in a sale for you and a profit for me is nothing but a blueprint for disaster and an invitation for unhappiness.

Today's trust is not yesterday's handshake. We have to teach our new sales leaders about the renewed value of trust. The foundations of today's trust are transparency, accuracy, and consistency. The building blocks for life-long clients are confidentiality, obedience, loyalty, disclosure, accountability, and extraordinary care.

Wright

Are there any characteristics that must be present in the lives of successful people? In other words, do people have *to be* before they *have*?

Mitchell

That is a good question. I believe that in order to be successful you have to:

- Be *present.* So help me, sixty percent of success is showing up—consistently, faithfully, and completely. Look your client in the eye, pick an eye, stay focused, and quit looking for the next quick deal.
- Be *resilient.* Redefine the rejection and focus on the reward. You don't stay down or you don't stay around people who bring you down.
- Be *attentive* to detail. Every day of my life, I live by three words—"read every word." It prevents many lawsuits.
- Be *faithful* to your calling. No regrets, no reserves, and no retreats. This is my post. I am going to find my acres of diamonds right here.
- Be *thankful.* Learn an uplifting prayer and pray it daily. Send at least two personally signed thank you notes daily.
- Be *ready.* You must be prepared. Early on I read a book by Dr. Billy Graham entitled, *World Aflame.* He stated he had only one regret—that he did not know how far-reaching his opportunities and influence would be or he would have become better educated to be better prepared.

Wright

Let's talk about success and strategies related to life's pursuits. Will you share with our readers what you think is the single most important step to experiencing material, proclaimed, or personal success?

Mitchell

That is an easy one for me. I believe you have to make the right decisions.

Wright

You must have in place a system or a guide to your decision-making?

Mitchell

Here are my seven steps to successful decision-making.

1. Is it good? ....The Smell Test
2. Is it legal? ....The Jail Test
3. What if it were published? ....The Newspaper Test
4. Is it ethical? ....The Peers Test
5. Does it make life better? ....The Stress Test
6. Does it make me money? ....The Profit Test
7. Does it take me where I want to go? ....The Map Test

I would like to tell you a little about each one of these.

Is it good? The Smell Test: Is it for the greater good; does it take you from good to great as author Jim Collins challenges?

Is it legal? The Jail Test: I am not sure but I think all prison stripes are some shade of gray. We need to learn what is black and white out there.

What if were published? The Newspaper Test: Early in my real estate career someone recorded all conversations that were going on in a house I was showing; that changed my behavior. Now I act as though everything I am saying is being bugged and photographed. What God overlooks, the paparazzi print.

Is it ethical? The Peer Test: In our real estate profession, there are ethics and now standards of practice—rules of behavior that guide our interactions with clients and peers. I would rather be *Chairman of*, rather than the *defendant before*, the Professional Standards Committee.

Does it make my life better? The Stress Test: There has to be a balance.

Does it make me money? The Profit Test: You can't go broke making a profit, but you can find yourself in need with a little too much greed.

Does it take me where I want go? The Map Test: Opportunity only knocks once is a myth!

Wright

Explain the opportunity myth or any other challenges that passionate and hard-working sales leaders must demystify.

Mitchell

A challenge facing our young sales leaders today is the reality that "opportunity just keeps knocking." Opportunity is like a bus—there is a different one every thirty minutes. The key is for us to get on the specific bus that will take us where we really want to go. Today's tragedy is too much peanut butter and jam, i.e., too many opportunities.

Researchers set up a table of thirty different jams in front of a gourmet market in California. Three percent of the shoppers who stopped at the table bought a jar. When they displayed six instead of thirty jams, thirty percent bought. In jam selections, as with many other opportunities, sometimes too many choices can cause brain lock.

In real estate, we are entering our ninth year of record growth, record sales, and dollars earned. We must keep focused and apply some *opportunity management* that ensures we are still headed to our chosen destination even if we did change buses.

Another challenge is the "just add water myth." I believe that there is such a thing as overnight success—it just takes twenty years to get there. We have proof of it every place we turn.

I read this wonderful little article in *Farmer*, a magazine for us John Deere tractor owners. The author said if you lift the lid off a pot of jasmine rice, as hard as you may try, you can't keep your mouth from watering. That nutty aroma can fill a room in moments and set the appetite on fire. It's not hard to see why the appeal of jasmine rice is so popular. It was no small feat to figure out the secret of that great aroma. In fact, a guy named Robert Henry and his research team at Australia's Southern Cross University in New South Wales pored over four hundred million DNA sequences to find the best aroma. I don't believe in the "just add water" syndrome. Success comes to the persistent.

Today's third challenge for sales leaders is the "vertical versus the horizontal rule." Image building is restrictively expensive. Successful agents only engage in effective and efficient personal promotion strategies. Find a niche; go vertical instead of horizontal. Find a specific area of expertise that is generally under-serviced, that is unprotected, and own it! Raise the barriers of that niche so no one can easily climb them. I am privileged to be involved in beautiful subdivision developments. Is there any correlation between the fact that I have tried to attend every monthly planning and zoning meeting for over fifteen years?

Wright

If I could wave a magic wand and grant you any two wishes for the future, what would you wish for?

Mitchell

The first one is easy. I would wish for a breakthrough cancer cure for Hodgkin's Disease, in the name of my dear brother. Second, I'd wish my book, *The Rocks Come with the Farm,* were already in print.

Wright

As we close this interview, do you have any last thoughts that you would like to share with our readers that would help them to be better, happier, or even more successful?

Mitchell

My parting thought comes from a most treasured personal note I have received. I would wish this blessing for all: "Your enthusiasm is so hard to contain that we all get to share in its overflowing. You inspire others to be motivated and to take the time to inventory their own lives. God truly uses you."

Wright

What an interesting conversation. It's always great to talk with you, Jonah. I have always enjoyed each of our conversations.

Today we have been talking with Jonah Mitchell, who has been a licensed Realtor® since 1974. He is a national speaker and consultant, and president of Jonah Mitchell Speaker & Seminar Leader. As we have found out today, he knows a lot about success...because in my definition Jonah Mitchell *is* success.

Thank you so much, Jonah, for being with us today on *Masters of Success.*

Mitchell

And thank you, David.

About Jonah Mitchell, Ph.D.

Jonah Mitchell has earned the reputation as a master Realtor, Broker, and Developer; marketing upscale subdivisions is his genius. He is President of Jonah Mitchell Real Estate & Auction Group. Jonah's heritage in majestic Eastern Kentucky impressed upon him that life is beautiful. As one of thirteen children, he learned the value of a balanced life, and time in an orphanage taught him that the "rocks come with the farm." His extensive education schooled him in prudent and practical decision-making. Jonah Mitchell, Ph.D., is a national speaker, and expert witness for real estate litigation, consultant, and author. In this chapter, Jonah shared with you his decision-making model, as well as the four seasons and the three forms of success. You will be enrolled in the "Mitchell's School of Lessons Learned."

Jonah Mitchell, Ph.D.
Email: jonah@jonahmitchell.com

Chapter Eight

JACK CANFIELD

THE INTERVIEW

David E. Wright (Wright)

Today we are talking with Jack Canfield. You probably know him as the founder and co-creator of the *New York Times* number one best-selling *Chicken Soup for the Soul* book series, which currently has thirty-five titles and seventy-eight million copies in print in over thirty-two languages. Jack's background includes a Batchelor's from Harvard, a Master's from the University of Massachusetts and an Honorary Doctorate from the University of Santa Monica. He has been a high school and university teacher, a workshop facilitator, a psychotherapist, and for the past twenty-five years, a leading authority in the area of self-esteem and personal development.

Jack Canfield, welcome to *Masters of Success!*

Jack Canfield (Canfield)

Thank you David. It's great to be with you.

Wright

I talked with Mark Victor Hansen a few days ago. He gave you full credit for coming up with the idea of the *Chicken Soup* series. Obviously it's made you an internationally known personality. Other than recognition, has the series changed you personally and if so, how?

Canfield

I would say that it has and I think in a couple of ways. Number one, I read stories all day long of people who've overcome what would feel like insurmountable obstacles. For example we just did a book *Chicken Soup for the Unsinkable Soul.* There's a story in there about a single mother with three daughters. She got a disease and she had to have both of her hands and both of her feet amputated. She got prosthetic devices and was able to learn how to use them so she could cook, drive the car, brush her daughters' hair, get a job, etc. I read that and I think, "God, what would I ever have to complain and whine and moan about?" So I think at one level it's just given me a great sense of gratitude and appreciation for everything I have and made me less irritable about the little things.

I think the other thing that's happened for me personally is my sphere of influence has changed. By that I mean, for example, a couple of years ago I was asked to be the keynote speaker for the Women's Congressional Caucus. The Congressional Caucus includes women in Congress, Senators, Governors, and Lieutenant Governors in America.

I asked, "What do you want me to talk about—what topic?"

"Whatever you think we need to know to be better legislators," was the reply.

And I thought, "Wow! They want *me* to tell *them* about what laws they should be making and what would make a better culture?"

Well, that wouldn't have happened if our books hadn't come out and I hadn't become famous. I think I get to play with people at a higher level and have more influence in the world. That's important to me because my life purpose is inspiring and empowering people to live their highest vision so the world works for everybody. I get to do that on a much bigger level than when I was just a high school teacher back in Chicago.

Wright

I think one of the powerful components of that book series is that you can read a positive story in just a few minutes. You can also come back and revisit it. I know my daughter who is thirteen now has three of the books and she just reads them interchangeably. Sometimes I go in her bedroom and she'll be crying and reading one of them. Other times she'll be laughing, so they really are chicken soup for the soul, aren't they?

Canfield

They really are. In fact we have four books in the *Teenage Soul* series now and a new one coming out at the end of this year. We have a new book called *Chicken Soup for the Teenage Soul and the Tough Stuff*. It's all about dealing with parents' divorces, teachers who don't understand you, boyfriends who drink and drive, and stuff like that.

I have a son who's eleven and he has twelve-year-old friend (a girl). I asked my son's friend, "Why do you like this book?"

She said, "You know, whenever I'm feeling down I read it; it makes me cry and I feel better. Some of the stories make me laugh and some of the stories make me feel more responsible for my life. But basically I just feel like I'm not alone."

One of the people I work with recently said that the books are like a support group between the covers of a book. People can read about others' experiences and realize they're not the only one going through something.

Wright

Jack, with our *Masters of Success* publication we're trying to encourage people in our audience to be better, to live better, and be more fulfilled by listening to the examples of our guests. Is there anything or anyone in your life who has made a difference for you and helped you to become a better person?

Canfield

Yes and we could do ten shows just on that. I'm influenced by people all the time. If I were to go way back I'd have to say one of the key influences in my life was Jesse Jackson when he was still a minister in Chicago. I was teaching in an all black high school there and I went to Jesse Jackson's church with a friend one time. What happened for me was I saw somebody with a vision. (This was before Martin Luther King was killed and Jesse was of the lieutenants in his organization.) I just saw people trying to make the world work better for a certain segment of the population. I was inspired by that kind of visionary belief that it's possible to make change.

Then later John F. Kennedy was a hero of mine. I was very much inspired by him.

Later, a therapist by the name of Robert Resnick that I had for two years was an inspiration for me. He taught me a little formula called E + R = O. That stands for Events plus Response equals Outcome. He said, "If you don't like your outcomes quit blaming the events and start changing your responses." One of his favorite phrases was, "If the grass on the other side of the fence looks greener, start watering your own lawn more."

I think it helped me get off of any kind of self-pity I might have had because I had parents who were alcoholics. It's very easy to blame them for my life not working. They weren't real successful or rich and I was surrounded by people who were. I felt like, "God, what if I'd had parents like they had? I could have been a lot better." He just got me off that whole notion and made me realize the hand you were dealt is the hand you've got to play and take responsibility for who you are and quit complaining and blaming others and get on with your life. That was a turning point for me.

I'd say the last person who really affected me big time was a guy named W. Clement Stone who was a self-made multi-millionaire in Chicago. He taught me that success is not a four-letter word, it's nothing to be ashamed of and you ought to go for it. He said, "The best thing you can do for the poor is not be one of them." Be a model for what it is to live a successful life. So I learned from him the principles of success and that's what I've been teaching now for the last almost thirty years.

Wright

He was the entrepreneur in the insurance industry, wasn't he?

Canfield

He was. He had combined insurance and when I worked for him he was worth six hundred million dollars. That was before the dot.com millionaires came along in Silicon Valley. He just knew more about success. He was a good friend of Napoleon Hill who wrote *Think and Grow Rich*. He was a fabulous mentor. I really learned a lot from him.

Wright

I miss some of the men I listened to when I was a young salesman coming up and he was one of them. Napoleon Hill was another one and Dr. Peale—all of their writings made me who I am today. I'm glad that I got that opportunity.

Canfield

One speaker whose name you probably will remember, Charlie "Tremendous" Jones, says, "Who we are is a result of the books we read and the people we hang out with." I think that's so true and that's why I tell people, "If you want to have high self-esteem hang out with people with high self-esteem. If you want to be more spiritual hang out with spiritual people." We're always telling our children, "Don't hang out with those kids." The reason we don't want them to associate with certain kinds of people is we know how influential people are with each other. I think we need to give ourselves the same advice. Who are we hanging out with? We can hang out with them in books, cassette tapes, CDs, radio shows like yours, and in person.

Wright

One of my favorites was a fellow named Bill Gove from Florida. I talked with him about three or four years ago; he's retired now. His mind is still as quick as it ever was. I thought he was one of the greatest speakers I had ever heard.

What do you think makes up a great mentor? In other words, are there characteristics that mentors seem to have in common?

Canfield

I think there are two obvious ones. One, I think they have to have the time to do it and two, the willingness to do it. And then three, I think they need to be someone who is doing something you want to do.

W. Clement Stone used to tell me, "If you want to be rich hang out with rich people. Watch what they do, eat what they eat, dress the way they dress. Try it on." He wasn't suggesting that I give up my authentic self, but he was pointing out that they probably have habits I didn't have. His advice was to study them—study the people who are already like you. I always ask salespeople in an organization, "Who are the top two or three in your organization?" I tell them to start taking them out to lunch and dinner and for a drink and finding out what they do. Ask them, "What's your secret?" Nine times out of ten they'll be willing to tell you.

It goes back to what we said earlier about asking. I'll go into corporations and I'll say, "Who are the top ten people?"

They'll all tell me and I'll say, "Did you ever ask them what they do that is different than what you do?"

They reply, "No."

"Why not?"

"Well they might not want to tell me."

"How do you know? Did you ever ask them? All they can do is say no. You'll be no worse off than you are now."

So I think with mentors you just look at people who seem to be living the life you want to live and achieving the results you want to achieve. And then what we tell them in our book is, when you approach a mentor they're probably busy and successful and so they haven't got a lot of time. Just ask, "Can I talk to you for ten minutes every month?" If I know it's only going to be ten minutes I'll probably say yes. The neat thing is if I like you I'll always give you more than ten minutes, but that ten minutes gets me in the door.

Wright

In the future are there any more Jack Canfield books authored singularly?

Canfield

Yes, I'm working on two books right now. One's called $E + R = O$ which is that little formula I told you about earlier. I just feel I want to get that out there because every time I give a speech and talk about that the whole room gets so quiet you can hear a pin drop. I can tell that people are really getting value.

Then I'm going to do a series of books on the principles of success. I've got about 150 of them that I've identified over the years. I have a book down the road I want to do that's called *No More Put-Downs* which is a book probably aimed mostly at parents, teachers, and managers. There's a culture we have now of put-down humor whether it's *Married With Children* or *All in the Family*—there's that characteristic of macho put-down humor. There's research now that's showing how bad it is for kids' self-esteem, and for co-workers and for athletes (when the coaches do it) so I want to get that message out there as well.

Wright

It's really not that funny, is it?

Canfield

No. We'll laugh it off because we don't want to look like we're a wimp but underneath we're hurt. The research now shows that you're better off breaking a child's bones than you are breaking their spirit. A bone will heal much more quickly than their emotional spirit will.

Wright

I remember recently reading a survey where people listed the top five people who had influenced them in their lives. I've tried it on a couple of groups at church and other places. In my case (and in the survey that's running) I found that about three out of people's top five mentors are always teachers. I wonder if that's going to be the same in the next decade.

Canfield

I think probably because as children we're in our most formative years. We actually spend more time with our teachers than we do with our parents. Research shows that the average parent only interacts verbally with each of their children only about eight and a half minutes a day. Yet at school you're interacting with your teacher for anywhere from six to eight hours, depending on how long the school day is. This includes interaction with coaches, chorus directors, etc.

I think that in almost everybody's life there's been that one teacher who loved them as a human being, not just as a student—some person they were supposed to fill full of history and English. And that person believed in them and inspired them.

Les Brown is one of the great motivational speakers in the world. If it hadn't been for one teacher who said, "I think you can do more than be in a special ed. class; I think you're the one," he'd probably still be cutting grass in the median strip of the highways in Florida instead of a successful presenter who can receive $35,000 as a keynote speaker.

Wright

I had a conversation one time with Les when he was talking about this wonderful teacher who discovered he was dyslexic. Everybody else called him dumb but this one lady took him under her wing and had him tested. His entire life changed because of her interest in him.

Canfield

I'm on the board of advisors of the Dyslexic Awareness Resource Center here in Santa Barbara. The reason is because I taught at a high school with a lot of kids who were considered "at-risk." They were kids who would end up in gangs and so forth.

What we found over and over was that about seventy-eight percent of all the kids in the juvenile detention centers in Chicago were kids who had learning disabilities—primarily dyslexia—but there were others as well. They were never diagnosed and they weren't doing well in school so they'd drop out. As soon as you drop out of school you become subject to the influence of gangs and other kinds of criminal and drug linked activities.

If these kids had just been diagnosed earlier, we'd have probably gotten rid of half of the juvenile crime in America because there are a lot of really good programs that can teach dyslexics to read and so forth.

Wright

My wife is a teacher and she brings home stories that are heartbreaking about parents not being as concerned about their children as they used to be or not as helpful as they used to be. Did you find that to be a problem when you were teaching?

Canfield

It depends on what kind of district you're in. If it's a poor district the parents could be drugged out, on alcohol, and basically just not available. If you're in a really high rent district the parents are not available because they're both working and coming home tired, or they're jet-setters, or they're working late at the office because they're workaholics. Sometimes it really takes two paychecks to pay the rent anymore. I find that the majority of parents care but often they don't know what to do. They don't know how to discipline their children. They don't know how to help them with their homework. They're not passing on skills that they never got. Unfortunately the trend tends to be like a chain letter. The people with the least amount of skills tend to have the most number of children. The other thing is you get crack babies. In Los Angeles one out of every ten babies born is a crack baby.

Wright

That's unbelievable.

Canfield

Yes and another statistic shows that by the time they're twelve years old, fifty percent of the kids in the U.S. have started experimenting with alcohol. I see a lot of that in the Bible belt. You don't see the big city, urban designer drugs; but there is a lot of alcoholism. Another thing you get, unfortunately, is a lot of familial violence—a lot of kids getting beat up and hit, parents who drink and then explode; as we talked about earlier, child abuse and sexual abuse—you see a lot of that.

Wright

Most people are fascinated by these television shows about being a survivor. What has been the greatest comeback that you have made from adversity in your career or in your life?

Canfield

You know it's funny, I don't think I've had a lot of major failures and setbacks where I had to start over. My life's been kind of on an intentional curve. But I do have a lot of challenges. Mark and I are always setting goals that challenge us. We always say, "The purpose of setting a really big goal is not so that you can achieve it so much, but it's who you become in the process of achieving it."

A friend of mine, Jim Rose, says, "You want to set goals big enough so that in the process of achieving them you become someone worth being."

I think that to be a millionaire is nice but so what? People make the money and then they lose it. People get the big houses and they burn down or Silicon Valley goes belly up and all of a sudden they don't have a big house anymore. But who you became in the process of learning how to do that can never be taken away from you.

What we do is we constantly put big challenges in front of us. Right now we have a book coming out in a month called *Chicken Soup for the Teacher's Soul*. You'll have to make sure to get a copy for your wife. I was a teacher and I was a teacher trainer for years. But in the last seven years, because of the success of the *Chicken Soup* books, I haven't been in the education world that much. I've got to go out and relearn how I market to that world.

I met with a Superintendent of Schools. I met with a guy named Jason Dorsey who's one of the number one consultants in the world in that area. I found out who has the best-selling book in that area. I sat down with his wife for a day and talked about her marketing approaches.

So I believe that if you face any kind of adversity, whether it's you lose your job, your husband dies, you get divorced, you're in an accident like Christopher Reeves and you become paralyzed, or whatever, you simply do what you have to do. You find people who have already handled this and how they did it. You find out either from their books, or from their tapes, or by talking to them, or interviewing them, and you get the support you need to get through it. Whether it's a counselor in your church or you go on a retreat or you read the Bible, you do something that gives you the support you need to get to the other end.

You also have to know what the end you want is. Do you want to be remarried? Do you just want to have a job and be a single mom? What is it? You need to reach out and ask for support; I think people really like to help other people. They're not always available because sometimes they're going through it themselves; but there's always someone with a helping hand. Often I think we let our pride get in the way. We let our stubbornness get in the way. We let our belief in how the world should be get in our way instead of dealing with how the world *is*. When we get that out of the way then we can start doing that which we need to do to get where we need to go.

Wright

If you could have a platform and tell our audience something you feel that would help or encourage them, what would you say?

Canfield

I'd say number one, believe in yourself, believe in your dreams, and trust your feelings. I think too many people are trained wrong when they're little kids. For instance, they're mad at their daddy and they're told, "You're not mad at your Daddy."

They say, "Gee, I thought I was."

Or you say, "That's going to hurt."

The doctor says, "No it's not." Then he or she gives you the shot and it hurts.

The doctor says, "See, that didn't hurt, did it?"

The result is you start not to trust yourself.

Or you ask your mom, "Are you upset?"

Your mom says, "No," but she really is. So you stop learning to trust your perception.

I tell the story over and over there are hundreds of people I've met who've come from upper class families where they make big incomes and the dad's a doctor, and the kid wants to be a mechanic and work in an auto shop because that's what he loves. The family says, "That's beneath us. You can't do that." So the kid ends up being an anesthesiologist killing three people because he's not paying attention. What he really wants to do is tinker with cars.

I tell people you've got to trust your own feelings—your own motivations, what turns you on, what you want to do, what makes you feel good—and quit worrying about what other people say, think, or want for you. Decide what you want for yourself and then do what you need to do to go about getting it. It takes work.

I always tell people that I read a book a week minimum and at the end of the year I've read fifty-two books. We're talking about professional books, books on self-help, finances, psychology, parenting, and so forth. At the end of ten years you've read 520 books. That puts me in the top one percent of people knowing stuff in this country. But most people are spending their time watching television.

W. Clement Stone told me when I went to work for him, "I want you to cut out one hour a day of television."

"Okay, what do I do with it?" I asked him.

He said, "Read."

He told me what kind of stuff to read. He said, "At the end of a year you'll have spent 365 hours reading. Divide that by a forty-hour work week and that's nine and half weeks of education every year."

I thought, "Wow! That's two months." It's like going back to summer school. As a result of that I have close to 8,000 books in my library.

The reason I'm on your show instead of someone else's is that people like me, Jim Rohn, Les Brown, and you read a lot. We listen to tapes and we go to those seminars. That's why we're the people with the information. I always say that your raise becomes effective when you do. You'll become more effective as you gain more skills, more insight, and more knowledge.

Wright

Jack, I have watched your career for over a decade and your accomplishments are just outstanding. But your humanitarian efforts are really what impress me. I think that you're doing great things, not only in California, but also all over the country.

Canfield

It's true. In addition to all of the work we do, we pick one to three charities. We've given away over six million dollars in the last eight years, along with our publisher who matches every penny we give away. We've planted over a million trees in Yosemite National Park. We've paid for hundreds of thousands of cataract operations in third world countries. We've contributed to the Red Cross, the Humane Society, and on it goes. It feels like a real blessing to be able to make that kind of a contribution in the world.

Wright

Today we have been talking with Jack Canfield, the founder and co-creator of the *Chicken Soup for the Soul* book series, which currently has thirty-five titles and I'll have to update this. It was fifty-three million. How many has it been now, Jack?

Canfield

We're almost up to seventy-eight million. We have a book coming out in just a couple of weeks called *Chicken Soup for the Soul of America*. It's all stories that grew out of 9/11—it's a real healing book for our nation. I would encourage your listeners to get themselves a copy and share it with their families.

Wright

I will stand in line to get one of those. Thank you so much for being with us today.

About Jack Canfield

Jack Canfield is one of America's leading experts on developing self esteem and peak performance. A dynamic and entertaining speaker, as well as a highly sought-after trainer, he has a wonderful ability to inform and inspire audiences toward developing their own human potential and personal effectiveness. Jack Canfield is most well known for the *Chicken Soup for the Soul* series, which he co-authored with Mark Victor Hansen, and for his audio programs about building high self-esteem. Jack is the founder of Self-Esteem Seminars, located in Santa Barbara, California, which trains entrepreneurs, educators, corporate leaders and employees how to accelerate the achievement of their personal and professional goals. Jack is also the founder of The Foundation for Self Esteem, located in Culver City, California, which provides self-esteem resources and training to social workers, welfare recipients and human resource professionals. Jack graduated from Harvard in 1966, received his M.E. degree at the university of Massachusetts in 1973, and an Honorary Doctorate from the University of Santa Monica. He has been a high school and university teacher, a workshop facilitator, a psychotherapist, and for the past thirty years, a leading authority in the area of self-esteem and personal development. As a result of his work with prisoners, welfare recipients, and inner-city youth, Jack was appointed by the state legislature to the California Task Force to Promote Self-Esteem and Personal and Social Responsibility. He also served on the board of trustees of the National Council for Self-Esteem.

Jack Canfield

P.O. Box 30880

Santa Barbara, CA 93130

Email: info4jack@jackcanfield.com

Chapter Nine

LINDA LARSEN

THE INTERVIEW

David Wright (Wright)

Linda Larsen is the founder and CEO of a successful communications company she started over sixteen years ago. She is passionately committed to helping people upgrade their thinking, improve their communication, and increase their bottom line. More than that, she is willing to do whatever it takes to get her message across and make it stick.

Linda's passion and spontaneous humor stems from over twenty years as a professional actress in film, television, and on stage. Her experience and training (she holds an undergraduate degree in Behavioral Sciences from the University of Florida and a Master of Fine Arts Degree from Florida State University) give her the unique ability to combine the entertaining, dynamic aspects of live theater with practical, high value content to produce lasting, positive changes.

In 1988 she began working exclusively with trial attorneys. As a highly respected trial consultant, she continues to provide CLE training for lawyers, helping them communicate more effectively and persuasively in the high stakes, high stress environment of the courtroom.

She is the author of the best selling audio program, "12 Secrets to High Self-Esteem," the critically acclaimed book, *True Power,* and *Linda Larsen's Power Tips.* She has also written or been featured in over 100 articles in such publications as *Investor's Business Daily,* the *Chicago Tribune, Women In Business, Personal Excellence,* CBSHealthWatch.com, and MSN.com, among others.

Linda, welcome to *Masters of Success.*

Linda Larsen (Larsen)

Thank you, David.

Wright

Since we're talking about success, would you tell us how you define it?

Larsen

I think at its most basic level success is the ability to achieve what it is that you set out to achieve, and what you set out to achieve is up to you. For me, it's about consciously growing and learning, expanding my capacity to give love, and making a positive difference for others.

And in some curiously ironic way, this definition doesn't tell the whole story. What I have found is that like almost everyone else on the planet, the things I have chosen to pursue have no "arrival date." They will forever be creating their own space for expansion. I don't expect to wake up one day and say, "Hooray! I have now successfully grown and learned a bunch of stuff. I'm finished! Bring on the margaritas!"

I think where we get into trouble—and this has certainly been true for me in the past—is when we believe that there *is* some success destination like, when we get that house, that car, that level of income—those symbols of success—*then* we will have arrived and we can coast after that. What an illusive, exhausting, deceptive pursuit *that* is! I believe we just have to understand that the arrival date, place, and experience are quite ephemeral and cannot be contained.

Wright

I know you are an international keynote presenter, but I understand you resisted the term "motivational speaker" for the longest time. Why is that?

Larsen

I think most people have a misconception about what the term "motivation" really means. When most people think of a motivational speaker, they imagine someone who comes in and creates a "pump and hype" experience—no real value—just a fun time. xxxThey believe they'll get all fired up, but then they'll go back to life as usual with the same set of problems they had when they walked into the room. And I can certainly understand why they'd think that, because that was my perception for a long time.

I no longer hold that definition to be accurate. I think that without motivation we don't have much chance of being successful at anything we want to accomplish. If I can't motivate myself to get up in the morning, then I'm going to have a bit of a problem. If I want to achieve more but can't motivate myself to take action, then I'm going to be stuck with the status quo forever. Motivation is the driving force behind all of our successes in life.

And yes, I am a motivational speaker, and I take my job very, very seriously. But the fact is that no one can motivate someone else to do anything. I cannot motivate you. What I *can* do is set up the kind of environment conducive to self-motivation; but I can't motivate anyone to do anything.

You might be thinking, "Wait a minute. If I put a gun to your head and said, 'clean up the house or I'll kill you,' wouldn't that motivate you to take action?" Well, only if I wanted to live. If I didn't want to live, you couldn't physically move my hands and feet and make me clean up the house. You can't motivate me to do that—only I can.

So it comes down to this. I believe that it is my responsibility as a motivational speaker to first find out what the issues of my participants are, and then to set up the kind of learning environment that is energizing and inspiring. Next I've got to come up with some great ideas to help them resolve their issues, and finally, present them in a fun, interactive, and entertaining way so that everyone can remember and apply them later.

That's my job. And I love it.

Wright

You say there's always one thing you address in your keynote presentations, no matter what the topic. What is that and why do you always talk about it?

Larsen

Have you ever had this experience? You attended a great seminar or read an amazing book, and thought, "Wow! This is it—the answer I have been looking for! My life is now whole, complete, and satisfied!" Then, three weeks later, you find that nothing in your life has changed. What happened? You were very motivated (there's that term again) to make a change, you knew what you should do and how to do it, but you didn't do it. Don't you wonder why that is?

In my work as a trial consultant I stumbled across some very interesting information published by Dr. John Bargh, Professor of Psychology at Yale University. His research focuses on the question, "How much free will do we really have?" He wanted to know the extent to which any and all social psychological phenomena—attitudes, evaluations, emotions, impressions, motivations, and social behavior—occur non-consciously (sic) and automatically. And the results were astonishing. Some of his studies, and those of his constituents, suggest that as much as 99.44 percent of our behaviors are automatic and unthinking. Wow!

That has profound implications for us! It explains why we may hear about a good idea and then never try it, or try it once, and then return immediately to the way we've always done things. It explains why we continue some ineffective action, or attitude, or behavior, even when it clearly doesn't serve us. We are just simply wired to keep on doing what we have always done.

I think this is very exciting information. If I know that every force in the universe is going to pull me back into my comfortable little, self-limiting, miserable rut, then I know what I have to do to overcome that—I have to get conscious and work hard! I have to learn a new skill and then practice it like crazy until *it* becomes automatic and unthinking.

So, I let every audience I speak to know first of all what they are going to be up against when they walk out of the room when I'm done. That way, they are aware of what they have to do to remedy this natural tendency. It's all about, "here are some really great ideas, here's what's going to happen when you try to apply them, and here's what you can do to actually make them happen."

Wright

Can you give me a specific example of how this might manifest for someone and how they could overcome the tendency to slip back into those automatic behaviors?

Larsen

Everyone would agree that the most effective people we know have really excellent communication skills. But unfortunately, most of us didn't get a lot of training in this arena. We learned how to communicate from our well-meaning parents, who learned from their parents. Our parents and grandparents may have all been told that, "If you can't say something nice, don't say anything at all," or that you should only "speak when spoken to." And those strategies are extremely counterproductive both personally and professionally. I would imagine that there were some folks at Enron who suspected early on what was happening but chose to adhere to those limiting beliefs. You can see where all that ended up.

So, let's say you want to become a very good communicator, but historically you allowed your emotions to get the best of you. Maybe it was a lack of confidence, or self-doubt or whatever, but frequently, when you wanted to speak up at a meeting, offer an idea, or question someone else's suggestion, you just kept silent. Here's what you could do:

1. Fully own your "automatic behavior" in this arena, and take full responsibility for having chosen this ineffective strategy. You can't let something go if you won't acknowledge that you have it.
2. Find a coach—a co-worker, trusted colleague, or family member—someone you believe has very good communication skills and is committed to your success. Tell her what you want to accomplish. Give your coach full permission to give you straight feedback when she notices you clam up. Also, use her to practice with. Got a big meeting coming up? Rehearse what you are going to say. Allow your coach to help you shape your thoughts in a clear, concise manner.
3. Be aware! In the meeting—during those moments before you actually get to try out your new skills—every instinct in your body will want to superglue your mouth shut. Just notice that feeling and let it go.
4. Keep breathing fully—this can sharpen your focus, help you slow down, and fully support your voice. It will also help you keep still.
5. Open your mouth and speak. Look people straight in the eye, and when you have said what you want to say, shut-eth (sic) your mouth. One of our biggest tendencies when we are nervous is to keep on talking after our point has been made.

And that's just one example. Maybe your problem is that you have an intimidating manner that puts people off, or you interrupt others, or talk about yourself too much, or don't exercise, or don't eat right. The list could go on and on. This strategy would work great with any habitual behavior that doesn't serve you, if you are committed to change.

Wright

You mentioned emotions—and for many people they seem to have a mind of their own—how can we control our emotions when necessary?

Larsen

And don't you wish more people you encounter during the day had that ability? Well, the truth is that if I can't maintain a calm state in the face of danger, a difficult person, or a boss who's screaming at me, I can create a greater problem than the one that already exists. But emotions are a prime player in almost every area of our lives, not just when there's a challenge.

We could spend a year on this thing called "emotion" and never scratch the surface, but here are a few things I've discovered.

First of all, in terms of decision-making, emotions are king (or queen). When I was working primarily as a trial consultant, I focused my research on the decision-making process. I wanted to understand how human beings (jurors, in this case) decide who's guilty or negligent and who's not. What I discovered was that the process they used is the same one we use when we decide whether or not to buy a product or service, or say "yes" or "no" to someone's request, or even whether or not we believe something is true or valid. And this makes sense when you consider the fact that we are wired (from our early days on the planet) to make an important assessment the moment we encounter a stimulus. In essence what we do is "decide" if what we are faced with is good or bad. Our early ancestors had to do this in order to survive. Good—I can eat it. Bad—it will eat me; and we got very, very good at this.

Here's how it works: decisions are made first, foremost, and incredibly quickly (within 200 milliseconds) from the emotional, feeling, intuitive side of your brain. Then, you will immediately jump over to the logical, analytical, thinking side of your brain to find the facts and data (and here's the cool part) to support the decision that *you have already made.*

So, in terms of controlling my emotions, I now understand that I'm probably going to have an automatic emotional response to anything that I perceive to be a threat. My fight-or-flight response will kick in very quickly. That doesn't mean I have to act on it, however, and that's where most of us mess up. We don't believe there is any space between the stimulus and our automatic response, so we just allow our emotions to do whatever they do. And from my personal experience, I can tell you, doing that can be ineffective, counterproductive, and, in my case, downright dangerous.

Wright

That sounds dramatic. Can you tell us about it?

Larsen

Yes. Go back with me to December, 1969. I'm twenty-one years old. I'm divorced and the mother of a two-year-old son. I'm working as a receptionist at a law office making fifty-five dollars per week and am desperately struggling to make ends meet. I am suffering the effects of having grown up in an extremely dysfunctional home with alcoholism, abuse, and abandonment, which now manifests itself in clinical depression, anxiety, and severe panic attacks. I have periods so filled with despair and terror that suicide seems like the only answer. And while I had seriously considered this option before, on the morning of December 6, 1969, I come perilously close to making it a reality.

From the moment I wake up, I hear the words resounding in my mind, "I'm ready to die. I just can't make it any longer. I'm ready to die." I feel sick. Hopeless.

But I look into the eyes of that beautiful little baby boy, and I know I have to try to make it just one more day. So I force myself to go to work, hanging on to my sanity by what feels like a thin silk thread.

At 11:30 in the morning, as I sit at the front desk in the law office trying desperately to appear normal, the front door bursts open and in runs a man in a prison uniform, brandishing a .357 magnum. It turns out that he is an escaped convict who, a few minutes earlier, had jumped the guard on the road gang where he was working, stolen the guard's gun, and fled on foot, only to wind up insinuating himself into my personal space.

He puts the gun to my head, grabs me by the arm, and demands car keys from one of the attorneys. He then announces that he is leaving and he's taking me with him. He goes on to warn the other people in the office that if they call the cops he will kill me.

Oh, there is a part of me—a very small part—that wants to say, "Wait, you idiot! I'm a certifiable crazy person! You don't want *me*! Pick somebody else!" Of course, I say nothing. Mostly I'm in some state of shock.

He jams the gun in my back and pushes me outside to the car. He puts me in the driver's seat and gives me directions to a remote part of town where he wants to wait until after dark. We get to the place only to find that there are construction workers there building a new subdivision. This turns out to be a good thing for me.

He then directs me to a home that belongs to a friend of his. We go inside and he tells her that she can leave to keep her children away if she promises that she won't call the police. She agrees and leaves. As she prepares to leave, I look into her eyes, silently begging her to please help me; but again, no words come out.

As the door slams behind her, my terror level soars. I am alone in a secluded, remote house with an escaped convict who has a loaded gun and nothing to lose. It is a dismal picture.

My emotions are running amok. Inside my head I am a blithering idiot. Inside my mind, I'm screaming, crying, begging for mercy, groveling on the floor—totally out of control. But somehow, on some level, I know that if I allow my emotions to influence what I say and do, it will be over for me. He is so nervous, intense, and jumpy that one wrong move on my part will send him over the edge.

And then the moment comes. I'm sitting on a chair, and he is sitting directly across from me about five feet away. There is total silence. He is just staring at me, saying nothing. I'm freezing cold, shivering from somewhere deep, deep inside. My heart is pounding, my mind racing. About a million emotions are slamming against each other in my head.

Finally, he slowly lifts the gun and points it directly at my face. He cocks the hammer, takes a deep breath and calmly says, "Are you ready to die?"

The exact words I had said to myself only six hours earlier.

And in this moment I get it. All the pieces of the puzzle seem to snap together as if all the unseen forces of the universe had suddenly magnetized them. I can see the answers to questions I haven't even thought to ask. And two very, very important things become exquisitely clear:

1. No, I am not ready to die. But isn't it interesting that it has taken this horrific experience for me to understand that?
2. If I am going to escape from this crazy man, then I *must* keep my emotions at bay. I *must* be calm (or at least *appear* to be calm). Only then will I be able to figure out exactly what needs to be said and done and precisely how and when I need to say and do them.

And that is exactly what happened. After five hours in what seemed like a suspended state of reality, I escaped. He didn't let me go; no one rescued me. I found the exact right moment and I escaped. It was like a giant, multi-dimensional, other-worldly chess game. Every single decision I made had to be factored in with a thousand other possibilities. It was so surreal.

But from that time forward, I really understood about the power of emotions and, more importantly, the power of being able to control one's emotions. I also knew—clearly, unequivocally knew—that if I could keep it together in that situation, then there would be nothing life could throw at me that I couldn't handle.

Wright

Linda, exactly what did you do to hold it together?

Larsen

Several things—all of which can be used in real life to help us be successful in spite of any emotional upheavals that may occur. I mean, hopefully no one will be confronted with the kind of experience I had, but the good news is that the strategies I used in my insane situation could be helpful across the board. Here's what I did. And as I mention these things, be thinking how you could use them in some area of your life where you keep getting stuck.

1. I focused on solving my problem—not on the problem itself. Every time I started thinking about how hopeless things seemed or how terrified I was, I would bring my attention back to finding a solution. I would also filter every action or communication through the question, "Is what I'm about to say or do going to help me or is it going to hurt? Will it get me the response that I'm looking for?"
2. I *acted* calm and in control, even though I didn't *feel* calm and in control. I figured out quickly that the only thing he

would be re-acting to would be my behaviors, not how I was actually feeling.

3. I absolutely knew that I had to build some kind of rapport with this guy. Somehow I had to get him to like me and trust me just enough to let his guard down a little.

4. I had to be very, very flexible in my thinking and my actions. I had to be extremely present in every "now" moment, gathering as much information as I possibly could in order to be successful in my endeavor to escape. I had to be able to recognize that when something I was doing wasn't working—I needed to shift gears and do something different.

Can you see how those strategies would help you overcome obstacles, solve problems, keep your emotions in check, and accomplish your objectives? And, by the way, this doesn't have to always be "work." It really can be quite fun.

Wright

Really? How?

Larsen

Okay, let's take the last idea—if what you're doing isn't working you have to do something different. We all know that this is true—we've heard it a million times—but do we really do it?

I came up with the following example to share with people who attend my presentations so I could do more than just *tell* them to do something different, I could actually *show* them. It goes like this:

Let's say that you have a son and you have told him over and over to clean his room, but he doesn't do it. Oh, he has a lot of great excuses, but the bottom line is it's not getting cleaned up. You yell, you bribe, you cajole, you demand. But it still doesn't get clean. It may be time for you to do something different—really different.

First of all, you need to speak a language that he can understand, and if he is a typical teenager then he probably likes rap music. You know what's coming, don't you? Yes. I suggest that if you want to be heard by the young man, then why not "rap" the request.

I actually wrote the lyrics to a rap song and got a musician friend of mine to write the music and we put it on a CD. It's real funky (although I'm not certain true rappers would even relate to the word "funky.") Anyway, the words go like this:

Yo' room, dude, it's looking real bad.
Yo' room, dude, ya better listen to ya dad. He's mad, real mad.
Better pick up ya clothes or the iPod goes.
Make up ya bed or the television's dead!
Well now you listen to me—I'll tell ya how it's gonna be.
This ain't the home of the free—there's a price, don't ya see?
I told ya 15, 25, 35 times,
That the money's gonna stop and ya bubble's gonna pop.
Ya better tow the line or yo' butt is mine!

There's another verse, but you get the point. And by the way, when you actually perform your rap song, you must do as I do in my presentations. You must don a backwards baseball cap, heavy-duty bling-bling, and sunglasses. You must also do your very level best to dance like Eminem or whoever's hot at the time. I know, I know—the very thought is scary.

Hey, listen, if I—a fifty-something, grown-up businesswoman—can do this, then *anyone* can. And will it get a different result? You bet it will! Your son may run screaming into the night, he may die laughing. But two things are absolutely certain: 1) he's going to listen! and, 2) he may never look at rap music the same way again!

Wright

It sounds to me like you're using creativity and innovation to solve an everyday, very real world situation.

Larsen

You bet. And I truly believe that our greatest successes in life will come when we get more creative, boldly step outside our comfort zone, and suspend our preconceived ideas about what will work and what won't, and about what is possible and what isn't.

There are thousands of great speakers out there, with useful information that they can deliver in an effective way, but that's the problem! How can you choose between great speaker number one and great speaker number 1001? I believe the question comes down to: what does one of them do that is *different*—how are they more memorable, fun, *and* consequently, more effective than all the others?

I am very blessed to have a dear friend by the name of Ben Vereen. You may remember him from the film, *All That Jazz*, or the television miniseries, *Roots*, or from any of his Broadway productions like *Pippin*, or *Jesus Christ Superstar*. Well, Ben has started speaking at events around the U.S., just as I do. Only *not exactly* as I do—or as any other speaker does. He is magnificent! It would not be unusual for him to break out into song in the middle of an idea, or run out into the audience, or leap across the backs of people's seats. He's different. He's bold. He's creative. And I think that's what it takes to be successful.

Wright

Well, you apparently do rap songs!

Larsen

Yes, and I've been known to shake things up rather radically if it will help me make a point. I was a professional actor for more than twenty years and have done everything from Shakespeare to Ibsen to Simon. I have a graduate degree in acting from the FSU/Asolo Conservatory and accordingly, some of the finest training available. I've done radio, television, and films. And from all that experience I believe I have learned what makes an audience listen, get fully engaged, and have a fabulous time.

Wright

And what is that?

Larsen

I believe it's really, really knowing your craft, learning absolutely everything you can, and then practicing over and over and over again until it just becomes a part of who you are. Then it's getting out there and giving it a thousand percent with all the passion and love you have. It's believing that what you have to share is *the* thing that will make your listeners' lives better, richer, and happier. It's sharing the very soul of yourself with no thought of whether or not you look good or sound smart. It's stepping out in total faith and with wild abandon and having one heck of a good time in the process.

And, after everything is said and done, maybe that's what would make us successful at any venture in life.

About Linda Larsen

Linda Larsen is the founder and CEO of a successful communications company she started over 16 years ago. She is passionately committed to helping people upgrade their thinking, improve their communication and increase their bottom line. More than that, she is willing to do whatever it takes to get her message across and make it stick. Linda's passion and spontaneous humor stems from over 20 years as a professional actress in film, television and on stage. Her experience and training (she holds an undergraduate degree in Behavioral Sciences from the University of Florida and a Master of Fine Arts Degree from Florida State University) give her the unique ability to combine the entertaining, dynamic aspects of live theater with practical, high value content to produce lasting, positive changes. In 1988 she began working exclusively with trial attorneys. As a highly respected trial consultant, she continues to provide CLE training for lawyers, helping them communicate more effectively and persuasively in the high stakes, high stress environment of the courtroom. She is the author of the best selling audio program, 12 Secrets to High Self-Esteem, the critically acclaimed book, True Power, and Linda Larsen's Power Tips. She has also written or been featured in over 100 articles in such publications as Investor's Business Daily, The Chicago Tribune, Women In Business, Personal Excellence, CBSHealthWatch.com, and MSN.com, among others.

Linda Larsen
Linda Larsen Communications, Inc.
3424 Tanglewood Drive
Sarasota, FL 34239
Phone: 941-927-4700
Email: linda@lindalarsen.com
www.lindalarsen.com

Chapter Ten

RIDGELY GOLDSBOROUGH

THE INTERVIEW

David Wright (Wright)

Today we are talking with Ridgely Goldsborough, author, speaker and producer of the acclaimed *Take YOUR POWER BACK!* CD and DVD series on personal empowerment. He has written five books, hundreds of motivational columns, produced many CD and DVD series, as well as created cutting edge Internet-based personal growth courses. He is the co-creator of *The YoungSlim Lifestyle™* *(www.youngslim.com)*, a wellness and anti-aging program based on an integrated approach to health and weight management that, as does all of his work, finds its roots in personal empowerment. He appears frequently on television and hosts his own radio show. Ridgely, thanks for joining us today on *Masters of Success*.

Ridgely Goldsborough (Goldsborough)

It is an honor to be here.

Wright

You have made personal empowerment a major part of your life's work. Why do you have such passion for it?

Goldsborough

David, I truly believe there is far too much suffering in our world today without any good reason for it. Most people suffer because they don't know how to make empowered choices—better choices—choices that lead them in the direction of fulfilling their biggest goals and dreams, to building a magnificent life of their own design. I find this situation completely unacceptable. We travel through life thinking heavy and negative thoughts, and as we do, *"thought particles"* get lodged between our ears, causing a condition affectionately known as *"truth decay."* We need to find a way to mentally *"floss"* on a daily basis, to take our power back, and get rid of any "stinking thinking."

Bad habits never miraculously disappear. Each is a kind of un-do it yourself project. The miracles that appear in our lives come not from the suspension of natural law but rather from the operation of higher laws. We need to learn those laws, tap those laws, use them consistently, and become empowered through them.

Wright

You interview and film leading authors and speakers around the world for your *Take YOUR POWER BACK!* series. What have you learned from that process?

Goldsborough

Two remarkable points: First, I find universal agreement that certain principles can and will make an enormous difference in the life of anyone who chooses to embrace them. I hear them over and over—the same principles over and over again—applied in diverse circumstances by incredibly successful people, each with their own legacy of victory after victory in finances, in relationships, with their health—there's no limit. For those of us who may be searching for the *"key to the universe,"* I have both good news and bad news. The bad news: there is no key to the universe. The good news: It has been left unlocked. We simply have to step in and walk the path.

Secondly, each person's unique journey brings a fresh perspective to every topic we discuss. Given that, we all have so many filters that cloud our ability to see and embrace new concepts that we need to hear many different takes on a particular topic in order to understand it and gain the benefit of that understanding. For example, if I have a challenge with listening, I need to hear about listening from a multitude of individuals, with different experiences, different ways of explaining and sharing their knowledge, until finally one of those points of view clicks with me. Then and only then will I learn a little bit more about how to listen better, in a manner that improves my relationships.

In the dictionary, they define the word *"empower" as "to give power to; to enable; to give ability to."* The masters we interview share their lives and do exactly that—they give power. We are the ones who need to make the choice to open up, learn and receive—a daunting task that requires a real commitment. Despite the universal application of these proven principles, our stubbornness and self-imposed blindness dictate that we need a multiplicity of perspectives and experiences in order for these principles to sink in.

Wright

It sounds like you gain something unique and different from each speaker.

Goldsborough

Absolutely. If I go to a seminar or listen to an empowerment CD or read one of your books, David, and walk away with just one nugget that improves my life, then I consider that a success. If I gain two nuggets then I hit a home run. Each of the people we interview gives us at least one or two nuggets, sometimes more.

One speaker taught me how to *"live in the mystery"* each day. Another reminded me that, *"repetition is the mother skill."* I scrounge for that nugget with every interview and get excited, confident that each person's particular life experience will birth a number of jewels for all of us. I make it my mission to create an environment conducive to exposing their lives, to sharing the challenges, defeats, lessons, and subsequent victories on video, in such a way that anyone watching the series can see in living color, with a full gamut of expression and a full range of emotions, the real story—the good, bad and ugly. I pull out everything I can and memorialize it for all posterity. Much unmapped country lies within each of us. I help gifted people draft maps for the rest of us to use at will.

Wright

This body of work sounds a lot like what Napoleon Hill did years ago with *Think and Grow Rich.*

Goldsborough

Thank you—what a compliment. Even though Napoleon Hill focused on a success philosophy in the area of wealth, the same principles apply across the board in all aspects of life. I feel the same way about personal empowerment. We did not have the benefit of getting Napoleon Hill on film because the technology did not exist in the earlier part of the last century. If we follow the same process now, travel the globe seeking out leading thinkers, speakers, authors and other accomplished individuals, and record their information, we can distill universal principles and share them with the world. As an added bonus, we make old truths fresh with each new person's experience—their varied and colorful backgrounds that paint the canvas of their journey. Logic makes people think; emotions make people act. Stories live in our hearts. We record peoples' unique stories and pass them on.

Wright

You also spend a lot of time speaking and writing on personal empowerment yourself. Would you tell our readers a little bit about that?

Goldsborough

If I split myself wide open, leave my blood and guts on a stage or a page, laugh, cry, and make a fool of myself, I build a small amount of trust. All of us hurt, fail, suffer, get back up and wonder what it's all about. By intimately exposing myself, I invite each person to relive their own experience, to go back to that sad or happy place and play with those emotions in raw form. I build a small bridge of trust and then share a take or an angle that may challenge an antiquated belief that silently cries out for reform. I am a messenger who tries to remove blinders through trust in order to revisit old notions with new eyes.

Every week, I agonize over my motivational column entitled *A View From The Ridge (www.aviewfromtheridge.com)*, and like a dog on a bone, will not let it go until I bite it, gnaw on it, play with it and work each fiber and sinew in every crevice. Only then will I release it into the cosmos.

For me, personal empowerment means life sharing—what I learn from someone who came before me, passed on through the emotion that makes the experience real for me. I'll rip it out and throw it out there. I want to know *your* story. I want to learn from you. I'll share mine first if that's what it takes to get you to open up.

Wright

So, what do you think of the primary components of empowerment?

Goldsborough

That's a profound question, though not particularly complicated. Its simplicity however should in no way be confused with *"easy."*

First, we must take responsibility, claim our lives as our own and make the powerful choice to create them according to our own design. The world is run by people who show up; we must flat out decide to be one of them. After internalizing that decision, we have to make a plan in writing, begin to execute the plan, and analyze one thing to determine its efficacy—the results. As the saying reflects: *"You can have reasons or you can have results. Reasons don't count, results don't lie."* Results or lack thereof dictate the next step. If our actions yield positive fruit, we continue, refine, and even accelerate the steps called for in the plan. If not, we go back to the drawing board and re-work the plan, always failing our way forward.

In addition, concurrently with boldly working the plan we must train our body and mind for success, constantly make an investment in ourselves as the most valuable of all resources, through personal development and embracing a success philosophy such as outlined in *Think and Grow Rich.* We can also add prayer, a form of focused thought.

As we make the courageous declaration *"this is my life—therefore I am in charge of it—in all aspects,"* all sorts of forces mobilize to support us on the journey. Those obstacles and challenges that we inevitably face bolster our growth; make us stronger and more able to overcome the next adversity, building an inner muscle that serves us in all areas.

We repeat the process over and over until the inner transformation that occurs manifests outwardly through fantastic results that paint our personal portrait of accomplished goals and dreams. The changes within us dictate new behavior that translates into new actions. These actions, by definition, produce new results. We tweak and tinker, play and grow, fall down and start over. Every time we get up we feel a little more em-power-ed, a little more power-full, a little closer to making our dreams come true. Once we venture down the path, persistence becomes our main ally. Let me share a favorite quote:

"Nothing in the world can take the place of persistence.
Talent will not;
nothing is more common than unsuccessful men with talent.
Genius will not;
unrewarded genius is almost a proverb.
Education alone will not;
the world is full of educated derelicts.
Persistence and determination alone are omnipotent."

— Calvin Coolidge

Wright
Who can do this?

Goldsborough
That's an easy one. Anybody who wants to—no exceptions.

Wright
I notice that you answered *"anybody who wants to"* rather than simply *"anybody."* What's the difference?

Goldsborough
Leopards don't change their spots. To open the creaking, groaning, and heavy door that is oneself, to look in and make modifications may well constitute the most difficult voyage a human being ever embarks on. It involves taking a true inventory, examining weaknesses as well as strengths, and admitting that we need to transform certain aspects of ourselves if we want different results.

The fact that *anyone can* do this in no way makes the process easy. It only makes it available. The missing ingredient is desire. Because of the difficulty, regardless of the pot of gold at the end of the rainbow, most of us would rather hide from stormy weather than brave the rain, wind, and lightning. And to complicate matters further, the tempest lies within, unseen. We don't know its shape—tornado, hurricane, squall—different and unique for all of us. Therefore, we have to discover it, bring it out into the open, shed light on it, accept it and then tackle it—each of these steps with its own degree of angst, not to mention the extraordinary amount of needed effort. We have to endure the discovery process, the acceptance of areas that call for work, the daily choice to challenge those areas, and the actual grind of taking the necessary actions.

Sometimes we will fail miserably and may even feel that we regress. Sometimes we will progress yet doubt ourselves and suffer lapses in confidence. Our desire must carry us—we have to want it. Without a burning desire inside, most of us won't walk the path.

Wright

It sounds as though you're suggesting that in some ways we have no real choice.

Goldsborough

If we want to lead a different life—an empowered life—we will have to do different things and take new actions that produce new results. This means we have to want it badly enough to go through whatever the challenge, whatever the obstacle, whatever the pain to help us adjust our belief system—the one that dictates how we act. The accumulation of different actions on a daily basis will yield astronomically different results over time. Anyone can do it as long as they want to.

Wright

You mentioned tools a few minutes ago. What tools are available for the average person?

Goldsborough

Every town across America has a library. For five dollars (and sometimes at no cost), anyone can get a library card and gain access to a wealth of materials on personal empowerment, personal growth, motivation, inspiration, and so on. The Internet opens up the world to us all with newsletters and other resources as well as direct mail access to tapes, video tapes, audio tapes, DVD series, books, magazines—all available to anybody who wants them. Any of us can go onto the Internet, run a search, and pull up fifty thousand sources for virtually anything. I can listen to an audio program while I'm driving. I can read one of your books David, instead of listen a trashy novel. I can watch a DVD like *Take YOUR POWER BACK!* instead of late night television. I can turn my car into a rolling university. There is an endless supply of tools for anyone willing to go get them and use them.

149

Wright

If I really want to take my power back as you have stated how long will this journey take me?

Goldsborough

That's not an easy question and I'll have to answer that in two parts.

Part one, I don't know. It will depend, from one person to the next, on how much effort goes into the process of taking that power back, how much new programming helps rewire the system through books, audio programs, videos, and from where each person starts the journey.

However, the second part of that answer is far more important than the first: *it doesn't matter how long it takes.* The question we have to ask ourselves is where will we be if we don't do it? In other words, five years or ten years from now, if we don't take our power back, we will find ourselves in exactly the same place where we sit now, except older, more jaded, more rigid and less able to make the needed changes. I'm reminded of a quote by Henry David Thoreau, *"If a man constantly aspires, is he not elevated? Did ever a man try heroism, magnanimity, truth, sincerity and find that there was no advantage in them—that it was a vain endeavor?"* The journey in and of itself contains immense value for the traveler. How long it takes is irrelevant.

Wright

I heard a motivational speaker tell a story about a lady who came up to him after his speech, all pumped up claiming, "You have changed my life and I'm going to go back and get my college degree." He asked her how far did she have to go. She answered: "Well, I graduated from high school and I'm going to go all the way back. It will take me four years." He congratulated her. He saw her about two years later and inquired about her college dream. She said that she decided not to do it. He asked why, to which she replied, "Well, I would be forty-four by the time I finished four years later." He pointed out that she would be forty-four anyway.

Goldsborough

Exactly right. All of us will be five years older five years from now. What will determine the difference in our lives? The books we read, the people we associate with and learn from, the audio programs we listen to, the videos we watch. The changes that come about because of all that powerful information (or the painful realization that no change has occurred because no effort was made) will determine the difference in our lives. If we do nothing the result is guaranteed—*nothing*!

Wright

I remember many years ago a man named Paul Myer, who owned The Success Motivation Institute in Texas taught me how to set goals. The last question I asked before I decided whether or not to challenge a goal was the question, "Is it worth it?" When I reflect on the things you have shared today, how long the journey might take, the tools I would need to use, things I would have to do, and so on, do you really think it's worth it for each individual?

Goldsborough

Is it worth living a full life? Is it worth loving with all your heart? Is it worth taking an amazing journey where you accomplish all kinds of goals and dreams that you don't even have yet because their sheer magnitude defies your current capabilities? Is it worth all of that? Or should we just wait until we hit the grave? Most people die early and young. They simply spend sixty or seventy years walking around without falling in the hole. That's not living. Harold Kushner once said, *"Our souls are not hungry for fame, comfort, wealth or power. Our souls are hungry for meaning, for the sense that we have figured out how to live so that our lives matter, so that the world will be at least a little bit different for our having passed through it."* In order for us to have any impact, we have to empower ourselves. Our greatest reward for our effort will not be what we get for it, but rather what we become through it.

The question, *"Is it worth it?"* is almost ludicrous. Consider the alternative. I coast, I exist, I fall asleep at the wheel, yet somehow I keep driving down the same old road, using someone else's roadmap—a map made without any of my goals and dreams in mind. As Napoleon Hill taught: *"It is always your next move"*—not someone else's—*yours.*

Wright

The best definition of a rut that I've ever heard is, *"a grave with both ends kicked out."*

Goldsborough

Absolutely.

Wright

Do you have any final thoughts you might give our readers and our listeners that would help them to develop themselves and thereby empower themselves?

Goldsborough

Dr. Daisaku Ikeda, a spiritual leader and modern day philosopher once said this: *"Even places that have been shrouded in darkness for billions of years can be illuminated. Even a stone from the bottom of a river can be used to produce fire. Our present sufferings, no matter how dark, have certainly not continued for billions of years—nor will they linger forever. The sun will definitely rise. In fact, its ascent has already begun."*

I find this: Diamonds are nothing more than chunks of black coal that stuck to their jobs. Anyone can turn their life around, achieve anything they want, and become the person of their dreams, happy, joyful, vivacious, dynamic, excited, and exciting. You owe it to yourself to do whatever is necessary to become empowered and live a powerful life. Then, give your gifts to others and the rewards return ten-fold. As Zig Ziglar once said, *"Be a go-giver not a go-getter."*

I want to thank you, David, for being such a *"go-giver"* yourself. I look forward to spending my life continuing that process.

Wright

Today we have been talking with Ridgely Goldsborough. He is an author, a speaker, and produces the acclaimed *Take YOUR POWER BACK!* CD/DVD series involving leading authors and speakers for the express purpose of exposing the journeys of personal empowerment of accomplished women and men. As we have found this afternoon, he knows what he is talking about. I know I'm going to start doing some things differently and perhaps this book might convince you to do the same.

Ridgely, you just can't imagine how much I appreciate you being with me today on *Masters of Success.*

Goldsborough

It was indeed a great pleasure. Thank you for spending this time together.

About Ridgely Goldsborough

Ridgely Goldsborough has written five books, recorded dozens of radio and television shows and publishes a free weekly inspirational column entitled, *A VIEW FROM THE RIDGE* that is read around the world. His greatest source of pride lies in his two acclaimed DVD series *Take YOUR POWER BACK!* and *MODEST TO MILLIONS!*, fascinating compilations on film of the philosophies of the titans of personal growth and some of the wealthiest people on earth. Ridgely records the legacies of industry giants and shares them with the world.

Ridgely Goldsborough

A View From The Ridge, Inc.

16264 North Shore Drive

Pensacola, Florida, 32507

Phone: 866.YOUNG00 (968-6400)

www.aviewfromtheridge.com

www.youngslim.com

www.modesttomillions.com

Chapter Eleven

KERRY DAIGLE

THE INTERVIEW

David Wright (Wright)

Today we're talking with Kerry Daigle, a proud Cajun from Opelousas, Louisiana. He's an entrepreneur, businessman, radio host, author, speaker, and the consummate Renaissance man. He shares his passion for personal growth with audiences around the world. His blend of wisdom, experience, and personal humility come together in unique and powerful insights that impact everyone he comes in contact with on a daily basis.

Kerry's tremendous knack for finding and developing talent extends beyond his core business of developing leadership in the direct sales industry and into his love affair with the sport of boxing. Kerry finds, coaches, and develops promising young boxers, helping them to excel and rise through the professional ranks and into the big leagues. He uses this special gift in all areas of his life—as a mentor, teacher, at home, in his business, and other personal pursuits.

His new CD, *Dreams, Fairy Tales, & Miracles,* recorded with his daughter, Angela, is available by contacting him directly or going to his web site. The CD consists of chapters of his upcoming book. Through his actions and accomplishments Kerry shows the world that one can truly "have it all." Kerry, welcome to *Masters of Success.*

Kerry Daigle (Daigle)
It's an honor, Dave, thank you.

Wright
You're a strong believer in the power of gratitude and you even mention that gratitude leads one to positive thinking. What do you mean by that?

Daigle
Well, David, let's think about that for a minute. Being grateful means being happy with yourself—that's the first step toward developing a positive self-image, which creates a positive attitude. Learning how to be grateful will bring an appreciation of things in your life that may be taken for granted. It recharges the mind and opens your heart. It releases you from stress and negativity.

My greatest mentor was my grandmother, Maw-Maw Daigle. She always told me to start with gratefulness first thing in the morning when I woke up because there are thousands of people who didn't wake up that morning. Be grateful for that opportunity and thank God for another day to make a difference in not only your own life but also in the lives of many others.

Wright
You mention your grandmother a lot in many of the workshops and talks you give as one of your mentors. Evidently she had a very forceful impact on your life.

Daigle
David, she definitely did. My grandmother raised me since I was three years old. I was born in 1952, so that tells you my age. Maw-Maw Daigle didn't have a Ph.D. nor did she have a B.S. behind her name. In fact, she was illiterate—she couldn't read, she couldn't write—and she could only speak French, which was her native tongue. What she did have, David, were the letters L.E. behind her name—meaning Life Experiences. It's amazing now, as I've attended some of the top workshops and seminars all across America and abroad, headlining best selling authors, and internationally known speakers, I've come to realize that Maw-Maw Daigle taught me some of the same things I learned at these seminars. She may have said these things differently but the meanings and results were exactly the same.

I have a new book I'm writing titled *Dreams, Fairy Tales, & Miracles,* which are the chapters of the lessons in life I've learned from my grandmother and my grandfather, Paw-Paw Daigle.

I have a CD titled the same with six of the chapters from my book available for sale at ten dollars including shipping. My daughter, who is only eleven years old, is doing some of the voice-overs and intros. I think you'll like this, David. The subtitle is, *Things I've Learned from Maw-Maw and Paw-Paw Daigle that You Won't Learn at Harvard or Yale.* I believe readers would enjoy the material. None of it is mine; it's all lessons I learned from my grandparents.

Wright

Would you share with our readers at least one lesson that your grandparents taught you?

Daigle

One lesson they taught me left a huge impact on my life. It was at a time when I complained to my grandparents about my misfortunes. We were living on state assistance, we didn't own a vehicle, and we didn't have any air conditioning. So many other people were so much more fortunate than we were. Paw-Paw Daigle immediately asked me to take a walk with him. I was about twelve years old, working in the neighborhood to make additional income to help myself with some of the expenses of going to school, and I was feeling sorry for myself.

Paw-Paw took me to a medical clinic in the small town we lived in, Opelousas, Louisiana. Interestingly, David, at that time you could actually walk right into the clinic without any visitor passes and there weren't any security guards. We would meet and visit with patients who were suffering from strokes, others were suffering from the results of life-threatening accidents, and some of them were in wheelchairs permanently. Other patients had terminal illnesses. Being only twelve years old at that time, it amazed and yet saddened me to see some of the patients were actually my age.

We walked home and Paw-Paw didn't say much. He remained very quiet until reaching the front porch of our home (we met a lot on that front porch). He then asked me in a very simple fashion, "After our visit today, Kerry, and your troubles you had this morning, I really need to ask you, do you really have a problem that can't be handled?" Immediately I started understanding the meaning of gratitude and that I was the lucky one and that I should be grateful for having such good, sound physical health and a strong mind.

David, it's so important to look back at lessons like these that may have been taught to you by your first mentors whether they were your parents, your grandparents, maybe a relative, or a friend, and be grateful that those lessons are treasures that have been given to us.

Also, it's important to understand that as we learn from these lessons our lives will change for the better. When I have a bad day now I look back and think about how grateful I need to be to have the opportunity to rid myself of those dark moments and learn from them.

Once more I began to understand Maw-Maw's and Paw-Paw Daigle's credentials, the letters L.E.—"Life's Experiences"—and what they really meant. It is now important for me to transfer these same experiences and lessons to others.

Wright

Gratefulness is something we've all heard about and obviously, whether it's a class on manners, or in church. I think we understand what the word "gratefulness" means but is it possible to train yourself to be more grateful?

Daigle

Absolutely, David. I really believe that everyone can do that and it's a very simple thing to do. One thing would be to always have a journal with you and write down each meeting you have with your peers and business associates. I think everyone should have a journal. Keep track of what you discussed that day so you can always look back at what you learned and what transpired. Remember, a short pencil is always better than a long memory. You've probably heard that many times.

Most importantly, however, in each day of writing in your journal, write something you are grateful about—just one sentence. That will create a habit of gratitude. Habits, David, become a way of life. Next share this powerful gift of gratitude with others and you can change—your life and many others around you. This way you become more grateful for the small things in life. It then becomes amazing how the bigger things in life just seem to happen if you just keep marching forward with a positive attitude. Many times the great things that happen in life come unexpectedly.

Wright

Are there any one-liners that your grandparents shared with you that you can pass along to our readers?

Daigle

That's a great question. I sure can. One of them is this: "You cannot be negative and grateful in the same moment." Think about what I just said. That stunned me when I learned that lesson. It made so much sense.

Of course, the most important lesson for me personally was Maw-Maw Daigle constantly mentioning that I should be grateful that I could read. That was a very impactful point in my life and a great moment. Maw-Maw always would tell me, "You will become who you are by the books you read and the people you hang around." If you read books on murders, robberies and crime, you will learn about the same. If you read positive thinking books, you will learn how to be positive. It's the same with the people you hang around. If you hang around a thief you will learn how to be a thief—you make that choice.

Life is that simple and really, reading books is so important. Just remember that the people who don't read books are no better off than the people who cannot read. Being that Maw-Maw Daigle could not read it left a solid impression on me of the gift of being able to read. I've read at least one book every two weeks in the last ten years.

There are little things many people may not think are important that they should be grateful for. One of those for me personally was the ability to read, but most importantly, using that ability by reading the right books such as all the books in your publishing company that promote good, sensible living habits and teach good, positive thinking skills.

Wright

What would you say to someone who lost a loved one early in life or who possibly lost someone they cared about through a breakup or divorce? How can you be grateful in those kinds of situations?

Daigle

David, that's a tough one. But then it's your outlook on life after a hard challenge and how you handle it is what makes the difference. This reminds me of something Maw-Maw Daigle told me before leaving us here on Earth to live with the angels. She always said to me that when she would pass away to always look back to mentally video those moments in time within our mind that we sincerely appreciated with her and not to dwell on her departure and the end of her life; but to remember when that time would come, to think she was in a better place. As we would say today, put those moments on video in our mind so we can replay the good times over and over and over again. Remember when we held hands, when we laughed with each other, when we hugged, or when we just sat next to each other and enjoyed each other's company. Remember the good moments and keep those alive. It will only make us so much stronger. Be grateful for those wonderful moments that will definitely outweigh the less than wonderful moments. Never, ever, ever, take *anything* for granted.

Wright

In your CD, *Dreams, Fairy Tales & Miracles*, you mentioned the power of the dream—the ability to believe in fairy tales and miracles. How does gratitude fit into a dream or a fairy tale?

Daigle

We should all be very grateful we have the ability to dream. The problem is, we as adults have quit dreaming and have taken the gift of dreaming for granted. Dreams can become fairy tales and fairy tales can turn into miracles.

I know it has for me. I've gone from state assistance as a child to financial success at the age of twenty-three, then bankrupt at the age of thirty-one, and then the ability to retire at the young age of forty-two, if I chose to. I now enjoy life and do all the thinks I love to do such as writing, speaking, radio, teaching others to be successful in their business, and working in the professional boxing industry. I am very grateful.

Gratitude changes the way we look at life and our challenges. Obstacles become opportunities in disguise once you learn the power of gratitude. Tough times will transform into challenges that make us stronger as we handle things with gratefulness. That's why dreaming is so important! Paw-Paw and Maw-Maw always said, "If you dream big, your world is big; if you dream small, your world is small."

Be grateful for things in life that you may take for granted and your dreams will return. Look for the good and your focus will automatically be drawn away from the bad.

Wright

What are some simple lessons to start accepting the power of gratitude?

Daigle

Well, at least once a day, David, preferably you should take fifteen minutes of your time and sit somewhere alone where you can look at the trees or what nature has given us—the snow-covered mountains, the beautiful colors of plants and flowers, the smell of the air after a rain, the chirping of the birds, or the simple sound of the wind. Be grateful for life and what it brings to you. Be grateful for nature. Love and appreciate everything in your life. Look for the positive in people. Gratitude is a special gift.

Secondly, don't forget about keeping a journal. It'll change your life personally and professionally. In writing down your meetings and experiences, always write in things that you are grateful for that particular day.

Thirdly, learn to say "Thank you" more often. And when you say it, mean it. Doing so will create a smile on the other person's face as you let them know you are grateful for something that person did. Say "Thank you" with eye contact. We choose what we receive in life. Choosing to be grateful and showing appreciation with a small, "Thank you," will you give you a fulfillment that you will want to experience over and over and over again. Say "Thank you" in a caring way and watch the results that will follow.

Wright

When do you start teaching this method of gratitude?

Daigle

Many of us as adults have been challenged in life with many trials and tribulations that have created doubt in our decision-making processes. This then creates self-doubt while losing self-confidence. It's at this time more than any other we must start looking at the good things that have happened to us. It may be that we have had a business failure. From that lesson we must learn from the mistakes we made and be grateful that we have learned so we can get stronger. That would be for the adults who have forgotten the gifts they were given in life, by having the opportunity to reach forward and start over again but in a grateful way.

One other thing that is generally missing in our lives is teaching our children the power of gratitude early in life while giving them the self-confidence and self-esteem they so richly deserve. I believe, if we start early with our children, we can instill strong, positive thinking skills that will grow with them into adulthood making them much more successful on every path they embark.

For example, if your child is slow in math, you want to do your best to teach them how to be better. The wrong way is to scold them into learning. You should look at their strengths and build their confidence up in what they are really good in. Should your child have great penmanship and have the ability to speak and read well, you must commend them on those strengths and tell them how grateful they should be that they are so gifted in those areas. To be thankful will create new inner strength and confidence that will move your child in the direction of becoming better in the areas they were weak in. It's amazing what the mind can do if it's trained to be grateful and positive.

My daughter, Angela, at this time is eleven years old. She was adopted at the age of six. She was virtually homeless—very little clothing, very unhealthy, and could not read nor write, although children her age were memorizing the alphabet and writing their names. She couldn't do either one. Entering school for her was quite a challenge; but through the power of having her feel good about herself and being grateful for her new life and the love she was receiving, she excelled in school and to this day, she is in the top of her class academically.

Every day we ask her what she did that day that she should be grateful for, plus something someone else did that she was thankful for. You can help by reminding children of the things they learned at school each day. You can also help by having them think of something they can appreciate in themselves that day. David, this will create positive thinking skills and self-esteem which in turn makes your child a happy child. Start with your children early and create strength through gratitude for the positive things happening in your child's life.

Wright

What do you think is a good way to express gratitude toward others?

Daigle

That's a good question, David, with a simple answer. There's nothing more powerful than a handwritten note letting a certain person who assisted you with something as simple as getting you a great table at a restaurant, or moving you quickly in a haircut appointment when you were in a hurry, giving you a smile at the cashier's counter, or buying you lunch, or just spending quality time with you. The list goes on and on. That handwritten note will be much more powerful than an e-mail, a fax, or a voice mail. It means you took the time out of your busy day to write a personal note to them, showing your gratitude for their assistance and their kindness. David, it's just amazing how that simple note will bring joy to the person's life whom you're sending it to.

I ask people on a regular basis in the seminars and talks I give if they remember the last time they received a personal, handwritten note from someone. David, it's amazing how each person remembers not only when they received the note. They also generally remember why and from whom they received it. I've asked these same people when was the last time they received a formal letter or an e-mail of the same type and they normally do not remember. Why is that? It is because these personal acts of gratitude of taking the time to write special "thank-you" or "appreciate-you" notes for acts of kindness are very seldom done and are very seldom forgotten by the receiver. These notes create rapport with these people who seldom get thanked and they will give you a personal sense of self-satisfaction, while at the same time creating a great sense of name recognition with your receiver. You can only win with this method of gratitude in so many different ways.

Wright

Do you have any closing comments for our readers—something that might wrap this up? I've really, really learned a lot here about the power of gratitude. I've made a decision that I'm going to start using some of your advice.

Daigle

Well, thank you, David. In wrapping this interview up it is important to understand practicing to be grateful will require that you slow down if you're speeding through the day, at least for a few moments to notice the simple things we take for granted. David, you've heard the old saying, "Stop to smell the roses." Most people overlook the blessings that are all around us—the food we eat, the book you are reading right now, the smile for the other person who is in need of making their day brighter by giving them a simple smile, the thank you, the stars in the sky. We should be grateful that we can give to others simple gestures of kindness and thanks that can change their lives while changing our own lives.

Paw-Paw Daigle always said, "Your future depends on many things, however, most of your future will be determined on your gratitude toward life and toward people."

Wright

What a great conversation. I really appreciate all the time you spent with me here today, Kerry. This has been enlightening to me and I know it will be to the readers of this book. Thank you for taking the time to express the power of gratitude.

Daigle

David, it was an honor just to be able to be involved with not only you personally but also Insight Publishing. I expect great things to happen from this interview. Thank you for your help.

Wright

Today we've been talking with Kerry Daigle. He's an entrepreneur, a businessman, radio host, author, speaker, and as we have found today, the consummate Renaissance man. His blend of wisdom and experience come together in unique and powerful insights that impact everyone he comes into contact with on a daily basis.

Kerry, thank you so much for being with us today on *Masters of Success*.

Daigle

Thank you very much, David. I appreciate you!

About Kerry Daigle

Kerry Daigle, a proud Cajun from Opelousas, Louisiana, paints the portrait of the ultimate Renaissance man. A successful entrepreneur since 1965, Kerry runs a number of businesses out of his home, while simultaneously hosting a radio show, writing books, keeping a hectic speaking schedule while operating and managing his RESIDUAL INCOME direct sales neutriceutical business. It is this RESIDUAL INCOME that has allowed Kerry to chase and follow his dreams giving him the time freedom so many people lack. Kerry's businesses take him literally around the world. He does speaking engagements each time he travels, sharing insightful presentations with worldwide audiences, full of revealing Cajun wisdom that he learned from his first mentors, his grandparents, Maw-Maw and Paw-Paw Daigle. Kerry's radio show *"KEEP PUNCHING WITH KERRY DAIGLE"* offers motivation and inspiration to a global audience that listens to archived shows at www.kslokogm-fm.com and www.keeppunching.com, twenty-four hours a day, seven days a week.

The KeepPunching Media,
Publishing, and Promotional Companies, LLC
PO Box 627
Opelousas, LA 70571-0627
Phone: 1.800.485.9323
Email: keeppunching@att.net
www.keeppunching.com
www.kerrydaigle.com

Chapter Twelve

DOUG DVORAK

THE INTERVIEW

David Wright (Wright)

Today we are talking with Doug Dvorak. Doug Dvorak is a professional humorous speaker and creativity consultant who believes that "laughter is the software of the soul." Doug assists clients with improving their bottom line through the use of humor and creativity.

Doug's clients are characterized as Fortune 1000 companies, civic organizations and service providers. Doug is a certified creativity consultant, management consultant and corporate humorist. He holds a Bachelor of Arts degree in Business Administration and a Master of Business Administration in Marketing Management. Doug is also a graduate of the Player's Workshop of the Second City, one of the oldest and most prestigious improvisational comedy schools in the world. In addition, he is also active member of the National Speakers Association (NSA).

Doug, welcome to *Masters of Success*.

Doug Dvorak (Dvorak)

Thank you very much David, I'm glad to be here and may I say, you look fantastic. Are those paten leather?

Wright

Here we go! I am in for it aren't I? I'm surprised you didn't crack up with my mispronunciation of the word improvisational.

Dvorak

This obviously isn't "Masters of Speech." By the way, I love the humble, self-effacing title—*Masters of Success*. Let me guess, Gods of Greatness was already taken, most likely by a morning AA group in Des Moines?

Wright

Okay, okay, its time for the Jay Leno in me to come out even though I have no idea what to expect with this interview.

Dvorak

Gee, David, let's see, I am a *professional* speaker; and we are talking about my favorite subject—ME. This could go on for a couple of days; did you bring enough tape?

Wright

To start, perhaps you can share with us how you became a "Professional Humorist" Have you always been funny?

Dvorak

Excellent opening question Jay—I mean David—very professional and smoothly done. In other words, "It's time to talk about being funny!" Let's see, how did I start? Well, I started out as a poor child living in a doublewide. Wow, that is probably not a politically acceptable joke any longer. Actually I was a rich child living in a doublewide; well, not that rich. No, truthfully I was just always a pretty funny kid, with a good wit and a knack for finding the funny in all situations. Growing up I tended to rely on humor as a means to overcome my shyness and insecurities. I wasn't necessarily the "class clown"—more the Ed McMahon to the class clown, mostly working the smaller rooms—the lunchrooms, the math halls, that sort of thing.

As I went through college and began my professional life I informally continued to bring humor into my everyday life. Throughout my twenty-three-plus years as a professional sales person, my sales people and my managers repeatedly told me I had a good sense of humor and I was very creative, sometimes maybe a little too funny (but what did they know?).

In some ways I've always tried to use my humor and creativity as a way to manage my sales staff and build relationships with my clients. I simply have always believed that being funny helped me better connect with people.

Wright

How did you begin thinking about doing this professionally?

Dvorak

I guess when I started to consciously use my sense of humor as a means to my approach to business started for me back when I was a regional sales director for Boca Research, a manufacturer of data communications and IP telephony products based in Boca Raton, Florida.

Once while working for Boca I found myself tasked with developing an interesting and creative theme for our trade show booth at Comdex Canada, which, along with the Cured Meats Expo, is still one of the largest trade shows annually in Canada. It was there I had the good fortune to meet a very creative gentleman named Jim Ince. Jim was a professional entertainer who owned a special events company in Toronto. I was interviewing different creative talent trying to hit on a funny idea or theme when I was introduced to Jim and his company—Interactive Entertainment. We chatted for bit and together hit on an idea for a circus theme for the show. It would turn out to be one of the most successful themes of the entire Comdex show. Granted, our competition may have been a Jarts catching contest and a Molson keg give-away but still, we were funny and the show was a success. We even won a few awards for the themed circus booth concept, including the prestigious "Funniest Booth" prize that I made up and awarded our team.

So, through the course of the four-day trade show as Jim and I bantered back and forth doing some slap stick improvisation, we became instant friends and I am pleased to say remain so today. Jim has been a comedy mentor for me, actually helping me to further develop the character I use in my speeches—Dr. Earnest Carpediem. Together we also wrote the original keynote speech I still present to this day all over the world, "Mega Motivation with a Twist," with an obvious emphasis on the "twist."

It was also Jim who first suggested I seek some professional help. Now *that* is mentoring! Truthfully, he wasn't recommending I see a therapist—I was already seeing one of those—but rather that I should explore formal creativity and humor training and what better place then Chicago, the hometown for some of the best improvisation anywhere—The Second City Playhouse. He gave me the old, "if you can make it there kid, you can make it anywhere," speech. So I decided to make some calls. Through good fortune, talent, and persistence I landed a spot at the Players Workshop of the Second City, one of the oldest and most prestigious improvisational comedy schools in the world.

Wright

The Player's Workshop of the Second City in Chicago? Isn't that where Bill Murray, John Belushi, Dan Ackroyd, and Mike Myers studied improvisational comedy?

Dvorak

That's correct David. I entered their two-year program, Creative Expressions Through Improvisation—more properly titled, "Acting like an idiot—on cue"! What an experience. It essentially forced me to check the left hemisphere of my brain at the door once a week for two years. "Sorry Doug, no inhibitions allowed here today. I'm sorry, are you feeling a little self-conscious today? Do the next skit with your shirt off." It literally forced me to focus on the right side of my brain where humor, emotion, and creativity occur.

I have to say, the formal embracing of humor in my life blossomed from there. No, no David, there are five e's in hemisphere. So, as I advanced through the workshop and became more comfortable applying humor to real life situations I found my effectiveness as a sales professional was also improving as I was connecting with people on a more personal level. And the sales increased as well. Ah, the almighty dollar—there's nothing funny about greed, is there?

Wright

Can you tell us more about the influence that workshop had on your approach to humor and creativity?

Dvorak

Well, the Player's Workshop has such a tremendous history and reputation that it can be somewhat overwhelming for new students.

The two-year program begins with a basic introduction to improvisation and then advances quickly through a series of eight highly advanced improvisational classes. The class culminates with each student writing, directing, and producing their own *Saturday Night Live* type of skit for the main stage at Second City. It was there I first developed my alter ego, Dr. Earnest Carpediem, an obvious spoof on "seize the day."

When I first created the good doctor, I had no idea what he would become; he was simply this crazy motivational speaker I developed for a skit. The skit was very well received and the doctor became a regular at the workshop. The two-years were rewarding on many levels. The experience helped me to understand how the human mind processes humor and creativity; it also convinced me that humor, in its purest form, is actually risk and achieving humor is risk rewarded.

Wright

Will you share an example of how you applied what you learned in the workshop to the business world?

Dvorak

There is one story I like to share about taking a chance on humor. While I was still with Boca Research we had a booth at the Comdex computer show in Las Vegas, this one attracted more than 1.3 million people each year—a big show—our biggest show of the year. This time I was charged with coming up with the Chochki (Yiddish for Chochki) the giveaway—the trinket—companies use to help those who attend their booth remember their products.

So the show is approaching and I have nothing! Not a single decent idea; just mostly lame stuff like "the Boca spongy finger" or a Boca bouncing ball. I was nowhere. We are in Vegas, two days before the show and I'm out to dinner with my wife Cathy. After a magnificent all-you-can-eat buffet at The Mint, we were strolling downtown when somehow we discovered a novelty store—clearly divine intervention that I was able to find a novelty store in Vegas! So we wander in and I come across this propeller beanie. Boom! It hits me—technical people in the computer world are often referred to as "propeller heads." Did I really have something here or was this just a surefire way for me to offend 1.3 million technology professionals? I admit I was torn but I decided to take the risk and bet on the humor. So I ordered 25,000, had them embossed with "Boca Beanies" and shipped to Las Vegas within twenty-four hours to be handed out at our booth.

Wouldn't you know it—we ended up having the hottest give away at the show! The big guys—IBM and Microsoft—probably had huge budgets and teams of marketing gurus focus testing the "Micro-Frisbee," and here was Boca Research, on the second day of the show, being interviewed by CBS Evening News, *USA Today,* and *The Wall Street Journal*, all fascinated with the "Boca beanies."

I tell you that story not just because it makes me look great, but because I remember to this day that I had a critical decision to make and ultimately, I placed my bet on humor. I passionately believe that in all facets of life, one surefire way to break down walls and find commonality with people is through humor.

Wright

So when and how did your transformation from sales professional to a Professional Humorist begin?

Dvorak

The success at the Comdex show really got me going. More and more I began to count on humor, looking for ways to bring humor and creativity to my sales presentations, my client interactions, and subsequently into my speaking engagements. Soon my sales clients began asking me, "Can you help us out with our conference theme or can we pick your brain." You're kidding? Sure! You bet, how can I help? It was really getting exciting.

Wright

What convinced you that you could leverage your sales career into a speaking career?

Dvorak

As I mentioned David, sales has always been my profession. I was drawn to the excitement of carrying a sales quota and achieving the financial and personal rewards that come with accomplishment. Looking back, I now realize what I truly enjoyed doing was presenting during sales calls and conferences and infusing humor and creativity into my sales presentations. I guess I fell backwards into the old adage: find what you love to do and do it the rest of your life.

I loved the performance component of presenting to clients which in turn led to speaking opportunities for me with my sales clients. I also began networking within the speaking profession, joining an organization called Toastmasters International which is designed to help people of all professions become better speakers and communicators. I began attending more speaking seminars and conferences, getting introduced to some of the industry's best motivational speakers who are always willing to share their thoughts and ideas. It is a very nurturing profession filled with great people who helped me develop my passion for speaking. I feel like I am one of the luckiest men in the world to be doing what I am doing!

Wright

So what convinced you to make the leap permanently to being a Professional Humorist?

Dvorak

Well it was 1998; my sales job was on cruise control and I was doing well financially. I was also conducting outside speaking engagements about once a month so I was living the good life...or so I thought. Then that May, two life-changing events happened to me within days of each other that caused me to totally reevaluate who I was. As I share in my presentations in May, 1998, my dad died suddenly after a fall from a third story window and literally days later I was diagnosed with cancer—banner month in the Dvorak household, let me tell you.

Faced with both challenges I naturally became very reflective, as would anyone dealt with two life-altering curve balls. I could either have allowed those events to negatively impact my life or I could somehow find a way to move forward with a positive attitude. I admit, I struggled for weeks; but as I recall, I spent most of that time looking for ways to feel better, rather than going down a destructive path that could make things worse.

So, after weeks of soul searching, talking with my wife, my friends, family, and most importantly, myself, I reached a disturbing realization. Outside of my marriage, I had only one other true source of satisfaction and pleasure in my life and it was my speaking engagements. My job had become just that—a job. I was only really happy at my work when I was speaking, which was just not happening enough. I was conflicted and depressed. So, I made the very scary decision to quit my sales job. This was the time—the right time—for me to make the leap. I decided from then on I would do what I loved to do—speak professionally.

Wright

What led you to choose to speak professionally about humor, creativity, and motivation?

Dvorak

While I was working through the issues I was facing with my dad's death and then being diagnosed with cancer, I began reading the works of renowned author Dr. Norman Cousins. I owe so much of my recovery and my approach to humor to the works of Dr. Cousins and his writings on the healing power of laughter. Within his books, he describes how when you laugh—a good belly laugh—your body creates and emits endorphins. Now, these should not be confused with their close cousins, the Miami Endorphins. (Oh, come on Dave, I'm giving you pearls here.) Anyway, endorphins are the body's natural healing element.

Dr. Cousins noted that ten minutes of healthy laughter is equivalent to two hours of restful sleep. In his most famous book, written in the early '70s titled, *Anatomy of an Illness as Perceived by the Patient,* he documents his battle to overcome his life-threatening disease through the use of laughter. His doctors ostensibly gave him a death sentence—just a few months to live. He checked himself out of the hospital, went to a friend's cabin armed only with humorous materials—record albums, audiocassettes, and books that would make him laugh. All he did for six weeks was read, listen, and laugh. He came back after six weeks, marched right into his doctor's office for an exam, and walked out with a clean bill of health. That is a true story.

I read that book twice in one month trying to squeeze out every bit of hope. I sought out humor everywhere I could, maybe not to the degree Dr. Cousins did but with the same conviction. He was obviously a huge influence on me personally and helped me find my voice in humor and creativity. In fact, I found that if I indulged in a daily dose of humor, the following health benefits occurred:

- Laughter is a stress buster.
- It reduces the levels of stress hormones epinephrine and cortisol.
- Laughter strengthens the immune system.
- The immune system is important in maintaining good health by keeping infections, allergies, and cancers at bay.
- Laughter therapy helps to increase antibodies.
- Laughter is anti-ageing.

- It tones facial muscles and expressions.
- Laughter causes an increase in blood supply to the face, which is why some people look flushed. This nourishes the skin and makes it glow.
- People look younger and more fun when they laugh!
- Laughter is aerobic exercise.
- Laughter stimulates heart and blood circulation and is equivalent to any other standard aerobic exercise.
- One minute of laughter is equal to ten minutes on the rowing machine.
- The singular benefit almost everybody derives is a sense of well-being because more oxygen is taken in during laughter.
- Laughter is internal jogging.
- Laughter is a natural painkiller.
- Laughter increases the levels of endorphins—the body's natural painkillers.
- Laughter can control high blood pressure.
- Laughter can help dump depression and anxiety.
- Laughter makes you sleep better.
- Laughter improves lung capacity and oxygen levels in the blood.
- Laughter just makes you feel good.

Wright

How did you apply Dr. Cousins' philosophies on humor to your situation?

As is my nature, I took a very philosophical approach. I began to "investigate" the humor component of living; how other people who had personal and professional challenges stayed positive and how did humor play a role? I was convinced there would be a common thread there—humor somehow must have played a role in their recoveries. I began to devour books, audiocassettes, video programs, and anything I could get my hands on. I visited therapy centers and recovery units where I met with many who were battling life issues every day. The more I spoke with them, the clearer things became.

When they shared what was still positive in their lives, almost every one of their stories would involve humor. Here were people fighting to hold on to something, anything that was positive to keep them going and what they were able to find and grab hold of was humor.

Now, what really did it for me was the realization that I was, in fact, working through my grief in exactly the same way. What did I do when I was deeply depressed? I reached out for my source of humor—my speeches. Talk about an epiphany—I had used humor to recover. I soon began to feel better, and it was becoming easier to gain closure with my dad's death. My cancer treatments were continuing and I was growing stronger every day. Looking back, I am convinced I was actually receiving two forms of treatment—medical and humor and I thank God, because today I am cancer free, stronger, and a heck of lot wiser.

Wright

I'll share that with my wife; she is an eight-year cancer survivor.

Dvorak

God bless!

Wright

That means you're going to make it.

Dvorak

Yes, I am.

Wright

So you decided to throw all caution to the wind and begin a new career. What happened next?

Dvorak

It was after this experience that I created my own company committed to turn my *avocation* into my *vocation*. You like that don't you David? Make a note to remind me to make a note. With all humility, I named my company, Dvorak Marketing Group, created to help companies and business professionals achieve their business objectives through the use of humor and creativity. That's really how it all began David.

Wright

So tell me about how you began to approach clients and earned business for Dvorak Marketing Group?

Dvorak

My trade secrets David? Wait! Do I have more then one? My belief is that humor, creativity, and motivation—emotions and feelings that occur on the right side of our brain tend to be somewhat absent in today's political correct business environment, not to mention in our post 9/11 society. People are just not laughing enough. Since its inception, Dvorak Marketing Group has developed a number of assessment tools and selective exercises that take people through the creative process. We all have an IQ—an intelligence quotient and an EQ—an emotional quotient; but I believe we also all have an HQ—a humor quotient. I developed and designed a humor assessment that through a series of questions and phrases helps determine a person's humor quotient. We also provide our clients with exercises and suggestions all designed to develop the right side of their corporate brain.

Wright

So let's say I'm a prospective client. How do you explain how humor can boost employee moral and productivity?

Dvorak

I think that the vast majority of businesses today are too focused on the bottom line—got to make the numbers. It's all about making the numbers. But how do they get that done? The best companies do it with people. My position is that people really are the most productive when their personal goals are aligned with the goals of the organization. That's rather obvious but much is easier said then done.

Almost every company I meet with mentions one of their top corporate goals is to attract and retain quality people. Almost none of them have as part of their game plan a formal approach for injecting humor or creativity into the workplace. Now compare that to most employees' own personal mission statement, which typically includes "gaining more satisfaction out of their jobs" as one of *their* goals. See the disconnect? Making that connection is where I come in.

Case in point, take Herb Kelleher, the former CEO of Southwest Airlines. I have flown with Southwest on a number of occasions and I am a huge fan. I also have a close friend who is a captain for Southwest. She makes a very comfortable six-figure income flying and probably works only ten days a month. She loves her job. Who wouldn't? Once she told me a bit of internal scoop that made me think. Do you know what the most cherished reward a Southwest pilot can earn? It's the brown leather bomber jacket—a trophy respected industry-wide symbolizing they work for one of the finest company's in the world. That's creative, clever, motivational, and simple—I love it. And it doesn't stop there as anyone who has flown Southwest Airlines can attest. How about the fun the flight attendants are having? Certainly not your typical stodgy announcements at take-off from *this* crowd—they are encouraged to add humor and creativity, which helps them connect with their passengers. As an organization, top down, they have embraced a culture of creativity and humor which is why Southwest is continually recognized as one of the best companies to work for. They have made that connection. Unfortunately, I am not seeing enough of this from other CEOs in Corporate America today. My work is never done.

Wright

I have to ask, I know what a consultancy is but I am a little unclear—what is a humor creativity consultant?

Dvorak

It's funny because I am asked that constantly. This curious designation is bestowed upon only those individuals who attended and graduated from The Players Workshop at Second City. And, as I mentioned earlier, the actual program is called, Creative Expression Through Improvisation. The two-year program helps prepare its members to view life and work through a more creative and humorous set of lenses. It wasn't all just fun and games—the program really focused on the human psyche and how laughter and humor affects the brain.

I often boast to women that I have a doctorate in humor and creativity. It's a good thing I am married because even *that* line doesn't work for me. What I was finding as I began proactively seeking clients was that organizations of all types are in need of and are looking for ways to bring more humor and creativity into the personal and professional lives of their employees. I mean, look at the pressures people face today. Our lives are so complex with two-income households, raising kids, paying bills, saving for college, and caring for family members. I have taken to calling it the "sandwich generation." With so much coming at us each day that needs to be compressed?

What I was hearing back from companies who were hiring me was validating all of these concepts. The demand for my services remains strong because organizations are under tremendous pressures to meet their business needs. They are now recognizing the value of add-ing humor and creativity to the workplace.

Let me share an example. I'm currently working with an interna-tional airline on ways to infuse more humor and creativity into their rather staid senior management team. This group makes a wax mu-seum look like a gymnastics competition. So we initially meet with their leadership team and discuss ways to customize the sessions to insure that it's fun and interactive while still meeting their specific needs.

We discussed a number of different types of exercises, even some that can take place outdoors, all designed to bring about different re-sults. So we settled on a full day workshop built upon a scavenger hunt theme. Each attendee is asked to complete a humor and creativ-ity assessment in advance of the workshop so going in they already have an idea of the areas where they need to improve. The assess-ment also gathers key personal preferences, such as an ability to communicate in a creative and humorous way, and what is the per-son's appetite for risk. This all becomes part of the session's key deliverable—our twenty-five-page individual profile—that we deliver at the end of the session. We call these "The Personality Owners' Manual." They are enlightening insights into each of the participant's psychological make-up that can hopefully benefit them well beyond the session. The Personality Owner's Manual focuses on helping the individual with:

- *Improved Communication* through a revealing explora-tion into the different ways team members send and receive information.
- *Reducing conflict*, tips on using humor and creativity to recognize and minimize unnecessary clashes be-tween dissimilar personality types.
- *Strengthened Management Effectiveness* through in-creased awareness of the team, various human needs, and professional preferences.
- *Decreased Stress*, discovering ways to sidestep anxiety-generating and time-consuming interpersonal issues through the appropriate use of humor.

Ultimately, the team members learn to develop better relation-ships, improve morale, and create greater camaraderie through the healthy insights harvested during the workshop. And the results are typically so hilarious the teammates openly share their personal

Owner's Manual with others, further fostering the bond the session establishes.

So if you find yourself flying an airline in the near future and their personnel seem giddy as they run around hugging each other—we did something right. Or you just may be flying Southwest—one of the two.

Wright

I see you also do some writing as well.

Dvorak

Yes I do David. I have written two Harlequin Romance novels centered on a medieval Lord named Fronk who is allergic to tin.

Wright

Seriously?

Dvorak

Hello, professional humorist here! Actually, I have written two humorous books, at least I think they are funny; they are: *101 Twisted Mantra's For The New Millennium*™ and its highly anticipated follow-up, *101 Severely Twisted Mantras - For The New Age*™. I am also working on a number of humorous pamphlets I can leave behind to help my clients maintain the humor momentum. And you never know when I may write something else about Lord Fronk.

Wright

As you have worked to refine your role as a Professional Humorist, are there any professional people you consider your role models?

Dvorak

Well David, I think as I mentioned earlier, I not only have tremendous respect for Mr. Herb Kelleher as a superb business man, but also as leader with a great sense of humor. Early on while in graduate school, I read a business case about Southwest and the influence he has had on his organization. He stated that one of the driving forces behind their success was they created a culture that placed high value on the soft skills in his employees—energetic, fun-loving, and personable. So, right from the beginning Mr. Kelleher saw the value in recruiting and hiring a certain type of person who fit into their culture. This was at the beginning, way before their decade of rising stock and company value.

Another business leader, Victor Kiam, who is since deceased, once owned the NFL Patriots as well as Remington® shavers. He has written two books, *Going for it! How to Succeed as an Entrepreneur,* and *Live to Win: Achieving Success in Life and Business.* Within both books he shares story after story throughout his life of how he has taken risks and incorporated humor and creativity into his personal and professional life. He is especially proud of the time he brought a live chimpanzee on a sales call. Neither Mr. Kiam nor I am suggesting that any sales professional bring a chimp to a sales call—besides, any good salesperson calls ahead to check to see if the client already has one available. So to answer your question, I would say these two business leaders definitely influenced me and my career.

Wright

What about comedy professionals? Are there any you have looked to as role models or for inspiration?

Dvorak

Well initially, like many of my generation it was the masters: John Belushi, Dan Ackroyd, Gilda Radner, and Chevy Chase and their work on *Saturday Night Live.* I was transitioning from high school to collage just about the time they hit it big, so their styles and voices really hit the mark for me. I couldn't get enough of them—the show, their comedy albums, even seeing them come to Second City. Along with them, I have always found the impov work of Jonathan Winters and Robin Williams to be very free spirited—risk taking in its truest comic form. It's their risk taking, the high-wire act without a net that connects with the audience. Fans recognize they are out there taking a chance.

Another legend would be Don Rickles. The first time I had the privilege of seeing Don Rickles perform live was in Vegas in the early nineties. I was really fascinated at how much of Don Rickles' show is pure improv—just him playing off the audience—the brilliance, the simple brilliance. I stand in such awe of these artists who discovered their comic gifts then took the time, the energy, and the risks associated with turning those gifts into their own form of art.

Wright

I know he is not here, but if he was, what would Dr. Carpediem say are his motivational "do's and don'ts"?

Dvorak

Well, I know for a fact his biggest "do" is quite simply, "DO." We see so many books on how to stay motivated—people giving advice on what to do. People spend too much time learning about the how but don't spend enough time on the doing. Anyone who has seen Dr. Carpediem speak knows one of his favorite phrases is "Don't be known for what you say, be known for what you do."

Let's see, what are some other motivational "do's" from the good Doctor? Ah yes—taking motivational risks. This means get out of your mental comfort zones and push yourself to discover your humor and creativity. If you want to have more fun, and be more motivated, you have to take some risks, appropriate risks. Simple suggestions include: go to different places for dinner, or introduce yourself to people you see every day but may typically ignore—the people on your commuter trains, those working at the restaurant you visit regularly, and especially people you work with.

One of the doctor's favorite exercises with clients is the "happy fun guy." He challenges the audience to say, "Hi," to at least one stranger every day for one week. He bets a dinner that by Friday, everyone will have least one very funny experience. Most are leery but hey, think about the worst thing that can happen—you become known as the friendly guy? Come on! Shame on us for allowing our human nature to see risks where none exists. David, what is the opposite of risk?

Wright

Reward?

Dvorak

Good answer, but no. The true opposite of risk is regret. If you ask a person to share with you their biggest disappointments in life they will invariably tell you a story that includes regret. If I could pick just one message to come across to my audience, it would be that they walk away encouraged to take more risks in their personal and professional lives. Today will be gone forever, make it great and seize the day!

Wright

Doug I really appreciate your spending time with me here today. This has been enlightening and extremely enjoyable.

Dvorak

That's it? I didn't get to share the period of my professional life when I was a nude piano player working a health club lounge? Oh well, maybe next time. But sincerely David, thank you very much, it's been a privilege and a pleasure to share with you my philosophies on humor, motivation, and creativity.

Wright

Today we have been talking to Doug Dvorak, a professional humorous speaker and creativity consultant who believes that laughter is the software of the soul. Doug assists clients with improving their bottom line through the use of humor and creativity. I'm convinced he's right.

Doug thanks so much for being with us on *Masters of Success*.

Dvorak

Thank you David.

About Doug Dvorak

Doug Dvorak assists clients with productivity training, corporate creativity and humor workshops, and other aspects of sales and marketing management. Doug's clients are characterized as Fortune 1000 companies, small to medium businesses, civic organizations, service businesses, and individual investors and entrepreneurs. Doug Dvorak is a certified sales trainer, management consultant and corporate humorist. Doug holds a Bachelor of Arts degree in Business Administration and a Master of Business Administration in Marketing Management. But Doug's sense of humor is no less refined, as he is a graduate of the Player's Workshop of the Second City, one of the oldest and most prestigious improvisational comedy schools in the world. Doug has presented to over 50,000 people on four continents. Doug conducts personalized presentations and workshops. He speaks to management groups, business owners, and professional associations that appreciate his customized programs which never fail to bring smiles to people's faces. But regardless of Doug's comical presentations, he is a consummate business professional whose primary goal is client satisfaction. In addition, Doug is an active member of the National Speaker's Association® (NSA®).

Doug Dvorak
1064 Bombay Way
Palatine, IL 60067
Phone: 847.359.6969
Mobile: 847.997.3454
Fax: 847.705.7157
Email: Doug@DougDvorak.com
www.DougDvorak.com

Chapter Thirteen

WILL CROSS

THE INTERVIEW

David Wright (Wright)
Will is a professional motivational speaker, mountaineer, and educator. He has spoken all over the world and to audiences of from thirty to three thousand. He has led expeditions to the ends of the earth. Will Cross can inspire your audience with rich tales, motivational messages and magnificent images that will move your participants to be refocused and more productive. Will's achievements have been covered by CNN, BBC, The Today Show, Discovery Channel, Voice of America, KDKA News and Talk Radio, and ABC, CBS, and NBC national affiliate stations. He has also appeared in publications such as *The Wall Street Journal, USA Today, The New York Times, Explorers Journal*, and *GQ*. During 2003 and 2004, Will delivered an inspirational Public Service Announcement viewed by over seventeen million people. Will's 2004 Mt. Everest expedition had a reach of over thirty-seven million people. Among his global expeditions, Will has successfully ascended the highest peaks of North and South America, Europe, Africa and Antarctica. In 2001 he was privileged to climb fifteen unmapped, unexplored mountains in Greenland. He received a Gold Congressional Award for exemplary service to the United States, granted for his initiative, achievement

185

and service. Will is a professional member of the National Speakers Association. Will holds a Bachelor of Arts from Allegheny College, a Master of Science in Education from Duquesne University, and Secondary Principal's Certification from the University of Pittsburgh, where he specialized in educational programs for troubled teens. Will, his wife Amy and their six children live in Pittsburgh.

Will, welcome to *Masters of Success.*

Will Cross (Cross)
Thank you.

Wright
How do you define motivation?

Cross
When discussing motivation—the setting of goals, overcoming fears and doubts, finding hidden strengths—we often deploy the imagery of mountain climbers inching their way to the top. We talk of reaching new heights. The most successful people are often described as having attained the pinnacle of their profession. Coaches and corporate CEOs stress the importance of peak performance.

Wright
Have you learned a great deal on these trips?

Cross
I can appreciate the potency of this imagery. Climbing some of the highest mountains in the world, as well as walking to both the North and South Poles, has taught me the importance of planning, teamwork, perseverance, and self-reliance. On expeditions and climbs these things become more than bulleted points in a motivational speech—they are essential to your survival.

Wright
What does it take?

Cross
To be a climber requires intense focus and absolute physical output that you can never imagine (you wouldn't want to because it can be so difficult). It also provides a tremendous sense of freedom and power and control in the world in which you are such a small part.

To stand on top of Denali, the highest mountain in North America, or to climb the south peak of Mt. Everest, where you're so high you can see the curvature of the earth as the sun rises over China, is to know an enormous sense of pride and accomplishment. In addition to overcoming the obstacles of altitude, bad weather, falling rock, and treacherous, man-eating crevasses, each summit gives me another victory over my diabetes. I like to think that it sets an example for others who may have my disease or other physical limitations—that they, too, can overcome them.

Wright
How has diabetes impacted you?

Cross
Type 1 diabetes is much more dangerous than Type 2 diabetes, which is often caused by age, a bad diet, and excess weight. The pancreas of a Type 1 diabetic cannot manufacture insulin, a growth hormone that breaks down glucose. The disease cuts life expectancy and renders sufferers insulin dependent. Diabetes is the leading cause of heart attack, kidney failure, amputation, and blindness. More people will die this year of diabetes than they will of AIDS and breast cancer combined.

I motivate others by telling my story as someone who has had Type 1 diabetes for twenty-eight years and someone who is trying to become the first American to climb the highest mountain on each continent as well as walk to both poles. I try to motivate by setting an example, telling a story well, and relating that story to my audience specifically, whether it is to a group of business people, a group of children, a group of parents, or a fundraising opportunity.

Wright
How did this all start?

Cross
My adventures really started when I was about nine years old and diagnosed with diabetes. I was told I couldn't do the same things that other kids do, particularly adventure sports. I didn't really accept that. As I grew older and learned how to manage the disease—in my early teens—a determination grew to prove that diabetics didn't have to remain homebound invalids.

As a Type 1 diabetic, I must inject myself with insulin at least four times a day. I must also monitor my blood sugar constantly, maintaining a careful balance of calories consumed, measured against the amount of exercise and medication in a given day. Obviously, the procedure becomes especially complicated when you're climbing a mountain or walking across a polar plateau.

Wright

Could you tell us about a big hurdle?

Cross

My first real test came when I was seventeen and I was accepted on an expedition to Patagonia, Chile. Diabetics were forbidden to go because it was thought their special dietary requirements and insulin dependence would prove life threatening. But I wrote to Prince Charles, who was sponsor of the expedition and asked if he would make an exception. He did.

About a week into the journey, rations were cut drastically when it was discovered that not enough food had been packed. I fought back the panic I felt and went along with the rations. I told no one about my diabetes because I did not want special treatment and besides, I had specifically asked his Royal Highness that I be included in this expedition; I was darned if I'd turn tail now. I forced myself to take it one day at a time and to concentrate on eating slowly. For the next two and a half weeks, we hunted and foraged. We ate birds, snails, leaves, grass, and berries when we could get away with it. I survived with no long-term damage to my health. The ordeal changed my perspective—It gave me a taste of the obstacles I would face.

Wright

How is planning part of leadership?

Cross

It's okay to change your game plan when things don't go as you'd hoped. For example, I wanted to become the first diabetic to walk to the South Pole. I grew up in England and I had a vision based on the cultural stories of England about Robert Scott and Ernest Shackleton going to the poles. These are classic odysseys, so I wanted to journey to the poles. I had no idea if I could do it, what it would cost, or who would do it with me; I just wanted to do it. I had a very clear vision but I had no idea how to execute it.

When I couldn't raise enough money, I set my sights on a more attainable goal—walking to the North Pole. I would use this polar hike to provide data to diabetes researchers at the University of Pittsburgh Medical Center. One of the researchers would accompany me and measure the effects of extreme temperatures and physical exertion on my body. I went there because I had no success convincing people I could do the South Pole without killing myself. I still had to overcome considerable skepticism, but with the help of colleagues such as Richard Danforth—also a Type 1 diabetic—I successfully walked to the North Pole in 2001.

Wright
What happened after reaching the North Pole?

Cross
Building on this success, I was able to achieve my goal of becoming the first person with diabetes to walk to the South Pole. It was a two-year process finding the right people, keeping them motivated, raising the money, and then getting down on the ice. Then it was a "mere" matter of hauling 150-pound sledges 730 miles, ten hours a day. During the sixty-day walk, which I began on November 18, 2003, with Jerry Petersen, my chief concern was making sure my insulin didn't freeze in the frigid temperatures, which sometimes reached sixty degrees below zero.

Wright
Tell us about the foundation of leadership.

Cross
I incorporate five specific elements of the climb into my motivational talks. Putting the first letter of each word together spells out the word climb:
Courage
Love
Imagination
Motivation
Belief

Wright
How does this fit into a business model?

Cross

The parallels between mountaineering and business are endless. Everyone has to have a common understanding of what it is you're going after. They have to share that vision you have. Teamwork is as vital in business as it is in being able to reach the summit of a mountain. You will run into difficult times and you need to be able to see those and account for them before you go bankrupt.

Success requires a good leader who can communicate effectively, think on h/her feet, make adaptations, and who possesses complex skills. All of those are important elements whether you're climbing a mountain or running a business.

On a mountain, successful execution means getting to the top and getting back down; but it makes no sense to summit if you can't make it home. That is why I turned around on Mount Everest in 2004 when I was fifteen hundred feet from the summit. Things were not going well; six people had died the day before. My partner and I believed we could make the top but we couldn't make it down, so we turned around.

Wright

How do you define success?

Cross

Success simply is attaining the goals you set out to achieve. That obviously becomes more complex as you look at it in terms of satisfaction. Satisfaction is physical and mental as well as emotional, and you become successful when you find balance in those areas.

Wright

How does motivation play a role in leadership?

Cross

My motivational philosophy perhaps can be summed up thus: You have no idea how you're going to do it, or if it can be done, but you know that it's something important to you and you go for it. Motivation is the engine that drives leadership.

(William Loeffler, a Pittsburgh based writer, helped with this story.)

About Will Cross

Will is a professional motivational speaker, mountaineer, and educator. He has spoken all over the world and to audiences of thirty to three thousand. He has led expeditions to the ends of the earth. Will Cross can inspire your audience with rich tales, motivational messages and magnificent images that will move your participants to be refocused and more productive. Will's achievements have been covered by CNN, BBC, The Today Show, Discovery Channel, Voice of America, KDKA News and Talk Radio, and ABC, CBS, and NBC national affiliate stations. He has also appeared in publications such as *The Wall Street Journal, USA Today, The New York Times, Explorers Journal,* and *GQ.* During 2003 and 2004, Will delivered an inspirational Public Service Announcement viewed by over seventeen million people. Will's 2004 Mt. Everest expedition had a reach of over thirty-seven million people. Among his global expeditions, Will has successfully ascended the highest peaks of North and South America, Europe, Africa and Antarctica. In 2001 he was privileged to climb fifteen unmapped, unexplored mountains in Greenland. He received a Gold Congressional Award for exemplary service to the United States, granted for his initiative, achievement and service. Will is a professional member of the National Speakers Association. Will holds a Bachelor of Arts from Allegheny College, a Master of Science in Education from Duquesne University, and Secondary Principal's Certification from the University of Pittsburgh, where he specialized in educational programs for troubled teens. Will, his wife Amy and their five children live in Pittsburgh.

Will Cross
1110 Morningside Avenue
Pittsburgh, PA 15206-1349
Phone: 412.606.7758
Email: wcross@willcrossmotivates.com
www.willcrossmotivates.com

Chapter Fourteen

JARIK E. CONRAD

THE INTERVIEW

David Wright (Wright)

Today we're talking with Jarik E. Conrad. Jarik is a professional speaker, trainer, leadership coach, and consultant. Jarik is a certified Intercultural Sensitivity trainer, a certified Emotional Intelligence trainer, and is certified as a Senior Professional in Human Resources (SPHR). He is currently an Executive Director with the Jacksonville Regional Chamber of Commerce where he leads "Blueprint for Prosperity," an initiative aimed at increasing the per capita income of Duval County residents in Florida. He is also the President of Conrad Consulting Group LLC, which is a leadership consulting organization that offers a variety of services aimed at maximizing the capabilities of an organization's greatest asset—its people. Jarik grew up in a housing project in East St. Louis, Illinois, a place once described as the most distressed small city in America. He went on to earn a BA from the University of Illinois, as well as MBA and MILR degrees from the Ivy League's Cornell University. Jarik has been a leader and trusted advisor to all levels of management at various Fortune 500 companies during his career.

Jarik, welcome to *Masters of Success*.

Jarik E. Conrad (Conrad)
Thank you for inviting me to speak with you today, David.

Wright
You know there are thousands of books and articles published annually about leadership. What do *you* think the greatest characteristic is for effective leadership?

Conrad
Emotional intelligence is key. Recent studies show that emotional intelligence is a much greater predictor of success than IQ. Most of the theories about leadership borrow from and build upon each other. Many of the theories include components of emotional intelligence such as confidence, self-awareness, empathy, assertiveness, and optimism. Confidence is everything! People will not follow a leader who is not sure of his or her abilities.

I want to note here, though, that confidence and arrogance are two very different things. We all know that any strength can be a weakness if taken too far. Self-awareness is also important. One of the biggest mistakes failed leaders make is thinking they can do it all. Self-awareness is necessary so that leaders can surround themselves with others who have better skills in some areas than they have.

Empathy is essential for effective leadership. Leaders who can understand the perspectives of others are in a much greater position to find collaborative solutions to vexing problems than those who are narrowly focused on their own needs and perspectives. Empathy requires a world-view that allows for differences in people. People have different personalities, different values and beliefs, and different dreams. It is important for leaders to avoid imposing their own personality style, values and beliefs, and dreams on others. Assertiveness refers to an individual's ability not only to recognize when actions need to occur, but the ability to step up and take the necessary action. Optimistic leaders are confident they can achieve their goals. Additionally, optimism is contagious.

Wright
So how would you describe *your* personal leadership style?

Conrad
I attribute a great deal of my success in leadership to emotional intelligence. In fact, I recently scored high on an emotional intelli-

gence test. Reuven Bar-On defines emotional intelligence as an array of capabilities, competencies, and skills that can influence one's ability to cope with environmental demands and pressures. I refer to the concept simply as emotional recognition and response. I have been able to understand and effectively channel my emotions in difficult situations such as growing up in East Saint Louis, competing at an Ivy League school, and facing challenges in Corporate America. I have also been able to read others and use that insight to solve problems. I am most excited about emotional intelligence because it can be measured and improved in a way that IQ cannot. IQ does not change much after adolescence, but emotional intelligence typically grows naturally through mid-life and can be accelerated with focused development. Emotional intelligence holds a great deal of promise for corporate and community leadership, which I believe is the greatest challenge society will face as it becomes more complex, competitive, and diverse.

Wright

You say that effective corporate and community leadership is the biggest challenge we will face in the near future. Explain why you feel that way.

Conrad

Now more than ever successful organizational decision-makers recognize that their true competitive advantage lies with their people. Constant change and rapid technological advances have made it impossible to compete on a product basis alone. Globalization has led to an increase in the speed and the quality of information one can obtain; and that has made it much more competitive.

Products and services can now easily be copied. If an organization once supplied the only product or service of its kind on the block its leaders could probably treat people with little regard and still be successful. However, when there are two or three other similar products on the same block, leaders have to change the way they view their employees. Creative, caring, hardworking, capable, and trustworthy employees are essential—especially in leadership positions—if organizations are going to keep their edge.

If what I have said thus far is true about the importance of people in organizations, the real key to all of this is managing the challenges and opportunities associated with diversity. I define "diversity" as the internal and external characteristics that make us different. The demographics of the workforce are shifting more rapidly than ever. The faces in our cafeterias, meeting places, and ultimately, our boardrooms are increasingly going to be different. From an internal diversity perspective, we are learning more each day about learning styles and personality styles that impact how individuals process information and interact with each other both within and across cultures. Leaders will have to be dedicated to getting the most out of each and every individual. Furthermore their success in doing so will be based not only on their cognitive abilities and technical skills; but primarily on their intercultural sensitivity and emotional skills.

Wright

Jarik, you talked a bit about diversity in your response to the last question. Do you think diversity, particularly race relations, is still major a challenge in this country?

Conrad

Of course we still have some major obstacles to overcome in this area, David. I am optimistic we can get there though. Two things must happen for us to get beyond racism, sexism, and all of those other *isms* that divide us. First, marginalized groups are going to have to avoid falling into "victimhood." Individuals from historically disadvantaged groups must be determined not to let institutionalized barriers prevent them from achieving their goals. It is unacceptable to take the position that "since racism might inhibit my success I won't even try; in other words, I am guaranteeing that I won't be successful since I might not make it anyway."

On the other hand, the other thing that needs to happen is for individuals in the dominant group to recognize that there are barriers specifically associated with being a woman or person of color that have to be removed. I believe very few people will deliberately discriminate against others; however, institutionalized racism is still a very formidable challenge for people of color in America. Even well meaning white people find it difficult to admit that institutionalized racism exists and these subtle biases result in privilege for them. I call this phenomenon "Buried Head Sydrome." It plays itself out like this: Things that come to our attention that fit our paradigms are let in but things that do not fit are ignored—so much so that we will not even acknowledge their existence.

Privilege does not mean that white people don't have to work hard. In fact, most successful people in America are hard workers. Privilege means that individuals from other groups might work equally as hard, but may face roadblocks related only to their gender or color of their skin that stunt their progress. Those who say we don't have a race problem in America, but we do have an economic problem are missing the point. Of course we have an economic problem—we have to work to erase the barriers to success for poor whites as well.

The challenge is that we see race; we don't see economics. For instance, if you took a wealthy Black man and a poor White man, dressed them alike and doctored similar resumes for them, and then sent them to apply for housing, start-up business loans, and mid-to-high level jobs, many Americans would be shocked to learn of the inconsistencies in terms of who gets the vacant apartment and for how much, who gets the business start-up money, and who gets hired for what job. Economics is part of the puzzle, but clearly a focus there won't completely solve the problem. If our nation is to be a true meritocracy, we must fight to give a fair shot to poor people, women, and people of color.

Let me share with you a little about my background for perspective. My friends and I grew up knowing that we were at risk. We were labeled as an "endangered species." It is very difficult for children growing up in those circumstances to believe that life has anything special to offer them. It is easy for people in this situation to either fall into victimhood or get angry and make poor decisions that lead to unfortunate consequences like jail or death.

I was able to overcome many challenges by focusing on education even though we had outdated textbooks, inadequate facilities, little to no extracurricular opportunities, no adequate science or chemistry labs, swimming pool, or even a cafeteria in some cases. Education afforded me the opportunity to finally see over the invisible fence around East St. Louis. Just because some of us made it out, doesn't mean that others with high potential will necessarily make it out as well. I am certainly a proponent of hard work and dedication, but this may not do it alone. Expecting kids to work hard and make it out of that situation is like saying since we saw one person win the lottery that means that if we play the lottery hard enough, we should all win.

Wright

Tell us more about your experiences growing up in East Saint Louis and how they've helped shape who you are today.

Conrad

I get this question all the time and I think it is impossible to go back and determine specifically what it was that made me who I am today. Let me say first of all, that I am extremely proud of where I come from. I was the youngest of five children and I had a supportive family, particularly my mother who did all she could to make me feel special. I grew up in one of the worst housing projects in America, but I recall at a very young age thinking there was something else in life out there for me even though I did not see that same expectation in the eyes of a lot of people I grew up with. Many people seemed to me to be content with the hand that life had dealt them. I know now that much of what I perceived as contentment was really hopelessness. People felt like the odds were against them to be successful in the traditional sense so they hardly even tried.

Somehow I knew there was something better out there and I felt like if anybody could have it, I could. I refused to believe that my future was already decided solely based on where I was born. We always hear the old adage, "If you can't beat them, join them," but I adopted the philosophy that, "If you can't join them, beat them." I used this strategy when I saw images on television of people who didn't look like me, read books by and about people who didn't think like me, or heard success stories of people who had not been born into the situation I had been.

I took education very seriously. I believed that education was the key to unlocking the door of prosperity. I signed up for any after school program, summer enrichment institute, and academic club I could. I was also fortunate enough to have a creative outlet that enhanced my discipline, confidence, and public speaking skills. I used to attend theatre rehearsals with my mother who was a member of an acting troupe at Southern Illinois University where she was taking some classes. At one rehearsal, one of the members was sick and could not attend the rehearsal so they needed someone to just stand in for him. When they asked for volunteers I raised my hand even though I was only nine or ten years old. They were at first skeptical, but grew more confident when they went to pass me the script and I said I did not need it because I knew the lines already. Not only did I know the lines, I delivered them with such passion and force that I ended up being added as the youngest member of the troupe (everyone else was at least collage age). I participated with the troupe for several years thereafter. The experience with the Unity Ensemble really implanted in me the idea that one could accomplish anything with desire, practice, and assertiveness.

Wright

So what do you say to kids growing up in a different environment as you did?

Conrad

Again, confidence is everything! Despite the considerable obstacles associated with growing up in difficult situations, anyone can be successful if they truly believe they can and are willing to put in the effort to achieve their goals. I think exposure to different places and different activities is critically important also. When you grow up in a place like East Saint Louis it's hard to dream beyond the city's boundaries and you become afraid to try new things. We see something on television and label it as a Black person or White person thing. Kids need to get exposed to new things and not self-select out of things based on stereotypes and ignorance. Such narrow-mindedness could never have produced Tiger Woods or Venus and Serena Williams to name a few.

Creative outlets are critical as well. Whether it is acting, dancing, playing an instrument, drawing, sports, or the countless other positive activities to get involved in, these activities serve as a foundation for learning important life-long lessons like discipline, hard work, teamwork, and communication skills. Kids must also have courage. Some people think that it is courageous to sell drugs, break the law, and stay in trouble at school; however, it takes more courage to go out and compete in a world that can sometimes seem so unfair.

Wright

Education is obviously important to you. In fact, by the time this book is published you will be closer to earning your doctorate degree. Tell us about your commitment to personal development.

Conrad

The importance of education cannot be overstated. It is just unfortunate that when kids grow up in difficult situations it is a bit of a stretch for them to focus on education when they are coping on the daily struggles of life. For many children in America, basic survival issues of food and shelter are foremost in their minds while they sit in overcrowded classrooms reading outdated books about people with whom they have nothing in common. As concerned parents and citizens, we need to work to make improvements in the education system of this country so that all kids have a *real* opportunity to learn. I believe wholeheartedly in personal development outside of the classroom as well. For instance, I wish more students from economically challenged backgrounds had the opportunity to study abroad. Studying in a different country teaches individuals not just about the specific coursework, but it teaches them about people and life in general.

Learning new things is intoxicating for me. The more new things I am exposed to the more I'm reminded of how much I have yet to learn. Even after the doctorate degree, I know I will be out learning new things and figuring out what else is out there. A focus on personal learning is key for corporate or community leadership.

Wright

Many would say that you took a major risk by leaving a successful corporate career behind to start your own company. What motivated you to take the challenge?

Conrad

It is amazing how concerned people were when I first left corporate America. Hardly anyone could understand how a fast-tracked young executive could suddenly leave a secure job and take such a huge risk. The choice was easy for me though. While I wasn't miserable in my last corporate position, I wasn't satisfied that my strengths were being fully utilized. I also looked around at some senior-level people in the organization and realized that was not the life for me. Many of them did not seem happy. And I didn't want to fall into that familiar routine.

I pride myself on having options—I simply exercised one of my options when I left my job. I have always believed that one will perform better doing something he or she really enjoys. Life is too short to be stuck in a position that sucks your energy, drains your enthusiasm, and kills your creativity. There are entirely too many challenging, meaningful, rewarding, fun careers out there to be focused on something that's not making a difference in your life and in the lives of others. I would encourage anyone to follow their passion as long as they have the credentials and the experience they need.

Wright

So what excites you most about the work you do with The Conrad Consulting Group, LLC?

Conrad

Not knowing what the next challenge will be is exciting for me. The opportunity to be creative and look for innovative solutions to challenging problems has been great. I enjoy working with and through people from various backgrounds. I am also very excited about speaking opportunities where I am able to discuss elusive concepts like leadership, diversity, emotional intelligence, and/or overcoming difficult circumstances.

Adjunct teaching at Jacksonville University and teaching in the Continuing Education Department at the University of North Florida has also been very rewarding. I really enjoy seeing the light bulbs light up over students' heads when they acquire new knowledge; it doesn't matter whether they are traditional juniors and seniors, or adults who've gone back to further their education. I know I am making a difference when I can see growth in my students.

Wright

Your wife Adrienne is a busy, successful lawyer. How do you guys balance your professional and personal lives?

Conrad

First and foremost, I am extremely proud of her and I know that she's proud of me. We made a commitment early on that we would make sure to spend quality time with each other regardless of how hectic our careers got—we have seen many couples struggle with this. We just try to learn from others' mistakes. No job is more important than my wife and I know she feels the same about me. We make a deliberate effort to spend as much time together as we can especially since we are planning on starting a family over the next couple of years. I know it's kind of taboo to some guys out there, but we golf together as well. We share in the cooking and grocery shopping and we even work out at the gym together. We also participate on some local boards of directors together in the community. We both believe that work-life balance is essential for good well-rounded leaders.

Wright

In addition to planning to have children would you tell our readers a little bit about your immediate goals and perhaps some of your long term goals?

Conrad

I look forward to a successful Blueprint for Prosperity initiative, which will improve the quality of life for the citizens of Jacksonville, Florida. I am also committed to finishing my doctorate degree. I will continue my professional speaking appearances and I plan to write more about leadership, intercultural sensitivity, and emotional intelligence.

There are a number of long-term interests I have, including developing a leadership institute here in Jacksonville, Florida, where professionals from across the globe could come and discuss issues relating to leadership, diversity, and emotional intelligence. Also, I want to do something major in East Saint Louis. It is important to me that I give back to that community because there are many young people there who have the potential to achieve well beyond what I have if they could only get exposure to the new things they need.

Another thing I haven't ruled out is politics. My background and experiences have left me with a unique perspective on a number of controversial issues, particularly issues dealing with race relations; I believe I can be a unifying force in this area.

Wright

Well what an interesting conversation, Jarik. I really do appreciate the time you've taken with me this afternoon in giving me some insight into some of the things you believe and some of the principles to which you adhere. It's really been enlightening for me. I really appreciate you spending the time with me.

Conrad

Thank you, David. I have enjoyed our conversation.

Wright

Today we've been talking to Jarik E. Conrad. He has a broad experience across a number of industries that include transportation, retail, food and beverage, financial services, sports chemicals, and aerospace companies. Through these experiences Jarik has been a trusted advisor and international consultant to all levels of management. He is currently a doctorial candidate of the University of North Florida.

Jarik, thank you so much for being with us today on *Masters of Success*.

About Jarik E. Conrad, SPHR

Jarik E. Conrad, SPHR is the President of The Conrad Consulting Group, LLC, which is a leadership and human resource consulting organization. He is also the Executive Director of Blueprint for Prosperity with the Jacksonville Regional Chamber of Commerce. Jarik has been a leader and trusted advisor to all levels of management at various Fortune 500 companies during his career including McDonnell Douglas, Pillsbury, Union Carbide, Dain Rauscher, Citibank, and CSX.

Jarik E. Conrad, SPHR
The Conrad Consulting Group, LLC
9838 Old Baymeadows Road, #325
Jacksonville, FL 32256
Phone: 904.565.1080
Email: jconrad@conradconsultinggroup.net
www.conradconsultinggroup.net

Chapter Fifteen

STEVEN W. EDWARDS, PH.D.

THE INTERVIEW

David Wright (Wright)
Today we're talking with Dr. Steven W. Edwards, recognized by *USA Today* for his innovative approach to leadership. Dr. Edwards implemented numerous programs to improve student performance during his sixteen-year tenure as a school administrator. He is an internationally recognized speaker, facilitator, and trainer for organizations including the United Nations and The World Bank. He is featured as a content expert with appearances on CNN discussing leadership, organizational climate, reform, and strategic planning. He has published numerous articles and has authored a book on conflict resolution. He's also served as a university professor as well as the Vice President of the National Crime Prevention Council in Washington D.C.

Dr. Edwards welcome to *Masters of Success.*

Dr. Steven W. Edwards (Edwards)
Thank you.

Wright
So would you tell our readers what is "reality leadership"?

Edwards

Reality leadership addresses one of the major components of successful leadership. It is the ability for organizations to clearly identify their challenges and the issues they face. Far too often organizations chase fads. I refer to them as "fad-aholics" chasing the current fad or trend. Not that the fad is bad but the particular fad of the moment may be something that may or may not assist them in moving their agenda forward. Reality leadership is the ability to deal in reality. It is about identifying and confronting your problems without hesitation or reservation.

Wright

So what are the essential qualities of effective leaders?

Edwards

Effective leaders are able to set a vision—a course—for an organization. Effective leaders are those individuals who can motivate others towards success. A leader without followers is basically someone who's just going for a walk. Effective leaders are change agents. They deal in reality and confront real issues as well as brutal facts. They lead the way, and they enable others to take action.

Wright

What do we know about organizational trust? We've had a lot of trust issues in the last few years, how do we build it?

Edwards

We build organizational trust by engaging others along the way. Too often we operate in organizations from a hierarchical approach which can contribute to mistrust. Trust is built when individuals from all aspects of your organization share in the decision-making process. When others are engaged in that process, they begin to take ownership for the organization, which is critical to building a strong foundation for organizational change. With organizational trust, we see the opportunity for effective change to take place; but without it no long-term sustainable change can occur.

Wright

In our company we had someone come to discuss some strategic planning and vision with us. Let me pose the question to you: What is vision and how do we go about creating it?

Edwards

Vision is the art of seeing the invisible. It is the "ideal state"—if everything was perfect this is what our organization would look like. How do we get there? We need to build vision collaboratively; but as leaders we need to help pave the way. And successfully engaging others in that process is critically important. But the *vision* is that driving force and that overarching goal that we're constantly trying to achieve. Although we may never get there, we're constantly moving in that direction. An organization without a clear vision is like a ship without a compass—it has no direction.

Wright

I was interested in the words you used: "the art of," that's a concept you rarely hear in the business world today.

Edwards

Right and I think it *is* an art. I think it's an art form and it's something not all individuals possess. A good leader can visualize the complete picture before it's painted, and has the intangible qualities that inspire others to help achieve this vision. We can all color, but we're not all artists.

Wright

So how do we foster an organizational culture that drives success?

Edwards

To foster an organizational culture that drives success we need to engage individuals from all aspects of the organization. We need to focus not only on internal stakeholders, but also on others externally who influence or have contact with that organization; they must be engaged as well. That will vary from organization to organization. Our customers, whoever they may be, are our external stakeholders who need to be engaged in that process.

Building that collaborative culture however, only happens when we have individuals working together and that takes time. It builds off trust. You need a clear vision. People need to have an incentive to do business a particular way and when those components come together we have the opportunity to build a collaborative culture.

Wright

How do we strengthen ourselves through strengthening others?

Edwards

This is really about empowerment. It's often said that the success of an organization is dependent upon what happens when that leader leaves. We judge the effectiveness of the leader after they've gone. In other words, a great leader is able to create a situation where he or she is no longer needed. By strengthening others, we become more effective. In the hiring process we need to think about bringing in people who have skills that are not similar to ours, so we can diversify our skill base. We need to give others responsibilities for leadership. We need to allow them to take risks without a fear of failure. When we do this, we create the opportunity to move an organization forward and build a strong foundation built on a solid, collaborative culture.

Wright

What's the role of collaboration in successful organizational change?

Edwards

Collaboration is a key element of organizational change. For a long time in our society we operated on a model that was very hierarchical. During the 1980s the Total Quality Management (TQM) movement was very popular as a result of Deming's work. Deming's work was based on a Japanese model of management that is highly collaborative. In the United States we struggled with this type of organizational model but we are making headway in understanding that we cannot operate in isolation—collectively we are much more effective. When we work in a team environment, we can build on shared resources and share our collective experiences and talents and minimize weaknesses. When we build that collaborative culture we completely change the effectiveness of the organization. Creating greater ownership builds a strong foundation for success.

Wright

What is the role of both internal and external stakeholders and how do we maximize both for organizational success?

Edwards

I firmly believe we need to build organizations from the inside out. We need to have our structure—our way of doing business—in place first. We need to create our own internal culture first before we move outside. In order to do this, however, we must have other people working collaboratively to create effective change and create a successful organizational model.

The role of internal stakeholders is critical. Moving from internal to external, we also need to engage individuals who are key to our success. Depending on the organization, that may vary; but it's very important to identify those key internal stakeholders and key external stakeholders who need to be involved in any change initiative right from the beginning. If they're brought in right from the beginning and we build that collaborative model, individuals will take ownership. We will build institutional trust and create positive and effective organizational change.

Wright

When examining organizational change, what is the impact on the individual in the organization and in society?

Edwards

In any change initiative, it is important for leadership to examine how that change initiative will impact individuals within the organization or individuals externally who may be impacted by that change. They also need to examine how that initiative will impact the organization as a whole and what the greater impact is on society. We also need to ask are we truly benefiting society from our efforts? This is important because for true success to take place we need to be providing a service to the greater community. When decisions are made, we must consider the impact on the individual, the organization, and society. All three are connected. Without examining all three, we will be shortsighted in our thinking and in our results.

Wright

For those readers who have difficultly changing, especially those who have the mantra that "if it ain't broke don't fix it," and for those who are trying to maintain the status quo, is there a danger in that?

Edwards

I've always believed that maintaining the status quo is, in reality, a move backwards. Individuals like to stay in their comfort zone. There's security in your comfort zone because there is security and comfort in what you know. There's often a fear of moving outside that comfort zone and in taking risks; but organizations that maintain the status quo in our rapidly changing world are doomed to failure.

If we are to get individuals out of their comfort zones, they need to be allowed and given the opportunity to take risks, and when they take risks, they cannot be chastised for failing. Failure must be thought of as an opportunity for growth. We need to create opportunities for individuals within all organizations to step outside the box, be creative, take some risks, and when we do that we create the opportunity for the organization to build capacity and move forward.

Wright

How do we use data to drive our decisions?

Edwards

Data is extremely important in driving decision-making. It is very important in making informed leadership decisions. Organizations must know where they are before they can decide where they need to go. When we talk about reality leadership we're really talking about identifying where we are, not our *perception* of where we are. The best way to clearly understand where we are is by looking at data, both quantitative and qualitative. Examining a combination of hard numbers, interviews, surveys and anecdotal information will help us garner the necessary information to identify our current state. Without effective data analysis and evaluation focusing on results, an organization would be operating without clear direction, and would be basing organizational decisions on perception rather than reality.

Wright

I think our readers would also like to know some simple rules or techniques for dealing with people who resist change. So the final question I would have for you is: how do we deal with resistance to change?

Edwards

First we must understand that resistors exist in every organization, and resistors resist for a variety of reasons. Before we look at resistance, let's examine some realities for a leader of any organization. Regardless of the circumstances, there will always be a group of people who are very supportive, who are "with you." There's also a group who appears to be against you, regardless of the circumstances. Then there's a large group in the middle who can go either way. The challenge is to get that large group in the middle to align with those people who are very supportive; this will create critical mass. Once you create positive critical mass, positive change can take place.

When dealing with resistors, the goal is definitely to shrink the number of resistors. To do this, you must identify who they are and why they're resisting. Once you do this, it is vitally important to engage resisters. Unfortunately too often, leaders do not engage the resistors and/or they let resistors influence the decisions of others. When that happens, we end up with a case of the tail wagging the dog. Too often a very few number of people drive organizational decisions that may not be in the organization's or employees' best interest. So shrinking that number— identifying them, having them involved in different aspects of the organization that are critical to the change initiatives, and having individuals who are resistors being accountable—is extremely important.

It is also critical to divide resistors so that they are not all engaged in one particular group within an organization. Spread them out among committees, task forces, departments or different initiatives. It is also important to recognize and praise resistors when they are correct; but also continually look at what their issues and challenges are, and look for ways to get them to become greater contributors to the overall success of the organization.

Wright

As a small business owner, are there any questions, any profiles or anything I might use that would give me a clearer idea of people who would be more willing to accept change as I go about the task of recruiting and hiring?

Edwards

When we think about recruiting and hiring it's vitally important to hire people who have the skills that are consistent with the skills you're looking for. Beyond that, we must also hire someone who has a positive personality that will enhance the culture of the organization. We know that people can be trained to perform certain tasks or functions in an organization, but I don't know that people can be trained to change their personality.

When we look to hire successful leaders and successful members of any organization, too often we hire folks based solely on their technical ability. But in the long run their interpersonal skills and ability to work collaboratively will measure their success, and in turn, the success of the organization. You can have all the technical skills necessary to perform a job, but if you do not have the ability to work collaboratively with others, an organization and any change initiative will definitely stall.

Wright

It's very interesting. Well, I really appreciate your time today, Dr. Edwards. It's really been informative for me and I'm sure our readers are going to enjoy your thoughts on organizational leadership. I really do appreciate all this time you spent with me.

Edwards

Well thank you, I enjoyed it.

Wright

Today we've been talking to talking to Dr. Steven W. Edwards. He is an internationally recognized speaker, facilitator, and trainer for major organizations in this country. He's also featured as a content expert and has appeared on CNN discussing leadership, organizational climate, reform, and planning. In addition to publishing several articles he's authored a book on conflict resolution. As we have found out today he knows a great deal about leadership and specifically reality leadership.

Thank you so much, Dr. Edwards, for being with us today on *Masters of Success*.

Edwards

Thank you.

About Steven W. Edwards, Ph.D.

Recognized by *USA Today* for his innovative approach to education, Dr. Edwards implemented numerous programs to improve student performance during his sixteen-year tenure as a school administrator. He is an internationally recognized speaker, facilitator and trainer for organizations including The United Nations and the World Bank, and is featured as a content expert with appearances on CNN discussing leadership, organizational climate, reform, and strategic planning. He has published numerous articles, and has authored a book on conflict resolution. He has also served as a university professor, as well as the Vice President of the National Crime Prevention Council in Washington, D.C.

Steven W. Edwards, Ph.D.

Phone: 202.359.5124

Email: stevewedwards@comcast.net

www.sai-dc.com

Chapter Sixteen

JOHN CHRISTENSEN

THE INTERVIEW

David Wright (Wright)

Today we are talking with John Christensen. John's story begins in the shipping department at Chart House Learning where he began working as a teenager for his father, Ray. He worked his way to the top the old fashioned way, having to prove to his father and the company that he was a real filmmaker who could tell moving stories. Today Mr. Christensen guides Chart House as playground director, which is business talk for CEO, with an inspiring vision of an engaged workplace that can be developed through the *Fish Philosophy*. Chart House Learning is changing the way business is done worldwide. Like his dad before him, John created an eloquent language to transform lives. In 1997, he translated what happens daily at Seattle's world famous Pike Place Fish Market's culture into a vital global learning program called *Fish* and changed the entire business film industry. In the process, John also achieved his lifelong dream of how to turn workplaces into energetic, creative, and wholehearted endeavors with the four simple principles embodied in the *Fish Philosophy*.

John Christensen, welcome to *Masters of Success*.

John Christensen (Christensen)
Thank you, David. I appreciate that.

Wright
John, obviously, my first question is what are the four simple principles of *Fish Philosophy?*

Christensen
The four simple principles are play, make their day, be there, and choose your attitude.

Wright
Play? In other words we're supposed to play at work?

Christensen
Yes. Play is the basis of where creativity and innovation happens. And if you look back into your own life and see where you were most creative, it was in those moments of play and inspiration where you got lost in the moment. We call that play. Now if corporations are scared by that, think of it as lightheartedness. Think of it as taking your work seriously, but take yourself lightheartedly.

Wright
So tell us a little bit about what you do at Chart House Learning.

Christensen
We are kind of like cultural anthropologists. We study things that are out in the world, then we help put a language to it. For instance, that's what I saw at the fish market. I saw these fish mongers being totally engaged in their work and said, "Wait a minute! Wait a minute! There's something deeper going on than just play and all this craziness that I see on the shop floor." So we interpret that, then put a language around things, and help get that out into the business world. It's not only in the business world, schools are using it, too.

Wright
When you say "language," you're talking about terms that can be understood universally?

Christensen

Yes, absolutely. In *Fish,* it's ancient wisdom that's been resurfaced and brought to you in a new way and in an unlikely place—a fish market.

Wright

While preparing for this interview, I read that the first film in your series titled, *The Business Paradise* is the best selling film of all time. Is that true?

Christensen

Yes.

Wright

My goodness!

Christensen

Yes. That was first created in the '80s, with my father and a futurist. It's been translated in many, many languages. *Fish* is creeping up there, though. It's going to surpass *The Business Paradise* someday.

Wright

When you speak and train, how do you motivate people to create workplaces that are joyful and innovative, lighthearted and whole-hearted?

Christensen

The interesting part of all this is when we tell them and they see the film or read the book, there's something that connects inside them that says either they had this in them or they were searching for this...this lightheartedness, this engagement of being at work and being engaged in what you do. We've made a film series with a poet named David White. David talks about being wholehearted. He has a friend, a monk friend, who said, "The way around burnout isn't necessarily burnout. It's being wholehearted in what you do." Now that's incredible. That says, if you come to work and you're totally engaged and enjoy what you are doing, the day goes by much quicker and you're going to be connected to it.

Wright

Do you find many CEOs, or especially upper management people, that are a little—

Christensen

Apprehensive of this?

Wright

Yes.

Christensen

Yes, there is. But the one's who embrace it and get it, stand back. Watch out for their organizations! For instance, the CEO of Aspen Ski Co., a ski company in Aspen, Colorado, who has embraced it said, "This is the pull; this is what we're going to be. This is the way we're going to service our employees. We're going to be engaged with what we do." They have 3500 seasonal employees. They teach them every year. They teach them the *Fish Philosophy* when the new group comes in, or even part of the old group comes in. They resurface this and say, "Remember, be engaged." And when they open that playing field and they give them the boundaries of saying, "Okay, safety is first in any business; here's the playing fields. Be safe. Don't do anything that's rude or crude." They saw things happening.

For example, like a guy—a young man—created his super hero called *Captain Iowa*. And he'd fly kids through the lift line up to the front and he'd help create an atmosphere in the lift line. When they're standing there for twenty-five minutes, that was engaging. They started karaoke in the waiting lines, and they do limbo in the waiting lines for the lifts. Now that created an atmosphere because, again, the CEO is saying, "Look, we have great snow and the same mountains as the other resorts. What separates us from the other people? What separates us from our other ski friends?" It was the way they engaged with customers.

That's the way, first and foremost, to have people engage in their work and be happy with where they are. I'm not just talking about making a "Pollyannaish" happy, happy workplace. I'm talking about people being engaged in what they do. Now if you have that and you create that kind of atmosphere, watch out! Your bottom line is going to go up. Your retention is going to go down.

Another thing that we find that's just really amazing is, when you step back and analyze it, we're in our places of work more than we are in our places of worship, more than we are in the great outdoors, and more than we are with our families. Now if we can't connect to that, be engaged and have a joyfulness to what we do, that's a sad statement saying, "Look at your life." Look at the hours you spend there, what are you giving it to? What are you spending your life's energy on? What are you giving, where are you giving your energy, your life energy too? Is this the place that you really want to be? Is this the place that's going to make you flourish?

Wright

What do you mean by "make their day?" Are these management theories that apply to employees, or are these employee theories that apply to customers?

Christensen

It includes absolutely everyone. It's employee-to-employee, it's employer-to-employee and it's employee to customer. It's the whole thing. I'm saying, if you come with that attitude, again, your life is about what you are giving to people. "Make their day" is just a new term of saying, be it, make people's day.

Serving others is when we really find joy. No matter if the CEO is talking to a vice-president or a president, or an employee is talking to a guest in a hotel, I'm saying make people's day! And it doesn't take much. It's really amazing the stories that we hear about the little nuances of what makes peoples' day. I mean, just being with a person— that moves into being there. What does "being there" mean? It means just being in the moment with a person. For example, if you're trying to talk to somebody in your office and you've got the phone ringing and a message on your cell phone, put all those distractions away. Let voicemail answer the phone, put the cell phone away, and be with the person. When you're in the presence of a person, they can feel it. Do I have time to share a story with you?

Wright

Sure.

Christensen

There was a policeman who was in the service area of a jail, the booking agent shall we say. The police department he worked for went through the *Fish Philosophy* teaching, and he got aware of being present and making people's day. The prison guard was totally in the moment with a shoplifter, who was being booked for shoplifting. He gave the person dignity and respect. The prisoner started to weep, saying, "I've never been treated this way in my life, much less I'm being booked for a crime I know I did." That's being present. That made that guy's day! That made that guy's life, maybe. Who knows?

Fish brings to the surface what people have in them. It gives them a way to say, "I can do this. I have permission. My organization has shown me the light of being "a day maker." Be private with people. When you're choosing your attitude, making people's day, and being present for people, guess what? The appropriate play comes out.

Wright

In reference to the third principle, choose your attitude, we're publishing a book for a man now about attitude. One of his favorite sayings is, "The difference between a good day and a bad day is your attitude."

Christensen

Absolutely. We all have magnificent stories about our lives. But if you look at people that have tragedies in some respect, and they come whistling in, what is that? How would we face some of these tragedies if they would happen to us? That is what we mean by choose your attitude.

Wright

John, I'd like to quote something you said referring to business. The quote is: "We need people who are passionate, committed, and free to live the organization's vision through their personal value." Would you explain what you were talking about?

Christensen

Yes. When you have an alignment with what you stand for as an individual and what the company, the organization, is standing for, step out of the way. Watch out! Watch the power that happens to that.

Wright

When you talk about businesses, you use words like "love" and "soul."

Christensen
Right.

Wright
Most people would think that spiritual values would not be appropriate in a business setting. Do companies accept your spiritual values as necessary ingredients to success?

Christensen
There's a whole new movement out there about spirituality. I want it to be clear. We're not talking religion. We're talking about the spirit and soul of people. And that brings the soul of a business alive. We made a film with Southwest Airlines. Southwest Airlines was founded on the following statement by Herb Kelleher and his two buddies: "We wanted to create a workplace based on love rather than fear." Now, if Southwest Airlines with 33,000 employees is based on love and is doing incredibly well in the airline industry, is that not a valuable statement to everybody in business?

Wright
Is there anything or anyone in your life that has made a difference for you and helped you to become a better person?

Christensen
I have a lot of mentors in my life. My parents have been incredible mentors. My mom was a social worker and a very incredible people woman, and my dad was an artist. And when you combine those two, they've been wonderful mentors for me. I've also had the blessings of having Ken Blanchard as a mentor and Spencer Johnson. So I've had great mentors in that respect, too.

Wright
I was talking to Jim Cathcart the other day. I told him that one of my mentors had no knowledge of his being a mentor, and that was Bill Gove from Florida who I have been listening to his talks and tapes and reading his books for probably forty years.
What do you think makes up a mentor? In other words, are there characteristics that mentors seem to have in common?

Christensen

I believe they're different for everybody. I mean everybody finds a different mentor. I think some of the beautiful mentorships happen when a person takes you under their wing.

Another inspiration for me is Norman Vincent Peale. Okay, he's got religion in there, but his being was a mentorship for me. His presence, the way he spoke so eloquently and so much passion, that's what mentored me. You can get inspired by many different things. If a tape or a book inspires you and becomes your mentor, fabulous. When it opens you up to the possibilities in your life, be it a book, a mentor, a tape, a film, they are all wonderful aspects of opening you up to possibilities.

Wright

I remember when I was in Seattle a few years ago and saw the people working in the company that you wrote about, I remember two feelings. One is a feeling that this would be a nice place to buy something. But the biggest feeling was these guys are really happy and fun. And they've got a tough job too. That's not one of your bank president's type jobs.

Christensen

No. Hey, they don't work in air conditioning in the summer and heating in the winter. They work with dead fish, ice and cold cement floors. I've wiped out there many a time. It's just showing you the possibilities that if they can do it with their hands in dead fish, cold ice, and twelve-hour days, that's what's so powerful about it. That's why we call it the *Fish Philosophy*. It's based on the fact that if the fish market can do it, you can do it. But the philosophy is ancient wisdom but it's coming alive on a fish market. And if a fish market can do it, we all can do it.

Wright

We've talked about three out of four of the principles; the last one I'd like to ask you about is the principle "be there." Do you mean come to work on time and be there? Or be there for people?

Christensen

Be there for people. I mean absolutely be in the moment. Like I was saying, when you're with somebody, put the other things down. I catch myself so many times sitting at my desk when people come in, and I'm reading something, or half with them or not. You have to take that moment and put what you're doing down and be there for them. Another good little exercise to do is when the phone rings, take a moment before you pick it up and just pause. Think about what you're going to do on the phone. It doesn't matter if it's a sales person or whatever, just remember to be there in the moment when you're on the phone with a person. It's an interesting little exercise of being present.

Wright
Most people are fascinated with these new television programs about being a survivor. What has been the greatest comeback you have made from adversity in your career or in your life?

Christensen
Wow! The biggest adversity? Well, there are two. We went through a stint with a company where some people tried to take over our business, and I made it through that. But one of the things was living up to my mentor—my father—and having knowing in my heart and my gut that I had the capacity to leave the company and to be a great filmmaker like my father. And I don't mean great in a cocky way. I'm saying bringing what we bring to the table of documentaries. Showing the world what possibilities are. That's what I mean by great. That was a high. That was a hurdle to work through.

Wright
When I was researching for this interview, I noticed on your website they also referred to Joel Barker, the futurist who helped your father.

Christensen
Futurist, correct.

Wright
And so your father started making what? Documentary films?

Christensen
Yes. He started off in advertising just when television was getting started in the late '50s. He happened to be in love with the documentary approach. He pursued the documentarian lifestyle and would go off and make films. What he brought to the table was this unique-

ness, this anthropological aspect into looking at things, studying it, and saying, "What can we do to show that?" For instance, when his career started off in Omaha, Nebraska, he made a film about the city of Omaha. But through the whole film, you didn't know where you were until the end of the film, *Come See Our City, Omaha*. But it showed you who the people were, what the organizations were like in Omaha, and you'd like to come and live here and build your business here. So he brought that approach to it. Let's study it. Let's bring it. Let's show people what it's about instead of telling them, Again, that's what happened with the paradigm idea. Let's look at a paradigm. Let's look at it all these different ways. If it doesn't get you this way, look at it this way. Look at it this way. If this story doesn't connect with you, look at it this way. Ah, and then you can relate to that.

Wright

The free-wheeling workplace of the 1990s is long gone. Companies are cutting perks. Employees are reverting from casual attire to business wear. How can employees really play at work when the reins are being pulled back so tightly?

Christensen

Well, that's our point. The reigns shouldn't be pulled back so tightly. Ken Blanchard calls it the tight underwear syndrome. We need to get rid of that. We need to free people up because when you're free is when creativity and innovation happens. I don't know where the quote comes from, but it was said, "If works were plays, Silicon Valley would not have been created." Because it would out the play. Two guys in their garage, I mean how many guys were in their garage playing, tinkering around, right? Hewlett Packard, Apple, I mean how many more can we list? They were playing!

See, it's the playfulness in which they react to each other and react to customers at the fish market. You can see what they're doing and make your own style. It opens you up to say, "What can *we* do that is about playfulness?"

Wright

I've heard about the impact that *Fish* is having on corporate America. Has it been used outside the business world?

Wright

Schools are one of our biggest clientele. It's amazing. We are now creating a curriculum for schools. We're working on creating how to bring this in. If you could talk about being present to what you are doing and making people's day to elementary students, imagine what possibilities lie in the future for that!

Wright

Are you having more success getting it into the private schools or public schools?

Christensen

Public schools are embracing it. First and foremost, what's happening is that the administration and the teachers are being brought into this, talking about how they can engage with their work. Again, you said the budget crunches and the tightening of the ropes, and with all that, how are we going to? It goes back to saying, "What kind of organization can we be that is going to help people be engaged in what we're here for?"

We have a roofing company that used this that turned their entire company around into roofing, and now they're a world famous roofing company. They get roofing jobs in different places in the world. They just showed up in a different way. They were being something different.

Now, back to education. If you are being present in the classroom for your kids as a participant, not even as customer you're saying, "They're the 'customers,' I have to serve them." They're there to teach you as much as you are there to teach them. My goodness! That was my first love. I wanted to be a teacher saying, "What can you bring to the table?"

John Keating in the film *Dead Poets Society* is the kind of teacher we need—people engaged in the minds of our youth saying, "How do I get to them? How do I reach them? How am I there with them? What do I do to make their day?" We're actually working on the concept of saying the four principles of *Fish* are the rules of the classroom. What am I doing today to play, to be playful? This works both ways. This is teacher and student, partner-to-partner. What are we doing to make the classroom fun? What are we doing to make each other's day? How am I being there for you? How are you being there for me? How are you being there for your other your peers? And first and foremost, how are you choosing to come to school? How are you choosing to be today?

Wright

Very interesting. Boy, this has been a fast, fast thirty minutes, and I really do appreciate your being a guest today. I really appreciate you taking the time.

Today we have been talking with John Christensen whose story began as he said working with his father as a great role model. You've heard the intelligent statements and how the *Fish Philosophy* can literally change you and your company's future, as it's changing some in America.

So, let me ask you before we leave, I'd like to shamelessly advertise the book. I think everyone should read it. I know you're making good at Amazon.com. Can people get it direct from you or can they find out more on your website? If you'll give us that information, I would appreciate it.

Christensen

Absolutely. It is available at www.charthouse.com. Inside of charthouse you can go to fishphilosophy.com, which is a whole website with all the fish information. You can purchase all sorts of our films including our ancillary products, our fishing gear, and you can purchase the books. Now there are two books on the market, David. There's *First Fish!* and our second one that came out in April called *Fish Tales*.

Wright

I hope our readers and our listeners will rush to the website and get this book. I've got *Fish Tales*. I'm going to get the first one.

Christensen

Thank you, David. Thank you so much. I really appreciate your time.

About John Christensen

John Christensen's story begins in the shipping department at ChartHouse Learning where he began working as a teenager for his father, Ray. He worked his way to the top the old-fashioned way, proving to his father—and the company—that he was a real film-maker who could tell moving stories. Today Christensen guides ChartHouse as "Playground Director" (CEO in business-speak) with an inspiring vision of an engaged workplace that can be developed through the FISH! Philosophy. The rest of the story is that Chart-House Learning is changing the way business is done worldwide. "The ChartHouse vision is an invitation to people to become fully immersed in their lives, using these four seemingly simplistic ideas," he says. "In many ways the FISH! Philosophy is really ancient wis-dom for modern times, a lifestyle choice to engage in life-long learning and self-improvement. The products we offer are really learning tools, from some of the best mentors one could have—real-life experiences that ultimately speak to the human spirit." Today John speaks to vastly different organizations about his journey—the serendipitous discovery of the fish market—and how that simple FISH! Philosophy he and his team poetically articulated on film four years ago can dramatically change the stories of companies and individuals.

John Christensen

www.charthouse.com

www.fishphilopophy.com

Chapter Seventeen

DONNA DOUGHERTY

THE INTERVIEW

David E. Wright (Wright)
Today we're talking with Donna Dougherty. Donna has an impressive record of helping organizations execute projects more efficiently. She engagingly translates *Project Management Institute* (PMI) based Project Management Principles into realistic action plans. She's conducted more than 700 workshops on project topics throughout the United States, Belgium, the Soviet Union, Ireland, and Scotland.

She holds an MBA from Fuqua Business School, at Duke, and has served as an executive for a Fortune 500 firm. She is an expert in the creation of collaborative project plans. She also specializes in mentoring people as they transition from independent solo contributor roles to the collaborative interdependent work style needed for project success.

Donna, welcome to *Masters of Success!*

Donna Dougherty (Dougherty)
Thank you, David!

Wright
Right up front let me ask you, what is a project?

Dougherty

A project is a temporary endeavor. It is not ongoing. It has a beginning, a middle, and an end. Everyone has project experience even if they've never had the formal title, project manager (PM). Life is full of projects.

Examples of projects are: Weddings, funerals, earning a college degree, buying a house, getting a divorce, healing from an illness, getting out of debt, raising children, and saving for retirement. Projects are goal oriented, and are multi-task endeavors. A project is a series of tasks when combined, create a roadmap for the completion of the project goal.

Wright

So what is the difference between project management and general management?

Dougherty

With general or functional management things are pretty much up and running. Managers make sure things stay up and running. They hire, they fire, and they manage problems and changes. In projects you've got to figure out the project goal, which can be a project in itself. Then you have to actually accomplish that goal and keep things up and running simultaneously.

Projects can be more intellectually challenging than managing ongoing operations. Projects will often require heightened creativity, innovation, and problem-solving capability.

Because projects are not "business as usual," you've got to create a road map to guide you. Since there's no proven procedure, there's a merging of the planned road map—how you think things are going to work out and the reality of what actually occurs.

Plan A doesn't always work. So, here's a good way to look at it, David: Being a PM is a bit like being a commercial airline pilot. Pilots are off course most of the time so they have to continually adjust their course in flight. We, as passengers, don't even know that's happening and we don't care. As long as we land in the right city, on the right day, safely, we are happy. In projects, you are often adjusting your course all the way through.

Wright

Why in your opinion, has project management become such a hot, highly marketable skill?

Dougherty

There are a lot of reasons. I think one of the main reasons is that organizations are continually downsizing, rightsizing, and shedding people. They're trying to look good in the earnings report or just stay in business, and they find themselves needing to do more with less. Doing projects more effectively really helps meet the challenge of doing more with less. Let me give you a statistic that's hard to believe—partially because it is such a powerful claim: people who manage projects according to best practice methodology can do a project in one third of the time it takes a PM who doesn't use proven PM methodology. Of course, this isn't always true, because some organizations are already masterful at doing projects. They've squeezed a lot of "fat" out of their timelines already. What it does mean is that many organizations could do three times the number of projects without spending more money or adding more people. This is quite a claim—a claim I've found to be true. This is one of the main reasons project management is a hot, and highly marketable skill.

Wright

So what are other benefits of executing projects well?

Dougherty

Beyond shortened timelines, increased profit margins, preserved resources, improved competitive advantage, and market share, there are the internal career opportunities that parallel effective project execution. Raises, bonuses, and upward mobility all typically exist when organizations do a good job at getting projects done.

Wright

Can a good PM overcome the barriers of a dysfunctional culture?

Dougherty

As organizations strive to do projects better, the organizations themselves are transformed in the process. Here's one real-world example: A start-up tech company of engineers fled a large, highly dysfunctional organization. When they left, they had several missions. They wanted to create a company that had a project friendly culture. One project goal was to design a faster semi-conductor chip. A big company invested in them so they were able to hire fast and furiously and hired mostly from the firm they fled. It didn't take them long to realize that they had inadvertently recreated the same dysfunctional culture they were trying to get away from. To fix this, they looked at what was getting in the way of their project productivity. What they discovered were typical organizational vulnerabilities such as scape-goating, a reluctance to delegate, inadequate communication across functions, and "bobble-head yes-people" who didn't tell the truth. The team created ground rules in an effort to do projects better. A few samples of the ground rules they created and adopted include:

- When problems arise, we problem-solve. We don't place blame. Scape-goating is not allowed here.
- We talk *with* each other—not *about* each other. Trashing the invisible person is not permitted.
- We assume best intention, no matter what the outcome— innocent until proven guilty.
- If your end of the boat has sprung a leak, speak up, or your end of the boat may take my end down. Spotlight trouble sooner rather than later!

They transformed their work place even though not everyone went along with the ground rules. In the end, the little start-up tech company sold for a billion dollars even before they created the faster semi-conductor chip! When the sale was made, reporters asked the acquiring company, "How could you pay a billion dollars for this fledgling little start-up?" Their reply was that out of all the start-ups they'd ever acquired, it was humming and buzzing better than any they'd seen.

The start-up reinvented itself so it could do projects better. They made a conscious decision to work with each other in a way that increased trust, productivity, and a willingness to take risks. By the way, the acquiring company did get their billion dollars' worth, in a faster semi-conductor chip. They were able to get the project done in record time! Not only did they have project success, the company and the team members involved were transformed in the process.

I don't care what kind of culture PMs find themselves in, they can create a healthier culture within a dysfunctional culture. They can do this by examining what gets in the way of productivity and then choosing more intelligent behaviors that support productivity better. These new ground rules need to come primarily from the team (i.e., bottom-up rather than top-down). The ground rules need to serve team members, so they need to come from team members.

Wright
Tell me, what is the Project Management Institute?

Dougherty
The Project Management Institute (PMI), www.pmi.org, is the largest global project management association. Formed in Philadelphia, in 1969, PMI represents more than 1,000 project management members from every major industry. It was formed to help recognize project management as a discipline. PMI has captured a body of knowledge about how to do projects effectively, and has published a guidebook called the *Project Management Body of Knowledge* (PMBOK® Guide).

They took project knowledge from many industries including the military and created a foundation framework for initiating, planning, executing, and closing out projects. The PMI process and structure sets you up for success by helping you know what to think through for the plan, and how to avoid predictable pitfalls throughout all stages of the project.

Wright
Is the PMI methodology really flexible enough to be used across industries?

Dougherty
Yes, it is. PMI has created the framework for how to do projects well. The PMI methodology liberates rather than bogs down PMs. It provides a basic structured approach, which allows PMs the flexibility to tailor their project work to their specific challenges and opportunities.

It's almost like building a house. Once you have the structure up, you have the freedom to decorate any way you want. That's how this methodology is, so PMs don't have to reinvent the wheel when providing the structure, or necessary phases for the project. They know that the bases are going to be covered and their general approach is solid. It gives PMs the confidence that they are moving forward in a best practice, road-tested way. At the same time, the PM is in charge of the methodology, the methodology is not the boss of the PM. The methodology is a tool. The PM gets to decide to what extent to use the tool.

Wright

When PMs use methodology, how does it impact their workload?

Dougherty

Before I knew PMI PM methodology I used my management and leadership skills to get projects done, because that's all I knew. It wasn't enough. What happens if PMs don't know PM methodology is that they end up working too many hours, which doesn't work long term. The PM experiences burnout and is not a good role model for the team. Those who don't take good care of themselves are going to eventually lose competence—not gain it—by working a ridiculous number of hours. In my case, once I learned how to plan well and execute according to the PMI approach, I tripled the number of projects I was able to handle—and I still had a life!

By using PM methodology, PMs manage the project more than the project is going to manage them. PM methodology actually provides a checklist of what to do at each stage of the project.

Wright

How can a PM possibly succeed when expectations are often unrealistic from the start?

Dougherty

The project originators ask for whatever they want, and chances are they don't realize the difficulty involved in creating what they are asking for.

What they want is often just a starting place—the place to begin to negotiate about what can be accomplished given the time, money, and resources available. A PM has to be an educator to help the project originator (internal or external customer) know what it's going to take and then match up what they want with what they can afford. This step is often short changed and expectations become unrealistic wish lists.

Wright

Since projects usually don't go according to plan, why waste the time planning?

Dougherty

That's the attitude most people have. As a matter of fact, I've heard it said many times, "With projects, planning is useless. But without planning you're dead." You'd never go on a long road trip without a map. When you get off course, if you have a map and a plan you can stop the car and see where you are compared with where you want to be. You can then figure out how to get back on course.

That's how it is with projects. If you have a blueprint—a road map—you know when you're veering off course. In projects, sometimes you've got to change course because the original roadmap just isn't working. In the "doing of projects comes more knowing." As you move forward on the plan you gain more visibility. You will see things you didn't see before—both risks and opportunities. It is necessary to be willing to adjust the roadmap to reflect the reality at hand. Without a roadmap it's impossible to tell when you veer off course, making it even more impossible to get back on course!

There's a prevailing attitude about planning, David. What is often said is, "We don't have the time to plan, but somehow we'll find the time to clean up the mess we make later." Planning takes time, and time is money. The investment in upfront planning is very small compared to the desperate and expensive, heroic efforts to put out fires in the final stages of the project. When you take the time to "kick the tires" on the plan and make it the best plan current knowledge allows, you'll avert most of your problems in the planning stage.

Wright

So what are the main things that go wrong with project execution?

Dougherty

There are many things that can go wrong, but there are three problems that plague most projects if you don't guard against them:

1. The first problem is not having a specific and measurable project definition. Projects are begun and the target is not defined. You know why that happens? Upper level management or external customers ask the PM to do whatever they want done. The PM doesn't want to be a pest so not enough questions are asked. Not obtaining clear information about the definition of the project target is a huge mistake. It is almost impossible to recover from this kind of mistake because the target keeps moving during the project. It is not possible to hit moving target(s)! The PM must be crystal clear about what is to be done before attempting to do it. It can take several rounds of interrogation before the PM really has the project defini-

tion nailed down. In addition to knowing what needs to be delivered, it is equally important to document what is *not* in the project. This protects the PM from expanding expectations once the project is begun, called "scope creep."

2. The second big problem is when we shortchange planning. We are very action oriented in this country and we haven't had much successful experience in collaborative planning. It doesn't make sense, really, because organizations hire the best and the brightest people, yet don't have a system of tapping into the collective IQ.

We've all been in meetings that last forever and the only thing decided is when the next meeting will be. The lack of collaborative planning is the second big mistake we make in projects.

3. The third major mistake PMs make is to drift into doing the tasks rather than managing the project. PMs sometimes have dual roles and may be more comfortable doing tasks. It's important to allocate sufficient time to managing the project, and not "hide out" in the more controllable task work.

Wright

Beyond understanding project methodology, what skills does a person need to be a successful PM?

Dougherty

PMs' success is fifty percent dependent on their ability to get things done through others, and about fifty percent dependent on utilizing PM methodology. Delegation, motivation, coaching, negotiating, problem-solving, and change management skills are needed. PMs need to be able to follow up on people and hold them accountable in a way that helps rather then hurts productivity. Facilitating project meetings is also very important. It, too, needs to be done in a way that supports rather than impedes productivity.

Wright

So what are the most frequent mistakes rookie PMs make?

Dougherty

Becoming a control freak. Rookie PMs are more comfortable in their area of expertise, they feel almost like frauds when they try to manage or lead people beyond their expertise at first. So, when there's a problem they get "pulled back into the weeds." They focus on what they know instead of keeping their head up and looking at the big picture. I've heard it said this way, "If you're the captain of a ship and you'd really rather be making soup in the galley, you could be heading for an iceberg!"

Wright

So how do you keep the momentum up on projects?

Dougherty

That is a really good question and we have great guru minds to help us out with that. Ken Blanchard is one of them. In his *One Minute Manager* series he provides guidance that works when you are working with people to get things done. The answer is to catch people doing something good, and acknowledge that specific progress. As the PM notices the success and makes it visible by praising the specific behavior, the PM is training the team in what to do more of. This really helps momentum.

The opposite is what some PMs end up doing. PMs often don't focus on what has been accomplished; they just see the mountain of work that has yet to be done. Many times project team members, particularly with a task technical focus, are very hard on themselves. They don't pat themselves on the back along the way. So, Ken Blanchard's guidance is great! Recognize specific and measurable progress—celebrate it, even though you're dragging problems with you along the way.

Wright

Why in the world would anyone want to be a PM when they're in the hot seat from start to finish?

Dougherty

That is true, you're "in the middle" as a PM. You feel like a warrior. You're trying to get what you need for your project team and you're the "go to" person to blame if things don't go well. When you do succeed, you'll get more projects as a reward!

When projects are planned well and executed well, project work is fun and very exhilarating. Most projects exist to make the world a better place in some way—a new or improved product or service.

Unless you're in the Mafia or up to no good, there's good intention behind the project, so it's easy to be passionate about project work.

In projects, we are often called upon to use more of our untapped potential. Team members learn new skills along the way. The innovative, creative experiments and learning along the way is like "mental chocolate." Learning and really using ourselves full throttle is energizing and just plain fun. I've seen organizations become "learning organizations" as a result of trying to do projects better.

Because project results are measurable, you can win at the game of project management, and keep score along the way.

Wright

To what extent should software be used as a tool?

Dougherty

You have part of the answer in your question, David. PM software is a tool—only a tool. Software can help you streamline reporting; you print project plans in a few minutes; and it can help with "what if" analyses as you explore different options. Software can do complex mathematical calculations instantly.

Frequently, rookie PMs buy the software, learn it, and think they know project methodology. Nothing could be farther from the truth. The methodology sets you up for success; the software is about data entry. The data entry should happen separately from, and after the planning. Data entry should be done prior to execution, when the plan has become relatively stable. It is a mistake to go to the software first, before doing the collaborative planning. Collaborative planning is more of a "right brain" kind of thinking process, while data entry is more of a "left brain" perfectionist process and can easily stifle new ideas.

Software can't communicate for the PM; it can't find errors in data input (i.e., junk in, junk out). It can't solve problems that require judgment, it can't facilitate collaboration, it can't make decisions, and it can't lead. You do need software, but it's important not to overuse it. It's just a tool. It does some things well, yet can't do, and never will do, the real project management work.

Wright

How can PMs protect themselves from overload and ultimate burnout?

Dougherty

The path of least resistance—the choice to work longer hours—does lead to burnout.

What efficiency expert psychologists say is that we can work up to about fifty-five hours a week without much fear of burnout. Beyond that, we're pretty much headed for trouble. It is important that PMs do not stay glued to the project days, nights, and weekends. I've read a lot about Ben Franklin and Thomas Edison and how they solved problems on their projects. Both say they often got their best ideas and solutions when they turned away from their work and were doing something totally unrelated.

PMs need to delegate, use methodology, and make sure they take care of themselves. They need to know how to say "no" and push back when they really can't take on any more work.

PMs are a finite resource and in every project there's an infinite number of things to do. So, PMs have to be very careful about how they spend their time and energy. That's why the methodology helps because it shows the PM the most important things to focus on. Project methodology is about prioritizing. It's about doing what needs to be done, to the extent it needs to be done.

The PMI approach reminds us to get clear about the definition, and hold people accountable for results. When PMs pay attention to the main things, they can utilize project leads to do non-critical work. When PMs are doing the most important things, not only can they get the project done, but they can also develop the capabilities of team members along the way.

Wright

So let me sum up, if I were to run an advertisement in the morning's newspaper to get a PM, it might read: "Intelligent person needed who loves pain and wants to sit in hot seat."

Dougherty

Yes, a PM is a person who likes adventure and who can take the unpredictable, make it as predictable as possible, and collaborate with others while they're doing it. A PM is also a person who likes to make progress against the plan, and who is willing to change the plan to reflect reality when Plan A just isn't working. Most importantly, a PM is a person who is interested in getting things done utilizing others, and developing people along the way.

Wright

Well, your ad sounds better than mine.

Dougherty

I don't know about that, but I do know that projects are great adventures. The faint of heart need not apply.

Wright

Well I really appreciate all this time you've spent with me, Donna. This is subject very, very interesting.

Today we have been talking with Donna Dougherty. She is an expert in the creation of collaborative project plans and mentoring technical people as they survive the transition from "solo contributors" to "collaborative PMs." As we have learned this afternoon, I really think she knows what she's talking about. Thank you for being with us on *Masters of Success*!

Dougherty

Thank you very much for this awesome opportunity. It's been my pleasure.

About Donna Dougherty

Donna Dougherty has an impressive record of helping organizations execute projects more efficiently. She engagingly translates PMI-based project management principles into realistic action plans. She's conducted over 700 workshops on project topics throughout the US, Belgium, Soviet Union, Ireland and Scotland. She holds an MBA from Fuqua Business School (Duke), and has served as an executive for a Fortune 500 Firm. She is an expert in the creation of collaborative project plans, and in mentoring technical people as they survive the transition from technical contributors to project managers.

Donna Dougherty
2452 South Carbon Street
Allentown, PA 18103
Phone: 610.797.8071
Fax: 610.797.0249
Email: DonnaLDougherty@aol.com

241

Chapter Eighteen

TERRI NORVELL

THE INTERVIEW

David E. Wright (Wright)

Today we're talking with Terri Norvell. Terri is the creator of the Inner Prize—A People Development Company, a training, consulting, and coaching organization. The Inner Prize provides personal development experiences which offer proof that expanded inner knowledge equals greater outer results. Terri is a positive, motivational leader who demonstrates what's possible when we trust in ourselves, believe in our inner knowledge and take confident action. She has a unique real-world approach and practical ideas that enable her to connect with people from the front line to the corner office. Her methodologies for personal effectiveness inspire action and notable results throughout organizations from coast to coast.

Terri draws upon her experience as vice president of a $1.2 billion property management and development firm, general manager for a $9 million temporary housing company, and product management with Frito-Lay, Anderson Clayton Foods, and Southland 7-Eleven stores.

She is committed to community service, serving as the youngest president of the Mountain View Chamber of Commerce, along with being a founding board member for the Housing Industry Foundation and the Center for Performing Arts in the Bay Area, California.

Terri assists people in going beyond what they previously thought possible, leaving her audiences profoundly changed. Participants gain physical experiential proof that whatever they focus upon can be achieved. Frequent comments include, "You helped me see that I can believe in myself" "Wow! I can do anything now!" and, "I experienced a total shift in my attitude."

She is a featured presenter with business organizations and associations across the country because she opens the minds of participants to see new possibilities, overcome obstacles, and focus on results. Additionally, Terri helps her audiences build their outer, or tangible, or substantive results through her nationally recognized *Inner Knowledge*™ e-Letter.

Terri, welcome to *Masters of Success*.

Terri Norvell (Norvell)

Thank you.

Wright

Let me start by asking, how does your intriguing company name, "The Inner Prize," tie into your success?

Norvell

There's a direct correlation between the name "The Inner Prize" and my definition of success. Let me start by defining what The Inner Prize actually means. It's that special something we each have within us. It's our inner vision, inner strength, inner trust, inner knowledge, and inner drive that allows us to do more than we believe we can. The inner prize is huge—it's like the sun shining brightly within each of us. Unfortunately, many people are experiencing 'cloud cover' and that's where I come in, to show how to get rid of the clouds and expose their inner light.

It can be tough to get one's arms around this concept because it's the process of exploration that enables us to figure out how to access and then attain our Inner Prize. It's like a series of muscles that must be developed and that strengthen with use. Over all, it's the qualities and abilities that make each of us uniquely special and enable us to be, do, and achieve whatever is important to us.

I arrived at this knowledge through my own life long questing, curiosity, and discoveries about success. My life and the people around me continue to be my primary exploration laboratory. People who influenced me greatly were my personal heroes, including my family members, close friends, mentors, and teachers; they inspired me to be my best.

In my questing, it often seemed that it's the simple, everyday things that can have the greatest impact on our lives. For a long time I searched for answers to my pressing questions outside of myself—then I had a life-defining experience. I received a special gift from a friend who gave me an "Ah-Ha!" moment. Yes, I found the meaning of life on a T-shirt. It had a Socrates quote on it: "Know Thyself." What I saw in that T-shirt struck a deep inner knowing.

I finally got it! I discovered that the answers were totally within me. I no longer needed to look outside of myself. I came to know that how I choose to think and what I choose to do truly do determine my view, not only of myself, but of the world around me. I realized even then that this was a huge revelation. I realized that the Inner Prize was both readily accessible, and was ready and waiting to guide me along the journey of life.

That was the key. All I had to do was to turn inward, access this inner knowledge, inner strength, inner trust, inner vision, inner drive, and then utilize them to create results in my life—my Inner Prize.

Yet, tapping into it on a daily basis can be elusive. It requires nurturing, ongoing attention, and focus. This has always been my motivating, driving force, and is what has made me successful. With each transformational shift I experienced, I was driven to explore further, document my results, and to share my findings with others so that they too could have transformational shifts and grow into their personal best. Developing methodologies helped me, and now others, to access and utilize their Inner Prize on a regular basis.

I decided to have fun with this approach and investigated what the Inner Prize meant to other business professionals. I asked this question: "How do you know if and when you tap into your Inner Prize?" People responded with such comments as:

- I do my best and I know I do my best.
- I discover an ability I doubted I had within me.
- I make decisions with more confidence.
- I see different possibilities rather than only one right way.

- I know what's most important and I let that guide my choices.
- I enjoy the process and not just the end result.
- I feel peaceful and calm inside even when chaos is all around me.

I thought, "Wow! Isn't that terrific!" When we are feeling at our peak, when we're feeling at the top of our game, when we're tapping into that inner uniqueness—that Inner Prize— we're poised to reach our personal and professional goals. Big steps toward success!

Wright

Regarding success, do people want to be successful?

Norvell

I've found that success can be defined in many ways, and is different for each one of us. People want to do their best. When we are doing our best, we achieve more and are more fulfilled. So yes, people do want to be successful. Yet here's a catch: Obstacles and challenges invariably come along.

When these obstacles and challenges do come, there are some people who have learned to triumph over challenges rather than letting challenges stop them. When we tap into our inner knowledge, we can see our challenges from a different perspective and learn from them, rather than feeling stuck or defeated. It takes us from a powerless victim role, to being players in our lives. When we are players rather than victims, success is more possible.

What I discovered on my Inner Prize research journey is that success is revealed in multiple areas of our lives. It's not a prize that we go after and claim once and for all. It took me quite a long time to learn this. For example, I absolutely love to be creating, assisting and achieving. I cannot imagine not working!

Prior to starting my firm I was vice president of a West Coast real estate development and management firm, and the stakes were very high. We held a leading market presence that required very long hours. During that time I prided myself on the fact that I hadn't used any vacation or sick time in almost three years.

By most people's standards, I was a success. I worked hard; I got results. I *felt* successful. And then I learned that there are other components to success than just working hard. I learned that success is much deeper than what society tells us.

I now know that success can be experienced in four different areas: mentally, physically, emotionally, and spiritually. I'm at my best when these four areas are in alignment. And, when we need to overcome obstacles in the process of experiencing success, that feeling is even more rewarding. I'll explain what I mean by the four ways.

First, mental success is determined by how we use our minds. It's how we think and what we think that contributes to our mental well-being and success. Oftentimes this is in the workplace, but it can also be whenever we are engaged in some intention or goal. Mental success comes from knowing that we have within us—right now—everything that we need to be successful. It's about having confidence in yourself. This includes knowing that if you don't have the immediate answers, you know how to get them.

I relate physical success to taking care of our health. It's so true that when we don't have our health it's tough for anything else to matter. When we're physically well, challenges are much more easily handled. Just think of how a nagging headache shadows your thinking and creating. Physical endurance also goes a long way in contributing to all success.

Then there's emotional success. This comes through building authentic relationships. When we stop and think of those people who are closest and dearest to us in our hearts, we need to ask if we actually give these people the time and care that they deserve. We have to assess whether we give them as much attention as we give to some of the other areas where we define success. Too often our emotional success is given a back seat in importance.

Spiritual success is reflected through living true to our values and ourselves. Some look at this as spiritual or religious beliefs. Defining spiritual success often requires deep reflection. It takes a lot of inner development to really clarify what's true for us. I know that I'm more successful when my daily actions reflect my core beliefs and what I value. The result is greater joy in my life.

The bottom line is that each of us needs to define success for ourselves. And in the process become what I call our own inner "Action Hero."

Wright

Action Hero? What does an Action Hero have to do with our personal or professional success?

Norvell

We each have an Action Hero or She-ro within us! Everyone does. Releasing the Action Hero within is a concept that I created to assist people in seeing themselves in a more capable, self-trusting, and self-reliant way. There's a quote by Marianne Williamson that includes the statement, "We ask ourselves 'who am I to be brilliant, gorgeous, talented, and fabulous,' when actually who are we not to be?" I agree and know that we each have a gorgeous, talented, and fabulous Action Hero within.

Action Heroes, in contrast to Super Heroes, are simply regular people who use their special talents, abilities, and techniques in their own pursuits. They're ordinary, everyday people and can include important people in our lives, acquaintances, or perhaps people we see from a distance. Most likely they are not widely known, yet we are inspired by their actions, attitude, abilities, approach, or caring. Often we look up to them for some remarkable quality or achievement. They inspire us and help us know what's possible. I think that can be said for each of us. Who do you think of in your life as an Action Hero? Who might look at you as one of his or her heroes?

When a person releases their inner Action Hero, they have taken the time to go on their own journey of discovery and have found the key...the key is access to their Inner Prize. Action Heroes achieve mastery in their success because they have attained the prize...they have gotten proof of just how powerful, talented, capable, strong, and creative they really are. They have learned to trust in their beliefs and instincts, trust in their knowledge and education, trust in other people, and confidently take action. We are often inspired to emulate them.

In my investigating I did an interesting exercise. I asked my ten-year-old twins whom they saw as an Action Hero—and what an Action Hero meant to them. As most children would do, they listed their mother and father. They also added Patrick Roy, who you might know is the most successful hockey goalie of all time, and Mia Hamm, who was already a soccer star at the age of fifteen.

When I asked them what qualities they thought of, they said (and this is so intriguing to me), "Strong, helpful, nice, generous, courageous, willing, intelligent, intriguing, loving, and supportive," all qualities that we each have within. I probed a little deeper and asked, "Why Patrick Roy?" My son responded, "Well, Mom, he inspires me to be a better goalie." Isn't that what life is about—helping inspire others to be the best that we can be?

I asked my daughter, why Mia Hamm? She said, "Mom, she shows me what's possible with focused work and dedication." Wow! Ten years old and she knows this already! This shows how other people can touch that deep desire within us to be our best, and can inspire us to take action.

To release the Action Hero, we need five things:
- An inner vision of where we want to go.
- An inner trust that we have the resources already available.
- An inner strength of focus and commitment to overcome challenges.
- An inner drive and determination to take action.
- An inner knowing of what's most important along the way.

Once that inner Action Hero is released we have more joy and success throughout our life. When that Action Hero is released in the workplace, we can begin to experience business ecstasy.

Wright

Tell me about business ecstasy. It sounds like an oxymoron—I mean, how many people experience *ecstasy* in *business*?

Norvell

I find that everyone either giggles or smiles at the concept of business ecstasy. I think it's the term "ecstasy" that does it because we don't often associate work or business with the concept of ecstasy. We know that ecstasy is intense joy or delight, and an inner feeling of immense fulfillment. We know that personal ecstasy is experienced when we feel really good about who we are and when we're making ourselves a priority. Business ecstasy is when we feel elated with who we are and with what we're doing or have done. It's being in the zone and on top of our game. It can include exceeding expectations at work, closing deals, forming new partnerships, and creating new opportunities. For me, it's also expressed through laughing, smiling, and feeling jovial or blissful (yes, *while I'm working!*).

Let's take these personal ecstasy feelings and describe them in the work environment. Ecstasy in the workplace translates to:
- I'm great at what I do and I love to do it.
- I'm passionate about the difference that I'm making.
- I trust and believe in my team.
- I'm appreciated and valued.

- My job isn't work but rather a purpose that I am fulfilling.

Business ecstasy is available to everyone. We spend too much time working to not feel good about ourselves and our contributions, and to not be having fun while we are at it. When we are experiencing business ecstasy, it's much easier for our Action Hero—the best we have to offer—to be released.

I like to think that when Coco Chanel started her empire, Pierre Omidyar started eBay, David Filo and Jerry Yang started Yahoo, and Jeff Bezos started Amazon, they and their team members were experiencing business ecstasy as they began as ordinary people, creating something bigger than all of them combined. Many entrepreneurs and intra-preneurs (entrepreneurs within an organization) express passionate, euphoric feelings about their work. Imagine if your work environment was just this exciting! It can be.

Wright

What is one technique someone can use as they move toward attaining success mastery and business ecstasy?

Norvell

A first step is to realize that we already possess a great variety of resources within us. And the one resource with unlimited potential is the power of our mind. Consider that the mind works around the clock whether we are awake of asleep. It will focus wherever we place our attention, and amazingly, it knows no difference between real and pretend. It's like having our own personal self-directed, energy-generating power plant in our heads. It's often said that we each have 50,000 thoughts going through our minds every day. That's a lot of energy. *The distinguishing quality in our results is how we choose to use this mind of ours!*

The process of acquiring the mental agility to produce favorable results and attract success goes by many names. Some call it mental programming, affirmations, visualizations, pre-paving, aligning your Reticular Activating System, positive thinking, personal power talk or self-hypnosis. Whatever you choose to call it, the process involves focusing on what you want, rather than on what you don't want.

It's interesting that professionals in the field of athletics have tapped into this resource much more fully than many other fields or industries. I read a quote by a sports psychologist predicting that, "Our professional athletes of today have reached the limit in their physical capacity to excel. The next level will be reached through tapping into and using the power of the mind."

I find this fascinating. He went on to give an example of a basketball team. It went like this: Two teams were given the goal of making the most perfect baskets at the end of six weeks. Now, here's the catch: Team One practiced on the court, and physically handled the ball. Team Two sat in chairs along the side and never touched a basketball. They physically visualized making perfect baskets in their minds. The results are astounding—the team that mentally practiced made measurably more perfect baskets.

Here's another example: Amy Van Dyken is a Coloradoan who won six Olympic gold medals in swimming. Prior to that experience she attended Arizona State University where she became so discouraged that she quit swimming and returned to Colorado to attend Colorado State University. Within one year she set a world record in the fifteen meter free-style—a very impressive turnaround. When asked how she could achieve this feat, she replied, "Before, I had a great coach and I worked on my stroke and kicking—the technical aspects of swimming. Yet at CSU, they gave me a sports psychologist. What I learned is that at this level it's more mental than physical." An athlete doesn't train for a world record the night before. Athletes train for it mentally as well as physically every single day. They achieve business ecstasy through visualizing success, positive self-talk, and having the expectation of being at their best.

I recently watched a movie that gave behind-the-scenes information and history about the Blue Angels—the Navy's air show team. Since I have seen and heard the Blue Angels many times in their F/A-18 Hornet fighter planes (they are amazingly loud), I was fascinated by their training regimen. Their flying acumen is breath-taking and awe-inspiring. Clearly they are releasing their Action Heroes at the highest risk-taking level and experiencing true business ecstasy, as they define it! What's interesting is that before each show all of the Blue Angels sit in a conference room and listen to the "Boss Man"—the man in the Number One flight position. The Boss Man verbally talks them through each maneuver as they visualize every stunt in the show as they fly within thirty-six inches of each other going hundreds of miles per hour. Using the mind to produce desired results and success is a powerful and life-critical technique for them.

In my seminars I often ask attendees if they use visualizations or affirmations—what I call "Personal Power Talk." Some hands enthusiastically go up. Yet, when I ask how many people worry, many more hands go up. Worry places our attention on what we *don't* want, and takes our attention off of what we *do* want. Using our mind to focus on achieving what's important to us is a powerful, success-building way of living.

When people begin to use these techniques it requires self-trust and belief. They need to trust themselves enough to try something new and believe in what's possible with focus and desire.

Wright

Why is self-trust so critical to success?

Norvell

I have found that trust in oneself is really the foundation of life—that trust gives us the confidence to use our knowledge and take confident action both personally and professionally.

When I became interested in what trust really is and what it means in my work, I took on a one-year research project about trust. In my exploration I discovered that there really are five different categories of trust and that we utilize these various categories at different times and for different projects. The five categories have to do with trusting: a higher power, our instincts and intuition, our experience, our education or training, and finally, trusting other people in our lives.

At the same time I determined that it's self-doubt that keeps us from trusting. Doubt keeps us from trusting ourselves—and from trusting others. That mental swirl of doubt can be agonizing when we don't trust that we have what it takes and that we know what to do.

In my investigation, I asked dozens of people 'do you trust yourself' and 'how do you know'? Across the board, most everyone mentioned trusting their instincts, or their gut-feel, as a way of knowing the best course of action. They use this as a barometer or indicator in determining their chosen actions. They had learned to trust their inner knowing to determine what is right for them, rather than what others might say or think.

A friend of mine is a director of a multi-million dollar division of a high-tech organization. She shared that, "I do trust myself and my intuition on business issues and with people, yet it has taken me a while to truly trust myself. What has made the difference is to reflect on how many times I am right about something...before others can see it." I call that gaining proof.

Last year she went against her intuition and took a risk on continuing an R&D program that she felt was not going to produce. Two months later she cancelled it. Had she trusted her instincts, she would have gotten a different program started two months earlier, would have disappointed fewer customers, and wasted less time and money. What great proof that her self-trust is on target. Sometimes "miss-takes" are even better trust motivators than a "being right" track record.

There are so many examples of people overcoming tough obstacles by trusting what is the best course of action for them. Think of Lance Armstrong. Doctors told him that he was crazy to even think about being on a bike again, that his attention ought to be placed on fighting his cancer and fighting for his life. Yet, he listened to his instincts. His seventh Tour de France win certainly provides proof that the inner Action Hero was more than ready to be released!

Oprah is another great example. Coming from her challenging upbringing, she followed her heart and profoundly listened to the voice within that let her know what she was capable of achieving. Self trust, absolutely.

When we learn to trust in ourselves and our abilities, anything is attainable. It's as if miracles happen right before us. How is this possible you might ask? Because with trust, it becomes much easier to break through whatever obstacles or doubts might come along.

Wright

Let's talk about breakthroughs. How do people have a breakthrough experience?

Norvell

Breakthroughs can occur whenever we overcome a challenge, a limiting belief or an obstacle of some sort. Obstacles sure can look like rocks or boulders on our path in life and yet too often we let the obstacles stop us or impede our progress. With an open-minded perspective, we can use those rocks as stepping-stones to move us toward achieving a project or a goal or something that is important to us.

Many times fear is one of the greatest obstacles a person can have. Often it is a fear of change, or taking a risk, or failure of some sort. In my "Break Through Your Challenges" sessions, participants learn a technique for conquering a fear or an obstacle that is holding them back. Everyone has an opportunity to write a challenge or concern on a twelve-by-twelve-inch wooden board and to break that board with their bare hand. The board is actually a metaphor for whatever obstacle is stopping or keeping them from feeling success in their personal or professional endeavors.

These breakthrough experiences are powerful. Imagine focusing every ounce of energy you have on the task in front of you—mustering up all your physical strength from the tips of your toes through every muscle in your being, focusing your total mental concentration on going beyond the board, aligning your breathing, affirming desire, knowing beyond a shadow of doubt that nothing can stop you...and then that quick strike, that release of all your energy in one strike as you experience that point of power when your hand goes through that board.

When you are totally aligned with every part of you—your hand goes through with sublime ease. Then the euphoric adrenalin rush permeates as you realize what you just did! Your confidence and trust in yourself are overwhelming. You have proof of just how powerful you really are when you focus on what's important to you. That's when people say and feel things like, "Wow! I can do anything!"

Physically putting your hand through that board results in so many mental breakthroughs. The results are nothing short of astounding. Here are a few examples of what people have overcome:

- A woman in property management broke through her fear of elevators; in that breakthrough moment she had a mental flash of what had caused this fear. Once she understood the cause, she was able to release its power over her.

- In that breakthrough moment another participant discovered just how powerful she really is and has parlayed that confidence into her daily work. She used to hold back on sharing her opinions, thinking that what others had to say was more important. Now she speaks up freely in meetings and with clients. The results include better relationships, additional sales, and feeling more successful.

- A maintenance supervisor found the courage to take the plunge to buy rental properties (three within the month following his breakthrough experience) and begin his own real estate portfolio.

- Another wanted to find a job closer to her family who was an ocean away. In that breakthrough moment she found the inner strength to look for a position back in her home state of Hawaii and landed an absolutely incredible management opportunity.

- One of my all-time favorite letters was from a woman who wanted to be an awesome mom and incredible wife. She said, "My breakthroughs are amazing both personally and professionally. First let me start with a personal one. I have become a great mother—we now splash in puddles after a rainstorm, I supply the picnic lunches for the neighborhood kids in the park across the street, and my children's friends ask to be invited to dinner because we talk about what's important in their lives. In the wife category, all I can say is look at the glow on our faces! I am now his best friend, fishing buddy, confidant, and business advisor. I broke through the 'traditional wife syndrome.' I have changed our family's lives forever."

In my seminars we break boards, we break arrows, we bend spoons—all to gain tangible evidence, to gain physical proof that we can do something that only minutes ago seemed unattainable. When you can break through a piece of wood with ease—it opens your mind up to what's holding you back and what's possible. You begin to imagine what other successes are now within the realm of possibility for you.

This goes back to focus and the power of our mind. Sometimes it takes something dramatic to demonstrate and prove to us that we have that Inner Prize within—that our Action Heroes are ready to be released.

Wright

What are the advantages of mastering success through the Inner Prize methodology?

Norvell

The Inner Prize methodology builds on the belief that all success, achievement, joy, and inspiration starts from within. Another core belief is that there are greater resources within us than we are currently using, and that once we access this inner knowledge, we are able to achieve greater outer results in all areas of our lives.

Access is the key in this process. And the prize is attainment—attainment of your inner vision, inner trust, inner knowing, inner strength, and inner drive and determination.

Action Heroes have found this key to attain and then use their unique Inner Prize. Action Heroes trust in themselves and we see this as confidence in what they say and what they do. We admire these Action Heroes because they inspire us. They inspire us by their accomplishments or contributions and enable us to see what's possible. They show us their best and inspire us to be our best.

There is a process we go through to get from questing to having that mastery of success. It takes more than hearing, agreeing, believing, and understanding the components of success. While these steps are important, it takes living them and integrating each small step into our daily lives. With each step we come closer to achieving the goals we've set for ourselves. This enables us to create new behaviors, new ways of interacting, and new results throughout our lives.

Another important component is reinforcement. Whenever we are incorporating new ideas or making a change, we need encouraging reminders as to what's important to us, what we want to do, who we want to be and what we want to achieve. Why? Because that's what helps us to overcome the inevitable obstacles and distractions we're bound to encounter.

When we each learn to tie all of these components together, the results are tangible, lasting, and contagious. Those who have accessed their Inner Prize are easier to spot. These characteristics are consistent:

- They know what's most important and set priorities accordingly.
- They live by their values and have a high level of integrity.
- They form authentic relationships with others.
- They want to continually learn—they're not afraid to ask for assistance or feedback.
- They don't let challenges paralyze them or keep them stuck.
- They ask targeted questions, then stop, pay attention, and listen to answers.
- They understand that business is personal, but they don't take it personally.

The results of living this way—of accessing your Inner Prize—are amazing and life fulfilling. This is my passion and mission: To assist people and organizations to trust themselves and tap into their Inner Prize. It often takes gaining proof of just how powerful we each are to thrive with change, and create the lives and careers of our dreams.

I'll close with one of my favorite quotes from Emerson:

What lies behind us
And what lies before us
Are small matters compared to
What lies within us.

Wright

What an interesting conversation! Today we've been talking with Terri Norvell who is the creator of the Inner Prize training, consulting, and coaching organization. They help companies tap into their true power source—their people, because the power in business starts with the power in people.

Terri, thank you so much for being with us today on *Masters of Success*.

Norvell

Thank you. Live and work inspired!

Terri Norvell provides a refreshing blend of life wisdom, business acumen, and expanding human potential to her clients nationwide. She brings twenty years of valuable real-world business experience and practical content to the podium and classroom through her speaking, training, coaching, and consulting. Participants leave her sessions energized and prepared to tackle the most demanding challenges with a keen focus on results. She is a highly respected contributor to many companies and associations including the Sales & Marketing Magic Companies, Prometheus, United Advertising/For Rent, Irvine Apartment Management Company, OMNI, Greystar, National Apartment Association, Society of Human Resource Management and RentNet.com. Her messages inspire people to thrive with change.

Terri Norvell
The Inner Prize
A People Development Company
11780 Perry Street
Westminster, CO 80031
Phone: 303-439-0077
Fax: 303-439-2466
Email: terri@theinnerprize.com
www.theinnerprize.com

Chapter Nineteen

JIM SMITH, JR.

THE INTERVIEW

David Wright (Wright)

Raised and coached by his mother, Nanci Gray, and educated in the Philadelphia public school system, neighborhood streets and ball fields, Jim Smith, Jr. personifies energy and passion. His speaking, facilitation and training style evolved from his ups and downs in life, corporate America, academia, college and professional sports, parenting and marriage.

Presently residing in Philadelphia, Pennsylvania, Jim's speaking engagements and workshops have taken him to both national and international audiences and for groups of all sizes. He is the president and CEO of Jimpact Enterprises (professional trainer development, leadership, diversity, and motivational speaking). Jim is also the author of *From Average to Awesome: 41 Plus Gifts in 41 Plus Years*. A member of the 1981 Widener University National Championship football team and an All Conference player, Jim was the first in his family to earn a college degree, receiving his Bachelor of Arts degree in English from Widener University (Chester, Pennsylvania), and his Master's degree in Journalism from Temple University (Philadelphia, Pennsylvania).

He belongs to the American Society for Training and Development (ASTD), the National Speaker's Association (NSA), national and Mid Atlantic Chapters. In addition, he has been an adjunct faculty member for Penn State University (Great Valley) and Rosemont College. He's worked with organizations like HBO, ADP (Dealer Services), Johnson and Johnson, Merck, Harvard University, MetLife, Abbotts Labs, Wilson's Leather, Astra Zeneca and The Melting Pot Restaurants.

Jim, welcome to *Masters of Success*.

Jim Smith, Jr. (Smith, Jr.)
Thank you.

Wright
Why the nickname "Mr. Energy"?

Smith, Jr.
The nickname "Mr. Energy" captures and personifies who I am professionally and personally. It depicts my drive, my spirit, and essentially how I go after life. The people who attend my workshops, trainings, and keynotes could attest to that. Not only do they feel my energy but they also feel the energetic environment that I create in the room. It's electric! They generally leave the sessions as exhausted as I do. One of my major goals during my sessions is to model, use, and share tips, techniques, metaphors, stories, and illustrations that create an energy level where people want to learn, experiment, play, and are anxious to use what's being taught when they leave the room.

Wright
I have heard of your keynote speeches. Could you tell our readers about the "fear factor" and about the "layaway plan" you discuss?

Smith, Jr.
The fear factor is that "factor or obstacle" we create (and strongly believe) that gets in the way of our pursuing our greatness, pursuing our dreams, and pursuing those things we really desire. The acronym for fear is:

False
Expectations
Appearing
Real

We create the fear factor monster. We create the hurdles and pot-holes. We create the reasons for our settling for second. Some may call these self-limiting beliefs. We play to keep the score close and our fear factors paralyze us.

I love Les Brown's quote, " 'But' is an argument for your limitations and when you argue for your limitations you get to keep them." Our fear factors help us to argue for our limitations, and we learn to argue well.

The layaway plan could be either positive or negative but in most cases it's the latter. Your typical layaway plan transaction involves someone putting down money on an item as an initial deposit, and then returning to the store periodically to make small payments until the total balance is paid off within the designated timeframe. The deposit, which is made in good faith, is needed to hold the item because the shopper generally does not have the required amount of money at that point. Unfortunately, in some cases, people stop paying on their item over time and it's put back on the shelf.

In life many of us put our dreams and goals on layaway. We make an initial deposit on the goal by making a mental note, writing it down, or by sharing it with others. We then periodically revisit that goal by making additional attempts to get closer to making it become a reality. Nevertheless, if our efforts are not consistent (i.e., if our payments are not regular), we generally lose out and lose sight, and our dreams and goals go back on the shelf with our other unfulfilled aspirations.

Now depending on how significant the goal is, some people use the layaway plan as a measured, strategic, and consistent approach to obtain what they want. I just wish those people outnumbered the myriad people who never pay off their layaways. I exhort and challenge people to take their goals and dreams off layaway. Also, consider this, we typically begin the whole layaway process by making it challenging. How? We usually put down the *minimum* amount (of money) that we can to get the store to hold it. If we put in the least amount of effort and planning into our goals or dreams at the outset then we're certainly getting off on the wrong foot. Successful people purposefully and intentionally go after their goals even if it means occasionally putting some of them on layaway.

Wright

You tell people to "get out of their own way" and to "get the junk out of their trunk." What's that about?

Smith, Jr.

To get out of your own way means simply to immediately stop talking yourself out of opportunities. It means to stop creating mountains of negative karma. It means to stop being your own firing squad. Two quotes come to my mind when I consider how people become their own personal roadblocks: "If you think you can or think you can't you're right," by Henry Ford, and, "The greatest conversation you can have is the conversation you have with yourself and the greatest belief you can have is the belief you have in yourself." With that in mind, during my sessions I emphatically stress to people, "Get out of your own way—you'll keep getting what you're getting as long as you keep doing what you're doing!"

With regard to the junk in one's trunk I believe we metaphorically carry tons of luggage and baggage around with us throughout our life. In our baggage are resentment, insecurity, jealousy, rage, bitterness, divorce, separation, hypocrisy, control, fear, bad habits, and the like. We seldom realize the toll baggage takes on our mindset, outlook, and well being. It's toxic, disintegrating our self-esteem every day. To successfully move through the world we have to rid ourselves of our junk.

The first step is to acknowledge that you have it—to own your stuff. Once that's accomplished you can seek help. There are plenty of self-help books, seminars, and the like, that speak to baggage discarding. Trust me—I know—I'm still emptying my trunk every day.

Wright

Your speaking and training style is both creative and empowering. Where does it come from?

Smith, Jr.

I have experienced an awful lot in my life and to me it has all contributed to what I bring to my presentations. At times during my life I have thrived and there have been other times when I have barely survived. Nevertheless, everything that has happened to me has played a critical role in who I am as a person, a father, a brother, a son, an author, a leader, a consultant, a speaker, and a trainer.

David, from being raised in a black, single-parent household, to attending schools that were either predominantly all white or all black, to my highs and lows in academics and athletics (high school, college, and professional), to broken promises, to silly corporate America games, to failed relationships, to routinely dealing with a number of isms (i.e., classism, racism, nepotism, etc.), I have developed an empowering, "put it all out there" style. I'm not afraid to make a mistake. I truly love what I do. People really feel me and feel my words. I'm all live—no Memorex here. Plus, I've always been somewhat of a ham and that helps.

With regard to my creative style, that stems primarily from my background in English and Journalism. My undergrad degree is in English and my master's degree is in Journalism. I create pictures with my words. My illustrations are rich in diversity. I want to give the learners ears eyes. Since a great majority of us are visual learners, I want to create pictures that you will marinate in today and tomorrow. I creatively move you from your head to your heart. Some would say that journey is the longest fifteen inches in the world. I appeal to left-brainers and right-brainers, kinesthetic learners and auditory learners—everybody.

I sincerely believe in the theories that suggest "just because I taught it doesn't mean you caught it," and, "just because it was said doesn't mean that it made it to your head." I have no fear in front of audiences. I view my learners as the most important people in the room and it's my goal to ensure that they leave with more than they come with. That means moving away from solely didactic, theoretical approaches to facilitation and speaking. I speak to express not impress. I want my learners to leave empowered, confident, knowledgeable, and inspired.

Wright

What would you say has been the biggest contributor to your professional success?

Smith, Jr.

I would say that several things have greatly contributed to my success. One significant contributor has been my mother who taught me to always step up—to overachieve. Because of her I attended kindergarten through twelfth grade without missing a day of school. Just watching her raise my brother and me, excel in her job, travel to all parts of the world, get her bachelor's degree after we both obtained our master's degrees and assume a leadership role in every situation she was a part of was the role modeling I needed.

Number two, I guess, is my risk-taker mentality. I'm not afraid to lose. I'm also not afraid to do what it takes to win. I can remember always being that way. Even in grade school I was always the daredevil—I always wanted to go first—I always wanted to set the standard and to get noticed.

Next I'd say is the number of "Titans" I've had in my life. Titans are people who always have your back. They are mentors and coaches, friends and colleagues, relatives, and teachers who always want to see you excel. I talk about them at length in my book *From Average to Awesome: 41 Plus Gifts in 41 Plus Years.* I believe you have Titans and "Titanics" in life. Knowingly or unknowingly, consciously or unconsciously, Titanics try to sink you and your dreams.

We should always remember our Titans. They remind you to give and to persevere. My Titans have always been a diverse group too.

Aside from my mother and other relatives, I've experienced a huge amount of diversity in my life. The schools I attended contributed to that. Because my parents were divorced when I was young I always attached myself to the male leaders in my life. This included my little league and high school coaches, teachers, and college professors, many of whom were not black. They played a significant role in developing my spirit, my passion for excellence, and my vision.

Finally, I'd say that I don't know any other way—I don't know how to settle for second—my eye is always on the prize.

Wright

Your personal Mt. Rushmore includes your mom, Mr. Sam (your little league baseball coach), Mrs. Brodie, and Kathy Cook. Could you tell our readers more about them and perhaps your other Titans?

Smith, Jr.

When I think of Mt. Rushmore I think of the people who have paved the way for our country and society. When I think of my personal Mt. Rushmore I think of the people who have paved the way for me. There are several but the top four include my mother, Nanci Smith, Mr. Sam, Mrs. Brodie, and Kathy Cook.

I mentioned my mom previously. She has always been filled with lessons, advice, tough love, and endless support. I call her my pulse.

Mr. Sam was my first little league baseball coach. Imagine Lou Gossett's character in *An Officer and a Gentleman* coaching age ten through sixteen youth—that was Mr. Sam. He was drill sergeant tough, extremely detailed, and very consistent. He used to always say, "Tuck that shirt in young man. Turn that hat around straight!"

What also made Mr. Sam important to me was his constant push for us to give more than we thought we had. He would yell from the bench, "Fire hard kid!" That was our cheer to take our effort to the next gear. No other coach, for the rest of my playing days, ever had to push me to give my all. Mr. Sam conditioned me so thoroughly in that mentality that I go after life with that same drive and spirit—I always "fire hard!" Mr. Sam also taught us how to win, evidenced by the number of little league championship trophies we won. Where have all of the Mr. Sam's gone these days?

Mrs. Brodie was my twelfth grade English teacher. She was, in fact, the reason why I pursued English and Journalism in college. She was another no-nonsense individual. You had to really study, complete all of your homework and be at your best to get at least a "B" in her class. Many seniors did not graduate on time because they took Mrs. Brodie lightly. She really spent quality time with her students coaching us and challenging us to develop an appreciation for poetry, prose, grammar, and essentially how to write. When I was in her class I believe she was in her late 60s but she never missed a beat and never missed a day of school. By the way, she mentioned to us that she was basketball great Wilt Chamberlains' English teacher when he was in high school. I'm blessed and grateful that I was in Mrs. Brodie's class.

Kathy Cook was my manager at one of my corporate jobs. She was a lot like my other Mt. Rushmore personalities—tough love and support. I reported in to her for three years and she taught me more about being a professional in those three years than I had learned in all my other years combined. Kathy was always three steps ahead of everyone else. She coached me on how to be strategic, how to read between the corporate lines, how to position myself for success, and how to avoid taking on bad business. She was huge on development and feedback and wanted to see all of her people stretch and excel.

My Mt. Rushmore members and Titans continue to make deposits into my professional and personal life bank account. They're extremely special and giving people, and I share with others what they have shared with me.

Wright

I have read that your favorite quote is from former baseball great Satchel Paige who once said that we should, "Love like we've never been hurt, work like we don't need the money, dream like we'll live forever, and dance like nobody's watching." Why is that?

Smith, Jr.

To dance like nobody's watching is so freeing. To get to a place in your life where somebody's opinion of you does not become your reality is so liberating. We are so consumed with what everyone else thinks or feels about us. There's a certain peace that comes with the ability to do your own thing. I believe that's what Satchel Paige was referring to. He wasn't talking about being a rebel or anti-establishment. He was talking about being so supremely confident in your ability and talents that you're not going to be knocked to your knees by dissenting opinions and views—you're not going to crumble from criticism.

You're not going to do it *that way* because that's the way it's always been done. This means creatively taking different steps, making steeper strides, acquiring special resources, going the extra mile, and doing whatever (of course ethically and legally) it takes to be successful. And by doing this you're going to separate yourself from the many others who let systems, traditions, politics, cultures, and social mores drive their every move.

A vivid illustration for this type of "dancing"—or living—can be found in the person at the wedding reception who is always the first to move to the dance floor. Upon hearing the music play, he/she gets up and starts to get his/her groove on. This person doesn't care who's looking, leering, or laughing—the sole purpose is to have a wonderful time. I believe Satchel was suggesting that we should go after our dreams and goals in the same way. I have to have fun in whatever I do. My audiences appreciate it.

Wright

Tell me, how did you get into speaking and training?

Smith, Jr.

You know, David, I stumbled into it. My first dream was to play professional football then write for Sports Illustrated. I then wanted to move into sports broadcasting and eventually work at my old high school as an English teacher and football and basketball coach. For myriad reasons, things did not pan out that way. For example, after college I got cut in my attempts to play pro football. I worked as a stringer for a couple of local Philadelphia area newspapers and after working briefly as a substitute teacher, I pursued a career in the corporate world.

Actually, my first official public speaking responsibilities came when I was President of my college's Black Student Union during my junior and senior years. Next, I made concept presentations when I was part of the marketing department at Prudential in what was my first real job after graduating from college. While at Prudential I next took a position in the Human Resources Department as a trainer. Since that time I have never looked back. I moved from a trainer to a training manager, to a training and organization development consultant, to eventually being vice president at the various companies I worked for.

People have always told me that when I speak to them I make them feel as though they are the most important person in the world at that moment. I was told that I really connect with people and I continued to receive that same feedback while working in corporate America for fourteen years. Because of that feedback and the success I experienced helping people to change their lives by pursuing their goals with vigor and zeal, I decided to make speaking and training my career. I love to give and to serve. I believe that I am a bridge to helping you reach your dreams.

Surprisingly, I still get nervous before I go on, but I'm doing what I love. Now as a business owner, I work with other trainers, speakers, and professionals to get them to raise their "speaking and training" bars. I couldn't imagine doing anything else.

Wright

You discuss challenges that minorities face in the corporate world. What are they and what advice do you provide?

Smith, Jr.

David, minorities face many of the same challenges that majority members face and many that are unique to them or that have a different impact. Some of the challenges are self-imposed and others are institutional.

If we took a look at our society we could clearly see that minority group members are not equally represented in top decision-making positions in most organizations. To that end the number of minority executive role models are limited. There's a certain level of confidence that comes from watching someone who looks like you and who performs like you in a position of power. Also, I don't believe that some minorities enter the workforce as prepared as we can be. I believe colleges could do more in the way of teaching business etiquette, business behavior, performance management, corporate politics, and self-development. I've seen where the best and the brightest minorities have not always been fairly rewarded and developed.

Minorities also face challenges when inappropriate behaviors, assumptions, stereotypes, and practices are at play and the contributors are not held accountable. In my role as a diversity consultant I facilitate a number of focus group meetings where minority professionals share a lot of the same unfortunate sentiments. They highlight the lack of consistent mentoring, information exchange, development, feedback, and support. Many have mentioned, however, that it makes them want to work harder to become the first or move on to work for an organization where they feel included and empowered.

As far as coaching is concerned I teach what I've been taught—to always take care of business and to "fire hard" in the meantime. That means always being on time, being purposeful, always completing assignments in a timely fashion, becoming a needed resource and team player, and always adhering to the organization's core values.

I explain that we can't spend time complaining and whining about what we feel is happening or not happening for us. We have to get additional training, education, and certifications. We have to learn the rules—those that are written and those that are unwritten. I tell them that we have to become invaluable, build relationships, become a subject matter expert, and become the best at our position. I tell them to listen for what's said and for what's not said. I tell them to learn from these experiences so that they can coach others. I tell them about the importance of image and exposure. I also tell them that by doing all of these things their behavior can help change the inequities (albeit some of them are very micro or clandestine) and organization traditions that are in place.

I tell them to not always consider race as the reason for their dilemmas. Sometimes race may be the problem but sometimes it's not. I encourage them to do some discovery work, to do some self-examination, and to elicit the support of their coaches and Titans. I also tell them to build a team of diverse mentors and Titans. I also tell them it may eventually mean having to move on. I believe that there is always someone or some organization that has a place for a talented individual.

Wright

You always encourage your audiences to "break through to awesome." What is awesome?

Smith, Jr.
Awesome is a state of mind—it's a belief. It's not a title or a position. It's not an income level. It's one person's belief that he/she can be anything he/she so chooses to be. Awesome is a mental, physical, and spiritual place that one achieves.

Awesome people don't see obstacles; they see opportunities. They don't see potholes; they see possibilities. They don't see dilemmas; they see developments. To break through to awesome means to break through to "no limitations thinking." You begin to believe that whatever you put your mind, your energy, and your spirit to you can accomplish. It means no more pity parties, victim vocabulary, or ordering from the whine list of life. It means no more playing to keep the score close or settling for second place. It means being resourceful, positive, intuitive, and resilient. It's personal accountability, personal responsibility, and personal empowerment rolled into one.

Wright
One of your keynotes is called "Bringing Out the Best." What do you discuss during that motivational talk or workshop?

Smith, Jr.
I typically talk about three things people can do to bring out the best in themselves, their customers, and their peers:
1. Be resilient
2. Be responsible
3. Be remarkable

There are so many additional factors associated with these three "R's" but they are at the root (another "R") for your being able to bring out the best in everyone you are associated with.

Here's an example: I was having dinner with a client not too long ago and our service was extremely slow. I motioned for the hostess to come over. I wanted to tell her about our sub-standard service in hopes that she would do something about it. After I explained everything to her she said they she couldn't help—that she was "just a hostess." I was extremely disappointed. It drives me nuts when people say, "I'm just a..." She could have said, "Let me look into it, I'll see what I can do." No. She wasn't interested in bringing out our best. She failed on all three "R's." She did not take responsibility to resolve the situation. Her level of customer service or service recovery was not remarkable. Resilient? No way, she just sneered at me when we left. Why? I was finally able to get the restaurant manager to come over to our table and I shared with her the two examples of poor customer service we had just experienced. I trust that her manager gave her some well-needed and poignant feedback.

Bringing out the best includes getting people to see and appreciate their genius. It's getting people to believe that they are more than a title or a description. It's getting people to value who they are. It's getting people to reinvent themselves. We have tons of opportunities to do this every day with our family, friends, coworkers, and customers. I encourage people to do more!

Wright

You talk about a lot of heavyweight subjects—mindsets, accountability, commitment, and results. Why do you think these factors are so important?

Smith, Jr.

I think they are important because to many people they are just words. I would like for them to become a way of life. We live and work in a society where people simply do not follow through—they don't even return your call when they say they will. I tell my learners to look in the mirror. I tell them to tell themselves that going forward, "I'm going to mean what I say and say what I mean."

Our mindset is huge! Our mindset generally determines our beliefs and our behaviors. Our behaviors generally determine the results we get. So in essence, our mindset determines our results. To that end we get who we are and what we think. So we have to be committed and accountable.

My mother used to always tell me to "wake up, get up, show up, and step up." I tell my learners to do the same. I want them to be honest and to be responsible to themselves and to others. Their results will be phenomenal.

Wright

What a great conversation Jim. I really appreciate the time you have spent with me here today. I have learned a lot.

Smith, Jr.

Thank you!

Wright

I might even start changing, who knows? I told someone this morning in a staff meeting that it has taken me sixty years to get as screwed up as I am today. I can start unscrewing.

Smith, Jr.

David, the older I get, the smarter my mother and the older folks in my life get. When I'm around them I'm just a sponge—I just listen. You know, when I was younger I used to think I knew everything. That's not the case anymore. A lot of what I talk about is basic—it's fundamental. Now, I do it very creatively and humorously, but I'm highlighting common thoughts that are not, unfortunately, common practices.

I tell people that I'm no one special. I'm just Jim Smith, Jr. I'm Nanci Smith's oldest son and Rodney Smith's older brother. A phenomenal woman who saw to it that I received an education and developed a passion for excellence and a giving spirit raised me. As a result, my goal is to help people break through to awesome—awesome trainers, awesome leaders, awesome parents, awesome friends, and awesome people. If *I* can do it *anyone* can.

Wright

Today we have been talking with Jim Smith, Jr., the President and CEO of JIMPACT Enterprises, Inc. He is one of the most spirited speakers and trainers to come along in a lot of years and we have seen today he has tons of tips, keys, and power points to help us improve in the areas of leadership, training and development, diversity and personal empowerment. Jim, thank you so much for being with us today.

Smith, Jr.

Thank you for the opportunity. I look forward to connecting again with you real soon!

About Jim Smith, Jr.

President and CEO of JIMPACT Enterprises Inc., Jim consults, writes, speaks and facilitates in the areas of motivation/inspiration, diversity, training trainers, leadership, professional and personal development. Previously, Jim was a Consultant for Simmons Associates (Leadership and Diversity Management) and a Performance Solutions Consultant for The Bob Pike Group where he consulted and trained in the areas of performance improvement, participant centered training techniques, motivation, high impact business presentations and customer service. Jim has also worked in a leadership capacity for Core States Bank (Vice President, Business Learning Resources), the Vanguard Group (Management and Organization Development Consultant), and the Prudential AARP Operations (Associate Manager, Training and Development). While at Vanguard, Jim received the organization's Award for Excellence, an award that recognizes outstanding contributions, professionalism and service. At Prudential he received the Minority Interchange, Inc. Constance O. Garretson Award for devoted and valuable service. INROADS/Philadelphia Inc. awarded Jim its Frank C. Carr Community Service Award in 1995. Jim is currently working on his next book, *Crash and Learn: Stuff Trainers Do in the Classroom that Make Participants want to Shout, Sleep or Sneak Out!*

JIMPACT Enterprises, Inc.
1530 Locust Street, #161
Philadelphia, PA 19102
Phone: 856.778.4778
Fax: 610.622.4488
www.jimpact.com